Hemingway and Italy

UNIVERSITY PRESS OF FLORIDA

Florida A&M University, Tallahassee
Florida Atlantic University, Boca Raton
Florida Gulf Coast University, Ft. Myers
Florida International University, Miami
Florida State University, Tallahassee
New College of Florida, Sarasota
University of Central Florida, Orlando
University of Florida, Gainesville
University of North Florida, Jacksonville
University of South Florida, Tampa
University of West Florida, Pensacola

Hemingway and Italy

Twenty-First-Century Perspectives

EDITED BY MARK CIRINO AND MARK P. OTT

University Press of Florida
Gainesville · Tallahassee · Tampa · Boca Raton
Pensacola · Orlando · Miami · Jacksonville · Ft. Myers · Sarasota

Copyright 2017 by Mark Cirino and Mark P. Ott
All rights reserved
Published in the United States of America

First cloth printing, 2017
First paperback printing, 2025

30 29 28 27 26 25   6 5 4 3 2 1

Library of Congress Cataloging-in-Publication Data
Names: Cirino, Mark, 1971– editor. | Ott, Mark P., 1966– editor.
Title: Hemingway and Italy : twenty-first-century perspectives / edited by
  Mark Cirino and Mark P. Ott.
Description: Gainesville : University Press of Florida, 2017. | Includes
  index.
Identifiers: LCCN 2017005525 | ISBN 9780813054414 (cloth) | ISBN 9780813081137 (pbk.)
Subjects: LCSH: Hemingway, Ernest, 1899–1961—Homes and haunts—Italy. |
  Novelists, American—20th century—Biography. |
  Americans—Italy—History—20th century. | Hemingway, Ernest,
  1899–1961—Criticism and interpretation.
Classification: LCC PS3515.E37 Z617755 2017 | DDC 813/.52—dc23
LC record available at https://lccn.loc.gov/2017005525

The University Press of Florida is the scholarly publishing agency for the State University System of Florida, comprising Florida A&M University, Florida Atlantic University, Florida Gulf Coast University, Florida International University, Florida State University, New College of Florida, University of Central Florida, University of Florida, University of North Florida, University of South Florida, and University of West Florida.

University Press of Florida
2046 NE Waldo Road
Suite 2100
Gainesville, FL 32609
http://upress.ufl.edu

GPSR EU Authorized Representative: Mare Nostrum Group B.V., Mauritskade 21D, 1091 GC Amsterdam, The Netherlands, gpsr@mare-nostrum.co.uk

Contents

List of Figures vii
Acknowledgments ix
"Torcello Piece" by Ernest Hemingway xi

Hemingway and Italy: An Introduction 1
MARK CIRINO AND MARK P. OTT

PART I. REMINISCENCES

1. Address to the Hemingway Society Congress: Venice, June 22, 2014 11
GIACOMO IVANCICH

2. Remembering Ernest Hemingway: And the Sad Epilogue of a Hero Described in the Novel *Across the River and into the Trees* 21
RUGGERO CAUMO

PART II. HEMINGWAY'S ITALY IN CONTEXT

3. Ernest, Hadley, and Italy 29
SCOTT DONALDSON

4. Views of Venice before Hemingway 47
SERGIO PEROSA

5. Torcello: From John Ruskin and Henry James to Ernest Hemingway 58
ROSELLA MAMOLI ZORZI

6. Hemingway at Lignano Sabbiadoro and in Friuli-Venezia Giulia 68
DAVIDE LORIGLIOLA

PART III. *A FAREWELL TO ARMS*

7. The Many Faces of Defeat: Italian Ideological Contexts in Frederic Henry's Caporetto 77
ALBERTO LENA

8. Reading and Not Reading *The Black Pig* in *A Farewell to Arms*   96
   MIRIAM B. MANDEL

9. "What If You Are Not Built That Way?": H. G. Wells and the Conflict of Science and Faith in *A Farewell to Arms*   108
   MICHAEL KIM ROOS

10. "I Was in Italy . . . and I Spoke Italian": The Cosmopolitan Battlefield of *A Farewell to Arms*   127
    JOHN D. SCHWETMAN

PART IV. ACROSS THE RIVER AND INTO THE TREES

11. Artifice and Reality: The Blending of Venice and America in *Across the River and into the Trees*   145
    ADAM LONG

12. *Across the River and into the Trees*: A Trigonometric Mirror   159
    MARINA GRADOLI

13. The Italian Translation of *Across the River*: Will It Ever Reach the Juncture?   177
    PIERO AMBROGIO POZZI

14. Across the Associate Editorship of the Harvard *Lampoon* and onto the Wall above the Urinal: The Reach and Legacy of E. B. White's "Across the Street and into the Grill"   195
    KIRK CURNUTT

PART V. THE FABLES

15. Dear Children (Good and Bad), You Are Cordially Invited to a Roasting of Instructional Literature   217
    CAM COBB

16. A "Very Complicated" Diet for a Lion: The Functions of Food and Drink in "The Good Lion"   230
    KEI KATSUI

List of Contributors   241
Index   243

Figures

12.1. Diagram of partnerships among institutions of Regione Lazio   164
12.2. The iceberg theory in *Across the River and into the Trees*   165
12.3. Whitman's connections under the surface   166
12.4. D'Annunzio's connections under the surface   169
13.1. Cover of the Mondadori translation of *Across the River and into the Trees*   180
13.2. D'Annunzio's Casetta Rossa on the Canal Grande   184
13.3. "Across the river and into the trees": the Ivancich villa at San Michele al Tagliamento   187

Acknowledgments

We would like to thank the generous and thoughtful readers of this manuscript, Linda Wagner-Martin and Linda Patterson Miller. We would also like to thank our friends and colleagues in the Ernest Hemingway Society that helped guide us through the planning and production of the XVI Biennial International Ernest Hemingway Society Conference in Venice in June 2014: James Meredith, Gail Sinclair, Cecil Ponder, Carl P. Eby, Suzanne del Gizzo, Alex Vernon, and Kirk Curnutt. In addition, we would like to thank Scott Donaldson and Gerry Kennedy for their continued support. We are especially grateful to Rosella Mamoli Zorzi for her wisdom and guidance. We appreciate the generosity of Gianni Moriani and the Ivancich family.

We would like to thank the supportive and professional team at University Press of Florida: Sian Hunter, Shannon McCarthy, Marthe Walters, Ali Sundook, and everyone who was so committed to this project.

We are enormously grateful to Susan Vandagriff and Loren Oboikovitz for their editorial expertise. We also thank Kerrie Maynes for her fine editorial work.

At the University of Evansville, Kathy Martyn provided essential administrative support. Dean Ray Lutgring, Larry Caldwell, and Lesley Pleasant also contributed in crucial ways.

Thanks also to Deerfield Academy and Dr. Margarita Curtis, John Taylor, and Brent Hale.

Mark Ott would like to extend his thanks and appreciation to his family, Lori, Claire, Anne, and Olivia. Without their infinite support, this book would not be possible.

Mark Cirino wishes to thank Matt Blank and David Davis, who provided steadfast support, as always.

He offers big thanks and bigger hugs to his family, Kristen, Luca, and Noah.

And he dedicates this book to Antonio Cirino and his entire Italian family.

"Torcello Piece" by Ernest Hemingway

In November 1948, Hemingway moved to Torcello, a small island in the north of the Venetian lagoon. During his several weeks in Torcello, Hemingway spent time with friends, hunted, and wrote. Presumably during this period, Hemingway sketched an evocative ode to his new home, "Torcello Piece," which has never previously been published, and which we reprint in full below.

TORCELLO PIECE

For we, who love the lagoon, it makes no difference if Atila[1] sat in the chair or if he did not. I doubt if he did. It is enough for me that Cipriani[2] sat in it.

It is a small village with canals and there are three beautiful buildings. The three monuments were made by men who believed in their God and in Torcello. It would be difficult to find a lovlier [sic] church[3] nor one where the mosaics expressed more doubt.

There is no doubt in the one mosaic of Our Lady. But the other mosaics always seemed to me to be made by boys from Caorle[4] who were accepting the product but did not know whether they really cared for it or not. Dom Francesco[5] who governs the Island and who writes the most beautiful latin that I have ever read will correct me if I am wrong.

But at night, with a fire of beachlogs burning almost to coals now, and you wake in the Locanda to hear the shots of the big punt gunners[6] who are working up to the free ducks in the night, you go to the window and you can see, through the mist, with the moon aiding you, the great tower and the glory of the town, reduced to a village through the needs of Venice, and you feel both humble and proud. You whistle to the turkeys and the gobblers (los machos) answer. They are Torcello boys[7] too; although they came from another country.

xxxxx

Notes

1. Attila the Hun ransacked much of northern Italy during the middle of the fifth century. Hemingway also mentions Attila humorously during his spoken-word performance "In Harry's Bar in Venice."

2. Hemingway refers reverentially to Giuseppe Cipriani (1900–1980), the owner of Harry's Bar in Venice and the inspiration behind the *Gran Maestro* in *Across the River and into the Trees*. Hemingway stayed at the Locanda Cipriani in Torcello. Cipriani is also honored in "The Good Lion," Hemingway's whimsical late fable.

3. Hemingway refers to the church of Santa Fosca, constructed in the seventh century.

4. Caorle is a small town on the coast north of Torcello. Hemingway hunted in the Caorle region in the winter of 1948–1949, often on the grounds of his friends, the Franchettis.

5. The priest of the church in Torcello during Hemingway's visit.

6. A "punt gun" is an enormous gun used for shooting waterfowl. A "punt" is a small, narrow hunting boat, so this gun was designed for hunting from the water.

7. Hemingway often referred to himself as a "Torcello boy," as does Cantwell, the protagonist of *Across the River and into the Trees*, in chapter 14.

Hemingway and Italy

An Introduction

MARK CIRINO AND MARK P. OTT

One of the strangest moments of dialogue in any piece of Hemingway's writing appears in *Across the River and into the Trees*, Hemingway's maligned 1950 novel about a dying American colonel and his doomed love for Renata, an eighteen-year-old Italian contessa. In this bizarre but pointed stretch of dialogue, by expressing his devotion to Venice, the dying Colonel Cantwell exchanges unspoken subtleties with Barone Alvarito, the young man who, it is implied, will assume a relationship with the love of Cantwell's life after he dies. In classic Hemingway style, the true issue is not confronted directly, but rather through suggestion. Their diction is striking, awkward, and a revelation. After some benign banter about the duck hunt they have just participated in, and then the weather, and then possibly eating something, and then the migratory habits of ducks, the Colonel penetrates deeper into the reality, which they almost, but never quite, discuss:

> "And I love Venice."
> The Barone Alvarito looked away and spread his hands toward the fire. "Yes," he said. "We all love Venice. Perhaps you do the best of all."
> The Colonel made no small talk on this but said, "I love Venice as you know."
> "Yes. I know," the Barone said. He looked at nothing. (277)

In the context of the novel, it is clear that the name Renata should be substituted for Venice on all three occasions, which would make for an unmistakable admonition from the Colonel to the Barone that he cares deeply for Renata and—even after he dies—what happens to her and who takes care of her. But it is the choice of his language that is so striking, whereby the city he loves and the woman he adores become interchangeable. Just as he associates visiting Venice one final time with being with Renata, he also describes his love for Renata in terms of his nostalgia for Venice.

A portrait painted of Renata, which takes on such dramatic importance to the point that it virtually becomes a character in Cantwell's imagination, is compared with Titian's *Venus Rising from the Sea* (ca. 1520), a painting synonymous with the city just as the painter is synonymous with Venice and sixteenth-century art. In an interview Hemingway conducted just before the publication of *Across the River and into the Trees*, he referred to Titian admiringly as one of the "old Venice boys" (Ross 83). It was Hemingway and his protagonist's wish that he could be considered similarly. As he wrote a friend around that time in 1950, "[I] am a boy with five home towns now—Paris, Venice, Ketchum (Idaho), Key West and Havana" (qtd. in Lyons 30). Any engagement with Hemingway's life and work must consider Italy—as Hemingway himself did—as essential to his life and artistic development.

As awkward and even passive aggressive as Cantwell's exchange with Alvarito is, coming at the end of *Across the River and into the Trees*, an occasionally stilted and forced performance itself, the exchange will remind us of the fundamental importance for Hemingway that Venice and all of northern Italy carried for the majority of his life.

Rather than attempt to offer an exhaustive view that encompasses every facet of Hemingway and Italy (for instance, canonical short stories such as "Now I Lay Me" and "A Way You'll Never Be," set at the Italian front during World War I), this book assembles representative papers that were delivered during the Hemingway Society's biennial international conference in Venice in June 2014, which gathered almost 275 of Hemingway's most esteemed scholars and devoted readers. By offering this collection, we hope to provide a sense of what the twenty-first-century landscape is of Hemingway's Italian life, career, and legacy. These essays present new perspectives on how Italy shaped Hemingway's writing, a topic that is now almost a full century old. The contributors to *Hemingway and Italy* reflect the current state of Hemingway studies. Each chapter contributes to celebrate the imbalance of the conference itself: of the sixteen essays, six are devoted to the historical background of Hemingway and Venice, eight focus primarily on Hemingway's Italian novels, and two address Hemingway's offbeat Italian fables, written in early 1950, "The Good Lion" and "The Faithful Bull," two short pieces not generally given critical attention.

Hemingway's lifelong engagement with Italy was carried out in distinct episodes. He first traveled to Italy in the crucible experience of 1918, as a volunteer with the Red Cross serving the Italian Army during World War I. His war experiences—particularly his July 8 wounding and his subsequent convalescence in Milan, where he fell in love with Agnes von Kurowsky, the American nurse—became the substance for the Italian fiction that would follow. Of the five full-length novels Hemingway published during his life, two are set in Italy. Although these novels, *A Farewell to Arms* (1929) and *Across the River and into the Trees* (1950), are not precise autobiographical renderings, they do draw from Hemingway's experience with the war, the Italian setting, and they mine his emotional investment in the culture, people, and events of his experience.

Hemingway's estimation as a short story writer, too, depends to a large degree on this Italian context. Early efforts such as "Cat in the Rain," "A Very Short Story," "A Canary for One," "The Revolutionist," "Out of Season," and "My Old Man," to say nothing of the interchapters 6 and 7—a significant portion of the *In Our Time* (1925) collection that would win him his reputation—concern Hemingway's involvement with Italy. Subsequent stories, such as "In Another Country," "Che Ti Dice La Patria?" "A Simple Enquiry," "Now I Lay Me," "A Way You'll Never Be," and "A Natural History of the Dead," depend on Hemingway's firsthand experience with the physical and emotional realities of war. Even the 1936 masterpiece "The Snows of Kilimanjaro" suggests that close to two decades later, the scenes of the war still played out in his mind images of *"the fighting on Pasubio, and of the attack on Perticara and Asalone"* (CSS 42), referencing villages that became synonymous for brutal World War I battles.

The resonance of this early experience, in fact, motivated Hemingway critic Philip Young to formulate his "wound theory," the notion that the impetus for Hemingway's entire literary corpus evolved from his July 8, 1918, wounding. This wounding, which Hemingway first dramatized in chapter 6 of *In Our Time* with Nick Adams as the protagonist, would for Young "serve as climax for all of Hemingway's heroes for at least the next twenty-five years" (40). Hemingway's Italian experience, then, and the early taste of war and wounding, would inform his entire life and career, whether a given work was set in Italy or not.

Hemingway returned to Italy intermittently in the 1920s, sometimes alone as a correspondent for the *Toronto Star*, and other times with his wife Hadley to show her in peacetime the Italy that he was able to see during the war. These early trips resulted in a clash between nostalgia and actuality that inevitably resulted in disappointment. Hemingway's riveting 1922 article for the *Star*, "A Veteran Visits the Old Front," warns that one can't repeat the past:

> So we walked along the street where I saw my very good friend killed, past the ugly houses toward the motorcar, whose owner would never have had a motorcar if it had not been for the war, and it all seemed a very bad business. I had tried to recreate something for my wife and had failed utterly. The past was as dead as a busted Victrola record. Chasing yesterdays is a bum show—and if you have to prove it, go back to your old front. (DT 180)

Hemingway was also able to see the fascist government that rose following World War I, resulting in some scathing journalistic pieces as well as the devastating "Che Ti Dice La Patria?," which chronicles the moral and physical wasteland of postwar Italy that he witnessed in 1927 with his friend Guy Hickock.

These sobering experiences from the 1920s, following the physical danger and emotional upheaval of his first Italian experience, combined to inspire the writing of *A Farewell to Arms* at the end of that decade, the defining novel of the Italian front during World War I.

Hemingway's writing on Italy presented a constant and relentless criticism of Italian fascism. For this reason, he felt unwelcome in the country until after World War II and the election of 1948 that democratized Italy. Soon after, he returned to Italy, but as a wealthy celebrity, perhaps the world's most famous writer, the author of *For Whom the Bell Tolls*, and just a few years away from being a Nobel laureate. His Italian experiences in the late 1940s, however, were not spent in trenches or war hospitals but in duck blinds at hunting reserves and in the best room of the ornate Gritti Palace Hotel in Venice. His friends were not fellow ambulance drivers but Italian aristocrats eager to show him a luxurious time. Hemingway, not surprisingly, took to this lifestyle with his fourth wife, Mary Welsh Hemingway, hunting frequently in the Veneto, sampling the Valpolicella wines from the casks of his friends, and visiting rich and well-connected Italians from the area.

This revivification of a love for Italy blossomed into his second Italian novel, *Across the River and into the Trees*, which Hemingway declared was devoted to "the city of Venice and the Veneto, which Hemingway has known and loved since he was a young boy" ("Hemingway Is Bitter about Nobody," 110). It was irrelevant to Hemingway that he had not actually entered the city of Venice until October 1948 (Reynolds 180); in his mind, it was a lifelong love affair, and it suffuses every page of the novel, along with his interviews of the period and his correspondence. As a writer who had already reached legendary status, Hemingway was aware that he was entering into the grand tradition of Venetian art, the city that Sergio Perosa (in the chapter he has contributed to this volume) argues as affecting Hemingway with a quality of "decay and death haunting the city," a sense of portent that would infuse Hemingway's Venetian novel.

Hemingway and his wife would return to Italy in March 1954, following two harrowing East African plane crashes. Photographs from that visit show a solemn, aged Hemingway meeting with concerned friends, showing burn marks and visible signs of the terrible toll of those crashes. During that visit, he reunited with Adriana Ivancich, the young woman on whom *Across the River and into the Trees'* Renata is based (and the sister of this volume's first contributor), and then left Italy, never to return.

Several essays in this book reexamine Hemingway's biographical ties to Italy, as well as the historical background of Venice and the arts. In our first essay, Giacomo Ivancich, the surviving brother of Adriana, offers his memories of Hemingway in Venice. Ivancich, who has served as an ambassador to various countries, delivered a moving presentation of his personal memories of Hemingway, eager to quell the salacious gossip that Adriana's friendship with Hemingway inspired. A sense emerges of Hemingway as a man rather than as a persona, where discussions revolve around hamburgers, rather than war, love, or loss. Ambassador Ivancich also gives a firsthand account of the shelling that his home suffered from Allied bombing during World War II, which is mentioned in *Across the River and into the Trees*. In a perspective from another friend, Ruggero Caumo—legendary barman at Harry's Bar in Venice—shares recollections of Hemingway and Giuseppe

Cipriani, who would be immortalized in *Across the River and into the Trees*. Caumo shares his memories through the lens of Hemingway as a drinker, holding court as a prominent figure in the bar he helped make famous.

Preeminent Hemingway scholar and literary biographer Scott Donaldson reviews Hemingway's early encounter with Italy during his first marriage, illuminating aspects of the Hemingway-Hadley relationship along with previewing Hemingway's future attitude toward Italy. Offering an Italian perspective, Davide Lorigliola investigates Hemingway's experiences in the village of Lignano Sabbiadoro and the region of Friuli-Venezia Giulia, northeast along the coast from Venice. Lorigliola gives a thorough account of Hemingway's postwar experiences there, his associates, and how his time there affected his Italian legacy and is reflected in his fiction.

For magisterial considerations of Hemingway and Venice, we turn to the observations of two of the most renowned scholars of American literature in Venice, Sergio Perosa and Rosella Mamoli Zorzi. Each of these scholars of Venice and the arts provides a background of the culture of literature and art in Venice; this culture is the world to which Hemingway responds. As these essays observe, *Across the River and into the Trees* directly enters this rich historical tradition of the arts, directly name-dropping the artists and writers that precede it, and indirectly alluding to a complex culture, the world of Byron, Henry James, Ruskin, Shakespeare, the Brownings, Sinclair Lewis, Wharton, and so many others that Perosa and Zorzi meticulously outline.

The conference also featured several striking presentations on *A Farewell to Arms*. In one highlight included here, Alberto Lena pays careful attention to the context of Caporetto, the devastating retreat that forms the dramatic centerpiece of the novel. Joining Lena's treatment of the backgrounds of the novel, veteran Hemingway scholars Miriam B. Mandel and Michael Kim Roos offer keen explications of arcane references in *A Farewell to Arms*. Mandel finds significance in a reference to the anticlerical novel *The Black Pig* referred to during banter early in book 1 of the novel. Roos, the coauthor of *Reading Hemingway's* A Farewell to Arms, explores the tension between faith and reason in the novel, with particular attention to another novel referenced: H. G. Wells's *Mr. Britling Sees It Through* (1916).

Following these extrapolations, John D. Schwetman introduces the notion of "cosmopolitanism" in a way that forces a new understanding of the context of Frederic Henry's attitude as an American abroad.

Adam Long embarks on a similar critical approach; however, his essay introduces the section dealing with *Across the River and into the Trees*. Long navigates the presence of America during this final weekend of the protagonist's life in Venice, showing how America and Italy form a chiaroscuro of meaning, a blend that lends new meaning to the novel. Perugian scholar Marina Gradoli gives an innovative reading of the novel, showing Hemingway's unexpected indebtedness to Walt Whitman and his other literary forebears. Gradoli's knowledge of Italy and its culture lead her fresh approach with some of the most insightful close readings that have ever been attempted of certain passages of the novel.

Next, Italian scholar and translator Piero Ambrogio Pozzi writes an iconoclastic piece, suggesting that the definitive Italian Hemingway translations—by Hemingway's friend Fernanda Pivano—are filled with errors and need to be redone. Pozzi traces these errors and the implications of these flawed editions: Italian readers have not read the "correct" Hemingway but rather a shoddy approximation of it. In the final treatment of *Across the River and into the Trees* in this volume, Kirk Curnutt offers the first critical piece ever written about E. B. White's notorious (and hilarious) *New Yorker* satire of Hemingway's novel, "Across the Street and into the Grill." Curnutt points out that Hemingway, who gained an early reputation as a satirist with his *The Torrents of Spring* (1926), has been paid back many times as the target of similar pieces.

The final group reads the most neglected fiction Hemingway would ever publish, his two 1951 fables, "The Good Lion" and "The Faithful Bull." As our contributors Cam Cobb and Kei Katsui point out, though these minor efforts are not masterpieces, they do reveal much about Hemingway's devotion to Venice and also Hemingway's state of mind around the time of the publication of *Across the River and into the Trees*. Cobb focuses on how these pieces allow us to include Hemingway in a discussion of children's literature, and Katsui shrewdly observes that Hemingway's role as a gastronome becomes prominent and worthy of analysis with this late fable.

For Hemingway, Venice and northern Italy were as rich and various as the assembly of voices in this volume. The region represented death and beauty and history and sadness, but also love, culture, and opportunity. It joined the binaries of war and peace, life and death, love and loss, and history and the future. William Wordsworth, in "On the Extinction of the Venetian Republic," asks us to "grieve when even the Shade / Of that which once was great is pass'd away" (192). In the legacy of Venice, Hemingway and his characters were able to contemplate their past, their regrets, and their triumphs. Just as Wordsworth was able to find glory in the defeat of Venice, Hemingway's career-long consideration of this region is a layered and complex literary project.

We are proud to offer these contributions to fellow scholars and to anyone interested in what Hemingway found when he first went to Italy as a war zone, why he kept returning and seeking the past, and why he kept writing about this country that he loved and thought about so much—from the innocence of his arrival of 1918 to the loss of that innocence to the pessimism, resentment, and distrust of Italy during fascism to the postwar reconciliation on his own terms, which yielded important new friendships and controversial new fiction.

Works Cited

Hemingway, Ernest. *Across the River and into the Trees*. 1950. New York: Scribner, 1996.

———. *The Complete Short Stories: The Finca Vigía Edition*. New York: Scribner, 2003.

———. *Dateline: Toronto: Toronto Star Dispatches, 1920–1924*. Ed. William White. New York: Scribner, 1985.

"Hemingway Is Bitter about Nobody—But His Colonel Is." *Time*, September 11, 1950, 110.

Lyons, Leonard. "The Lyons Den." *New York Post*, March 10, 1950, 30.

Reynolds, Michael. *Hemingway: The Final Years*. New York: Norton, 1999.

Ross, Lillian. *Portrait of Hemingway*. New York: Avon, 1961.

Wordsworth, William. "On the Extinction of the Venetian Republic." *The Selected Poetry and Prose of Wordsworth*. New York: Signet, 1970. 191–92.

Young, Philip. *Ernest Hemingway: A Reconsideration*. University Park: Pennsylvania UP, 1966.

Reminiscences

1

Address to the Hemingway Society Congress

Venice, June 22, 2014

GIACOMO IVANCICH

As the one and only surviving person here in Venice among those who have been friends with Ernest Hemingway, I have been asked to give a talk to this learned but captive audience, who probably knows it all, anyway.

As I was incautiously given no clear terms of reference and no limits, I could go on for hours about all what I have seen, heard, or read. But rest assured: I will try to restrain myself somewhat.

I'd like to start by describing Venice in the year 1948, when Ernest Hemingway came to this city.

The war had ended barely three years before, leaving a wake of death and destruction that was still raw and present. My family had been badly hit by the war: first, our country monumental residence in San Michele al Tagliamento was totally destroyed by sixty senseless carpet-bombing American raids that also razed the nearby undefended village—San Michele al Tagliamento, 10,000 inhabitants. What the bombings failed to destroy was their target: the bridges over the Tagliamento River.

Later my father was brutally murdered.

However, in spite of the war and of its tragic toll, the prevailing atmosphere of those early postwar years was one of unrestrained joie de vivre, in Venice just as in the rest of Italy and of Europe. About everybody was impoverished, of course; anyhow, social differences were still significant.

My family belonged in the higher, aristocratic-bourgeois stratum of Venetian society. This was a rather selected world of rentiers—mainly landowners, but also penniless has-beens. It was a fairly cosmopolitan society, and one with a boundless capacity for gossip on just about any kind of event or happening.

I believe Hemingway hadn't spent much time in Venice before 1948. He probably paid a quick visit after the First World War, in 1923. That's when my mother and my aunt Emma casually met him in Cortina d'Ampezzo.

Personally, I first met Hemingway when I was sixteen years old, at a formal lunch in our house in Calle del Rimedio, a historical Venetian palazzo which was then known as one of the most hospitable houses in the city. He hadn't been in town for long; he had just arrived from Friuli, where he had been a guest of the Kechlers, whom he had probably known in Cortina. The Kechlers were good friends of the Ivanciches, and our neighbors in the country; they had spent the last ten months of the war in our house in Venice, hiding from the Nazis during their occupation.

After that first meeting, naturally I started reading Hemingway's works, and I became a fan of his distinctive way of writing, and of his tauromachy. And I saw Ernest and Mary again on several occasions, treasuring these meetings, from that first time until 1954, when they came back to Venice after the terrible plane crashes in Africa and I saw him in bed in his suite, all covered with bruises. Most often we met at Harry's Bar, where I learned to appreciate the first Montgomery dry martinis (Hemingway affirmed that the field marshal wanted to fight only when he had a superiority of fifteen to one), or at the Gritti; I was always treated very kindly, affectionately I would say, as if I were family. The precise details of our many conversations are lost, but most of them—I have the impression—must have been on such topics as war, bullfights, hunting, and similar themes. I remember better his judgments about people. He liked people (from all walks of life) who were straightforward, generous, brave, sincere, and righteous. He strongly disliked the opposite, people who were ambiguous, deceitful, pharisaic. And he did not like a person that would not look straight into his eyes, as was the case with Eugenio Montale, great poet and journalist for the *Corriere della Sera*, who had secured an interview with him only through the intercession of Adriana, my sister . . .

When they drove from Havre to Pamplona with my elder brother Gianfranco, I tried to join them, hitchhiking my way, but I had to give up and stopped in Paris. And still, after Ernest's death, we saw Mary a number of times. We were her guests—my wife and I—on the yacht she had chartered to cruise in Yugoslavia in 1966, having decided to finally spend some of the royalties Ernest had earned through the years. Gianfranco was also there. And we saw her again in New York in 1968, and were her guests in Ketchum in 1969.

While staying in Friuli in 1948, Hemingway had gone duck hunting in the Franchettis' "valle," as a guest of Nanuck, also a friend of ours. There, he had met my sister Adriana, who was then eighteen years old and had just graduated from her Catholic high school. She hadn't read a word of Hemingway's books but quickly connected with this older but friendly and likable person. Anyway, after the party's return to Venice, it didn't take long before a small group of people—Venetian friends who could speak English, young and not so young—coalesced around this unusual writer, whom they found so *simpatico* and such good company. This was reciprocated by Hemingway and his wife Mary, and they all saw a lot of each other.

Adriana was one of this group.

I must here point out that in those times, and mainly also nowadays, young women and men would meet in ways that had nothing to do with the American custom of the "date," in which a couple goes out alone. Young people would meet in small groups, at parties, excursions, or going to shows. And, of course, sexual behavior was much stricter than nowadays. In this context Adriana, after her coming of age at eighteen, and her entrance into society, was quite popular among her contemporaries as well as with older people, not just because of her beauty, but mainly because of her lively, distinctive spirit, her intelligent and passionate conversation, her quick mind, vivid imagination, and sense of humor.

Well, after that lunch at our house, I guided Hemingway back to the Gritti. He was alone that day, Mary having stayed behind in Cortina. As we walked to the hotel, Hemingway talked all the time, mumbling with his half-closed mouth, in an English I strained to understand: it was all about the secrets of boxing or driving racing cars around bends.

Hemingway came to our house several times after that, and got to know the whole family. One day my elder sister Francesca challenged him, saying he would be incapable of writing a book for children. A few days later he brought back his answer: it was his short story "The Good Lion," which he dedicated to Francesca's baby son Gherardo, who was then one year old.

During his visits to our house, he also gave two short stories as a gift to Adriana. The first was "The Faithful Bull," which had the inscription "For

Adriana with love from Mr. Papa. Venezia 26/1/1950." In this tale, love is really present for "a cow, a heifer, that was young and beautiful and slimmer and shinier and more loveable than any other" (this is a rough retranslation from memory), a love the bull is unwilling to share with any other, ending up because of this in the arena where he fights beautifully and dies. His death puts an end to all his problems and recalls to mind the closing of *Across the River*.

The second one was "The Story of the American Hemingstein," this being a pseudonym Papa used in his private life, a compound of Hemingway and Frankenstein. In this story the main character has a friend, a Venetian horse, "a champion, the fastest horse in the world," whom he would take to Harry's Bar, creating a lot of scandal. But the American and Black Horse (one of Ernest's names for Adriana) didn't care.... This story was never published, because the characters were easily recognizable, and it was considered a game between Ernest and Adriana. I just heard there is another, longer and satirical version of the black horse story, but it was written many years later.

My memories, however, are not limited to what I directly saw or heard when I was actually meeting the Hemingways. This is true because Adriana was a great extrovert, and we were very close; she would tell me practically everything, day after day, or each time she came home from a trip, and she let me read the letters that Papa continuously sent her, for years, most of which I twice saved from destruction, I should add. So I was there, close by, an indirect as well as a direct witness of all the events and occurrences in her life.

And, as you know, the events and occurrences in Adriana's life have all too often been misread and distorted by a certain type of gutter press and by unscrupulous biographers, all too eager to entirely identify Adriana with the lascivious character Renata in *Across the River and into the Trees*. And that still happens nowadays.

My sister got so sick and tired of all the lies and falsehoods that for years she kept seeing in print, that she decided to write a book herself, to state the facts. By then she was married, and had two sons.

This book was published by Mondadori in 1980, and I can testify that it is a truthful rendering of her life in those years, and of the special relationship she had with her friend, Ernest.

Incidentally, my brother Gianfranco in his later years—he was then eighty-eight—also wrote a book of personal recollections. Gianfranco, who had behaved heroically in war and in the Resistance, was a man with something of an artist's temperament, adventurous, passionate about Africa; he and the Hemingways had immediately connected, and they were friends for life. Well, he wrote this small book of memoirs—the title is *Da una felice Cuba a Ketchum: I miei giorni con Ernest Hemingway*—which includes the long period he spent in Cuba, working for a shipping company, and living for a while at the Finca Vigía. Gianfranco's book goes on to recall the days in Pamplona, Venice, Málaga, and Madrid, and finally his breakneck trip to Ketchum, to get there in time to attend Ernest's funeral and to comfort Mary. Ernest wrote him fifteen letters, which are now in the Kennedy Library in Boston.

Back to Adriana's book now. The title of her poetic memoir, *La Torre Bianca*, actually comes from the company, a sort of club, that Papa Hemingway jokingly proposed to create as a society for mutual assistance. It was to be called the White Tower, Inc. (named after Papa's hideout in Finca Vigía) and would be composed of—I quote—"creative and sensitive members," including Mary Hemingway, Marlene Dietrich, Ingrid Bergman, Gary Cooper, Ava Gardner, Gianfranco and Francesca Ivancich, and, as honorary members, all the cats and dogs of the house. The statutes of the W. T., Inc., signed in blood by the founding members, Ernest and Adriana, were buried in the grounds of the Finca Vigía.

Adriana's book is, I believe, both entertaining and interesting, also because of her descriptions of a now vanished society, Italian and international. Besides giving a detailed account of her special friendship with the Hemingways, she also writes about the many famous people she met in different countries.

The book covers the period from 1948 to 1954, until the Hemingways last came to Venice after the African plane crashes.

La Torre Bianca had a marked success when it was first published, and is still much appreciated by those who come to read it. They must read it in Italian, though, because for some strange reason no American publisher has yet been willing to get it translated and published, the reason given often being that they are unable to appraise it, since it's not in English!

Anyway, a few short quotes appeared in Bernice Kert's book, *The Hemingway Women*.

Adriana's memoir has an inscription on its first page, an excerpt from one of Hemingway's letters; I could not find the original text, which roughly translates as "I'm writing all this because always, from my books, they try to create 'escandalo.' Then, ten years later, they are university textbooks. I'm not saying this to boost my self-importance. If I should die, you can tell everyone how fond of you I was; and you have letters very clear to prove it." The book (for the few who haven't read it) starts on a rainy autumn day, with the chance encounter of Adriana and Hemingway near San Michele al Tagliamento. After exchanging civilities, Hemingway's first words express regret for the destruction, by American bombing raids, of that beautiful villa across the river, among the trees: "War is a damn dirty bitch," he says. Adriana is then eighteen years old. They and their friends are on their way to a duck shoot, near Venice.

The book goes on recounting the day out shooting, and the following weeks when Adriana and her friends show the Hemingways around the city.

Later Hemingway avows his feelings for this young friend who has restored his ability to write after eight years of bleak unproductivity. It is thanks to Adriana, he says, that inspiration has come back to him and that everything seems now easy. The friendship between Adriana and Ernest deepens, certainly of a different nature on Ernest's side, who clearly has a crush on Adriana. The meeting of two different cultures and two different generations: they call each other Papa and Daughter (or, later, Partner or Black Horse).

All along Adriana is worried and careful to protect the Hemingways' marriage and tries to reassure Mary. Hemingway asks Adriana (who is good at drawing and also writes poems) if she would care to draw the jacket for his next novel, of which she knows next to nothing. After some hesitation she accepts. Later her design is adopted by Charles Scribner for the first edition of *Across the River and into the Trees*.

Adriana will again meet the Hemingways in Paris, where she was staying with a friend of ours, Monique de Beaumont. At some point, Hemingway casually asks Adriana for permission to clothe the character of his new novel, Renata, with some of her real features, permission which she rather ingenuously grants.

Later our older brother Gianfranco is offered a job in Havana with a Venetian shipping company. With that in mind the Hemingways invite

Adriana with our mother and another friend to be their guests in Cuba for Christmas 1950.

Follows the description of festive and hectic life in Cuba: their daily conversation, the Hemingways' friends they meet, Mary, a romantic flirtation of Adriana with a Cuban boy, cruising on the yacht *Pilar*. When Hemingway presents her with a copy of the freshly published *Across the River and into the Trees*, Adriana gives him her candid critique of the book's faults. It is unthinkable that a Venetian girl would behave like Renata, she objects, inter alia. Hemingway replies that that just happens. He is first disappointed by her remarks, then feels challenged. The following weeks bring the first premonitions of *The Old Man and the Sea*, and Hemingway tells her, "For you I will write the best book I have ever written. Wait and see . . ."

Suddenly the so-called scandal breaks out: *Across the River* is finally published and rumors fly, starting from the press, of Adriana being the lascivious Renata of the novel, and therefore the presumed mistress of Hemingway. Our mother decides to leave Cuba immediately, while young and naive Adriana protests that one should not care about nasty, unfounded gossip. Ernest is very sorry for this unintended outcome, and as an atonement decides to forbid the publication of the book in Italy and says he will not return to Venice, although it is a city that he loves most dearly, "a town," he writes in a letter, "I left my heart in . . . and haven't been able to find the son-of-a-bitch since."

In the following years Adriana and Hemingway don't see each other but entertain a very intense correspondence: many letters are now in the archives of American foundations and universities and show their delicate sentiments, different but profound. The "scandal" does not subside completely. Adriana leads a normal life, meets new people in Venice, Milan, and Paris, draws, and writes poems, a good number of which are finally published by Mondadori in their best collection of Italian poets—the title is *Ho guardato il cielo e la terra*, that is, "I gazed at the sky and the land."

She is still in love with her distant Cuban boyfriend Juan, but after a while this feeling subsides and she meets other young men, with whom she has platonic relationships.

One day, Venice is suddenly hit by tragic news: the Hemingways have died in an air crash in Africa. Adriana cries, deeply grieved. Just as suddenly, this news is corrected by the report of their survival.

The last chapters describe the arrival of the Hemingways on a ship from Africa and the last moving encounters of the old friends.

I believe that neither Ernest Hemingway's last years nor some of the deeper significance, metaphorical and literal, of his two last books can be fully understood without taking also into account what Adriana writes, in her straightforward, seemingly naive prose, in *La Torre Bianca*.

This point seems to have been well understood by Piero Ambrogio Pozzi, a talented Italian scholar who casually began translating bits of *Across the River and into the Trees*, was captivated by the story, and little by little acquired a full and balanced knowledge of these events, of which he is nowadays, in my opinion, one of the best experts and commentators.[1] He presented a paper in 2011, in Cuba, at the Thirteenth Coloquio Internacional Ernest Hemingway. This essay, which was quite successfully received, was on "The story of Ernest and Adriana through the metaphors in *Across the River and into the Trees* and *The Old Man and the Sea*.

Mr. Pozzi later published, both in Italian and in English, an e-book as intriguing as a novel called *Il fiume, la laguna e l'isola lontana*; this was a title that Hemingway himself had suggested when Adriana's book of poems was about to be published. He had written to her saying:

> I also thought "The River, the Lagoon, and the Distant Island" was a good title, but more suited to a novel than a selection of poems. It would be the right title for our story, Partner, for the story that I will never write, because no one would believe it. Some will think this and some will think that and only you and I will know, and we will be dead.

Pozzi collates every line of *Across the River* with *La Torre Bianca*, with Ernest's letters to Adriana and to other friends, with Adriana's poems, and with just about every other document of significance, highlighting analogies and differences, and identifying a number of metaphors used by Hemingway throughout this book, and possibly also in *The Old Man and the Sea*.

With your permission I shall quote just a few excerpts from Mr. Pozzi's works, which I find agree with my experience.

Among other things, Mr. Pozzi states that "*The Old Man and the Sea* was written for Adriana alone, and was completed when she was no longer close to him after having been hit by the scandal. But in Hemingstein's heart, everything is far more clear and simple, re-written under the pain of separation and a sense of guilt. Clarity and simplicity are poured into the small masterpiece, so different from the rest of his work."

Mr. Pozzi analyzes Hemingway's books on the trail marked by *La Torre Bianca* and finds ample evidence to support his statement that (I quote) "the American writer saw Adriana as his muse and the woman of his life, so much so that the two books are clearly inspired by her, and are secretly dedicated to her, through numerous metaphors which are present in both works but can be decoded only by those directly involved." Or, indeed, by those who, like Pozzi, did have the patience to begin with a new translation and search for these hidden references, spotting them and finding the links between them. Again, I quote:

> Once the literary mechanism of *Across the River* has been identified, other hidden dedications become evident: notably to Marlene Dietrich and to Mary Welsh, Hemingway's fourth wife. These are significant, if one is to understand Hemingway's story as a human being. The dedication to Marlene Dietrich of the "scandalous" chapters 13 and 14 is of particular importance. Critics and readers have maliciously supposed that the book was a novelized version of the relationship between Adriana and Hemingway. This slanderous supposition set off the "scandal" and malevolent gossip which ruined Adriana's private life...

On the contrary, Mr. Pozzi's essay clearly shows how the most unseemly incidents in *Across the River* were actually inspired by an episode that Hemingway had really experienced with Marlene Dietrich, and which he evokes as a surprise tribute to her, having discreetly told her about it before the novel was published.

Mr. Pozzi also emphasizes that some points of *Across the River* were inspired by Gabriele D'Annunzio's lyric novel *Notturno*, in which, by the way, the principal female character, nicknamed "la sirenetta" (the little mermaid), is called Eva, Renata, Adriana. Indeed, Colonel Cantwell mentions, with some note of admiration, D'Annunzio and *Notturno* when passing on a launch in front of the house in Venice, La Casetta Rossa, where the Italian poet used to live. Several other sources of inspiration and telling metaphors emerge from Mr. Pozzi's meticulous comparisons.

But I think I have taken up too much of your time; I do hope not to have bored you excessively.

Thank you for your patience.

Note

1. See Pozzi's chapter in this volume.

2

Remembering Ernest Hemingway

And the Sad Epilogue of a Hero Described in the Novel *Across the River and into the Trees*

RUGGERO CAUMO

TRANSLATED BY MARK CIRINO

Of Ernest Hemingway, whom I knew and served personally several times (even though it was [Giuseppe] Cipriani's[1] privilege to serve his first drink), I have told many times, to the point of exhausting my memories. As long as Mr. Cipriani remained in business, every question by journalists, columnists, correspondents, historians, and the simply curious came to be promptly answered by him while I listened and gathered the news. But since his son Arrigo took his place in 1960, the task to satisfy the curious about the great writer was passed to the undersigned. For anyone who happened to ask, the young Arrigo used to confess that while having known Hemingway, he had met him only sporadically (at that time Arrigo attended the Università di Padova). He used to point in my direction to the questioner, saying, "Roger, our barman, who has been here since 1946, is the person most suitable to answer your questions." This request did not always come at the most opportune moment. In the middle of almost always frenetic activity, between orders of drinks and cocktails, it was impossible to respond fully to the request of interlocutors. The requests often varied from the search for racy particulars to the indiscreet. I remained often until the following day or until the late evening, relaying facts, memories, and anecdotes of my knowledge. I have to say that I never permitted myself to comply with the requests to the morbid extreme or to add something more than I had assimilated and heard from the testimonial of Mr. Cipriani. And so I used to say that . . . "For all of us at Harry's, Ernest Hemingway was not only the famous writer but above all a friend of our employer. Something else that did not hurt: he was also an ideal client. He knew how to drink; he held his alcohol well; he could drink for hours without one noticing even minimal discomfort. It was above all his way of living and his mighty physical presence (well known in every good bar in half the world) to create around him and him alone a cluster of impenitent drinkers. He could be a proper part of the Club 'Bar's Fly,' which is to say 'bar fly,' French recognition that was given only to exceptional drinkers as such. You would recognize one if you see a simple brooch depicting a golden fly at a lapel buttonhole. Attention, however. It was not of a drunkard, as many argued. He was an exceptional drinker, yes, but not a drunkard." And of this I tried to convince the interlocutor, remembering news, reports, readings, and adding my thoughts.

Since he was young, Hemingway was dedicated, pushed by his father, a distinguished Chicago medic, to practice outdoor sports, fish, hunt, and do some boxing in a gym with sparring partners. In 1918, at twenty years old,[2] he joined the American Red Cross to follow as a witness the intervention of the United States in the First World War, on the Italian front. He assisted at the retreat at Caporetto[3] and was gravely wounded. From this experience much later he drew the inspiration to write *A Farewell to Arms* (in this atmosphere of war he made the acquaintance of Italian assault troops and of the Grappa of the Alpines). Then in the twenties he toured Europe as a journalist. He spent brief periods in Germany, Switzerland, and Spain, while holding happily to his residence in Paris (cognac, champagne, and sidecar cocktails at Harry's Bar on rue de Nou[4]). Of this period he later wrote *The Sun Also Rises*. In 1933 he was in Africa to satisfy his passion for big game hunting and to test the sensations and the anxieties of the hunter face to face with the wildlife of the savannas and of the African forests (gin and tonic, more gin than tonic, and whisky and soda). From these experiences, always in the first person, he drew material for the book *Green Hills of Africa*. Then in Spain he lived for months in the world of the matadors, hanging out with them before and after the corrida (sherry, wine, and Spanish brandy), presenting then the literary world another of his books, *Death in the Afternoon*, almost a treatise on bullfighting.[5] He returned for a brief period to his *finca* near Havana, frequenting the famous Cuban bar La Floridita, first known by the name The Silver Pineapple or La Piña de Plata, cradle of the international cocktail daiquiri (there are five, to be truthful, all of them numbered). And in this famous bar he spent whole days with journalists and writers passing through, local importers and exporters, with memorable drinks of Bacardi rum and good ice cream until the sun disappeared on the horizon, plunging into the ocean. For his assiduousness at the Floridita, the famous Cuban barman Constantino Ribalaigua dedicated a daiquiri (number six) with this recipe (that follows a bit of daiquiri number three):

Ernest Hemingway Special

40 grams of rum
15 grams of grapefruit juice
15 grams of maraschino
juice of half a lime
ice, chopped finely

Shake well and pour into double cocktail glasses.

In 1937 Hemingway returned to Spain as a correspondent for the Civil War. He lived through adventurous moments that were transposed into his literature in his compelling novel *For Whom the Bell Tolls*. In 1950 he would write the somewhat sad novel *Across the River and into the Trees* about Venice and Torcello, where the hero of my stories and memories entered. And here one can remember that when he stayed at the Locanda Cipriani in Torcello to finish the drafting of his penultimate literary effort, the waiter had orders to prepare in his room some bottles of Valpantena.[6] In the middle of the night, during the long hours of vigil, he awoke his wife Mary, who, now used to it, got the typewriter, and he dictated. He would intersperse typed pages with gulps of Veronese wine until he exhausted the bottles. Then at dawn they lay down to sleep for a few hours. Two years later (perhaps the swan song) came *The Old Man and the Sea*, which was a great critical success, also as a film with the masterful interpretation of the old man by Spencer Tracy.

In '54 the Nobel Prize followed by the serious airplane crashes in the jungles of Kenya[7] that caused the physical decline of the man, first, then the writer. The advice of his doctors to break off with alcohol, the recurrence of old wounds, the exasperation, led him to end to his life prematurely.

I apologize to the reader if my memories have taken me far away from the theme that I had set out at the beginning of this book. It overpowered me, this will to state and clarify and even to bear witness that the writer Ernest Hemingway was simply a large, good, potent drinker.

And now, the person that for the publication of the penultimate novel finished prematurely and sadly his earthly life: He was the maître of the Hotel Gritti Palace at the time that Hemingway lived there in the months of autumn 1954.[8]

The writer immediately noticed the professionalism and elegance with which he carried out his work, moreover it was noticed and appreciated by the directors of the hotel and from the upper hierarchy of the company (CIGA).[9] Hemingway watched him for a long time, during every occasion of the day, and finally consecrated him in his book with the appellation of *Gran Maestro*. When the novel was finished and put to press, it arrived in the hands of a very rich American widow, Mrs. Lena Usinger, proprietor (of the Hot Dogs of America).[10] Her attention and interest in meeting the *Gran Maestro* in person was such that she booked a suite in the Gritti and, arriving full of energy (although she was more than seventy years old), began her observations, initially with discretion, then with more and more interest to see for herself if the writer had truly described this man so elegant, deferential, cultured. In short, he was a personage of another time, with whom she, two thousand miles away, had fallen in love with at first "read." Not to dwell over it, within three years he would retire to his native Treviso, and without fanfare or any loss of precious time she professed her love and her intention to marry him. The terms were very precise and did not involve reciprocating the affection that she had already expressed. To her it was enough that he became a faithful and devoted companion for the project of long trips around the world in the most beautiful places.

Mr. Vittorio Calzavara ("Victor" for the English clientele) for a moment was silent, stayed without breath, contrary to his otherwise imperturbable security and sense of humor... He was certainly a free man, also a widower, although he had a married daughter, and two sisters that loved him and cuddled him as if he were still their baby brother. He had finally decided to retire in his small villa of Treviso with a garden and greenhouse; that dream unfortunately remained unrealized.

Mrs. Lena, the rich American, insisted, showed a vitality and an enthusiasm for life and travel (to say nothing of her inextinguishable resources), did so much to undermine little by little the resistance of the *Gran Maestro* that after two months of assiduous courtship he decided to consent.

After the season he resigned, and they left together for the United States, where he was presented to the entire patriarchal family. The marriage was celebrated, and the honeymoon was a two-month-long cruise. In the spring followed another trip, and during the next summer they went again to Venice, lodging at the Hotel Danieli, interspersing trips and excursions to Torcello, Treviso, Asolo, and the Ville Venete.

This change of life that for any other person would have represented the realization of a cherished dream, for our "groom" signaled first a decline, then slowly a bitter and undeserved end.

For he that after years of work arrived at the apex of a brilliant career, with enormous satisfaction and recognition, by now used only to giving orders, obeyed and respected by an entire brigade of colleagues, to find himself out of the blue, albeit in wealth, having to think, advise, plan, materially help to select even the toilettes suitable for the evening galas and in short to help her to doll up, almost dress her (from the moment that they were married, she had fired her lady companion). It was too much.

All this new life for him—insignificant, empty, stressful, and a little degrading—brought him slowly to a debasement so profound that it undermined his strong fiber; in two years he fell ill. He requested and was able to return and stay for a brief period in his Treviso, while she stayed and tanned herself on the beach of the Excelsior.[11] In his Treviso he found a little serenity, but it was only for a little while. He died in his style, simple, dignified, surrounded with the affection of his two sisters and of his daughter back from her London home. A premature end. This is not the only sad memory that followed the penultimate work of Ernest Hemingway. Another inexplicable mourning occurred perhaps as consequence of this novel, and this time did not go unobserved in the "Venezia Inn" as that of the anonymous *Gran Maestro*, that I wanted to remember here. This last that crushed a much younger life was for a long time the most-discussed topic in the parlors of Venice.

Notes

From *Ricordi del barman Ruggero Caumo all'Harry's Bar* (Venice: Vin Veneto, 1999), 69–77.

1. Giuseppe Cipriani (1900–1980), the owner of Harry's Bar in Venice, was immortalized by Hemingway in *Across the River and into the Trees*. The legend is that Cipriani never drank with his clientele; Hemingway was the only exception.

2. Hemingway was eighteen when he joined the Red Cross.

3. The retreat of Caporetto was in November 1917; Hemingway did not arrive in Italy until June 1918.

4. Harry's Bar in Paris is located at 5 rue Daunou, where it has been since its inception in 1911.

5. *Death in the Afternoon* (1932) was published before *Green Hills of Africa* (1935).

6. In the novel, the characters drink copious amounts of Valpolicella wine, from the Valpantena area.

7. The Hemingways suffered two plane crashes in East Africa on January 23 and 24, 1954. The Nobel Prize announcement was October 28, 1954.

8. Hemingway stayed at the Gritti Hotel beginning on March 23, 1954 and stayed until early May.

9. Compagnia Italiana Grandi Alberghi, the company that owns some of Italy's most prominent hotels.

10. Lena Usinger was the daughter of Fred Usinger, the founder of a successful sausage company in Milwaukee.

11. The Excelsior is an opulent hotel on the beach of the Lido in Venice.

Hemingway's Italy in Context

3

Ernest, Hadley, and Italy

SCOTT DONALDSON

When Ernest Hemingway came back from the wars in January 1919, it was with the expectation that Agnes von Kurowsky would soon follow and that they could be married. The "Dear Ernest" letter arriving in March put an end to the marriage plan but not to Hemingway's enthusiasm for Italy and the Italians—he'd written his parents from the Milan hospital about how much he admired the country's war effort, showing no signs of the disillusionment so vividly on display a decade later in *A Farewell to Arms*.

Eighteen months later, when Ernest met Hadley Richardson and began their courtship, he was still very much an Italophile. During the interim, he had made friends within Chicago's substantial Italian-American community. A group of them gathered at the Hemingway house in Oak Park to honor Ernest as a warrior wounded in their homeland, shocking Dr. Hemingway with their spirited drinking and boisterous behavior. In Chicago, Ernest made repeated visits to the Venice Café, an Italian-American hangout, and boxed on rooftops with Nick Neroni, who, like him, had served in Italy during the war. He folded some of these people and places into the apprentice fiction he was writing. Those stories were immature, unpublishable, but the rejections did not discourage him from his drive to pursue a writing career. When Hadley came along, devotedly supportive of this goal, he was eager to show her where he had been stationed and wounded and recovered, to visit other cities in Italy as well, and, quite possibly, to become full-fledged expatriates living there.

Hadley harbored some practical reservations about that prospect, but was reluctant to dampen the enthusiasm of the young man eight years her junior. From the beginning she recognized that Ernest would play the dominant role in their marriage. She would love him, take care of him, invest all of herself (and her trust fund) in his writing career. But she knew that her handsome husband-to-be, charged with vitality, was wonderfully attractive to men, women, children, and even dogs, and that there would always be rivals for his affections.

Jim Gamble, for instance. Gamble had befriended Hemingway during wartime service in Italy. A captain with the Red Cross, the wealthy Gamble drove Hemingway to Fossalta di Piave, where he was severely wounded in July 1918. He visited Hemingway in the Red Cross hospital in Milan where he was recuperating—and falling in love with Agnes. In October, Hemingway went back to the front but almost immediately came down with jaundice. Once again Gamble was there, driving him back to Milan to recover. Then he invited Hemingway to spend part of the Christmas holidays with him in a villa he'd rented in Taormina, Sicily.

In a letter to E. E. (Chink) Dorman-Smith, the Anglo-Irish officer he'd encountered at the officers' club in Milan, Hemingway denied that he'd ever reached Taormina. He'd set out for that destination, he claimed, but was waylaid by his hostess in the first hotel where he stopped. She'd hid his clothes and kept him to herself for a week. This was fiction, not fact, for Hemingway and Gamble spent that week together in Taormina, and bonded there. The war was over, and Gamble made the young ambulance driver an offer that was difficult to refuse: that he stay on in Italy for a year as his secretary and companion, all expenses paid.

Agnes scotched that plan, fearing that it would turn Ernest into a bum, a sponger, a floater. She sent him back to the States on the understanding that she would join him when her term of duty as a nurse was over. Meanwhile, Hemingway stayed in touch with Gamble. On March 3, shortly *before* the devastating breakup letter from Agnes arrived, he wrote his former Red Cross captain, rhapsodizing about Taormina and their nighttime strolls, pleasantly "illuminated," through the beautiful Sicilian city, watching the moon path on the sea below and Mount Etna fuming above. He yearned to be back there, and raised a glass in memory to Gamble, his "Chief."

Gamble was in Philadelphia by that time. When Hemingway's letter, which had been mailed overseas, finally reached him in mid-April, he responded immediately. Not a day had gone by when Jim had not thought of him, he told Ernest. Italy was out for the time being, but he invited Hemingway to join him at "his place in the mountains" at Eagles Mere, Pennsylvania (qtd. in Griffin 116). Jim would paint, Ernest should bring his typewriter along (Jim had a few stories to suggest), and together they could enjoy the beauty of springtime, with "practically nobody" around to disturb them (116).

Emotionally undone by the jilting, Hemingway did not accept that invitation. He kept the door open, though, and in December 1920, just as Ernest and Hadley were agreeing to an engagement, Gamble once again asked Hemingway to join him for five months in Italy, this time in Rome. At the time Ernest was editing and writing most of the material for the *Cooperative Commonwealth*, the house organ of what turned out to be a fraudulently run organization. It was scut work at best, and used up much of the energy he wanted to invest in his fiction. Jim Gamble's proposal sounded wonderful to him.

Quite naturally, he wanted to know Hadley's reaction before making any commitment. Ernest must have mentioned the overture from Gamble before Hadley's December 20 letter, with its comment that "Jim Gamble sounds great if you like him so." On December 23 Ernest replied, apologizing for not being able to accept her invitation to come to St. Louis for a New Year's Eve party. He was broke, he explained, having spent too much on Christmas presents for his younger siblings, and couldn't afford the trip. Then he added, by way of reassurance, that "Jim Gamble is great, and I love him a lot. But not like I love you."

The prospective journey to Rome came to a head with Gamble's cable and letter of December 27. Jim proposed that they sail on the *Rochambeau*, leaving New York Tuesday, January 4, 1921, but was prepared to adjust plans to conform to Ernest's wishes. He also inquired what had been going on in Ernest's life since they last communicated—"Married? Writing? Making money, or what?"—and added that the trip would be inexpensive, with the lira "only worth three cents."

In his cabled reply of the 27th Ernest did not say either yes or no. Here's how the wire read: "Rather go to Rome with you than heaven Stop." Then, crossed out, "Not married." "But am broke stop Too sad for words stop Writing and selling it stop." Then again, written on the side of the page and crossed out, "Unmarried." "[B]ut don't get rich stop all authors poor first then rich stop. me no exception stop Wouldn't we have a great time stop Lord how I envy you" (*Letters* 1: 260; signed "Hemmy").

In pleading poverty with Gamble, Ernest may have been seeking further confirmation of the exact financial arrangements. No record survives of his reply, but two days later, Ernest wrote Hadley that things were "all up in the air" and he was liable to leave Tuesday for five months of writing under ideal conditions in Rome. He could send articles to the *Cooperative Commonwealth* about the cooperative movement in Europe to help make ends meet, at the thirty-lire-to-a-dollar exchange rate. Y. K. Smith, his landlord in Chicago, said he was "an utter damned fool" if he didn't go (*Letters* 1: 262). His father favored it, too. What did Hadley think?

Hadley must have been distressed about the proposal, but struck exactly the right notes in her comments about it. Earlier, she had written Ernest that she would miss him "pretty frightfully" unless the five-month absence resulted in a "great gain" to his work (qtd. in Reynolds, *Young Hemingway*, 171). Still, she commented in her Christmas day letter, "I suppose it would be just as much fun to write and hear from you in Rome as in Chicago" (qtd. in Griffin 151). But in her special delivery letter of December 31, responding to a specific query about five months with an ocean between them, she wrote, "I hope you can tell me the reasons for and against Rome" (*Letters* 1: 262fn3). So far Ernest had insisted on the pros, and ignored the cons.

If he was still in doubt about whether to accept Gamble's offer, it may have been Hadley's report on New Year's Eve that settled the question. She went to the party with Dick Pierce and told Ernest all about it. At the University Club "there was so much to drink you never saw the like" and dancing to a ragtime band. After midnight Dick and a few others came back to her house for more to drink, and she'd kissed him "in the quietest way" (qtd. in Griffin 151). Suitably jealous, Ernest wrote back that he was afraid of leaving her alone, and thereafter they began to talk of going to Italy *together*.

On January 12, Ernest wrote Hadley about making a "bold penniless dash for Wopland" (qtd. in Mellow 132), specifically to Milan. They'd find an apartment with a piano for her music, he could devote himself to his fiction, and whenever they wished they could go to the massive Duomo where, he hoped, Hadley would join him in prayer as Agnes had not, or to the convent of Santa Maria delle Grazie to see da Vinci's *Last Supper* flaking away on the refectory wall.

"To hell with the beaten path" (qtd. in Griffin 153), Ernest commented, so it became Hadley's job to become the sensible partner. Their Italian plans had "to be thought out, not felt out" (154), she cautioned. If they had to live in poverty overseas, she feared she might become a hindrance to him instead of a helpmate. Thereupon Ernest began converting much of his fifty-dollar-a-week salary from the *Cooperative Commonwealth* from dollars into lire, and at least once Hadley sent him a "filthy lucre check" for the same purpose (173). And he also spent more time practicing demotic Italian with Nick Neroni.

In March, when Ernest spent three days in Saint Louis visiting Hadley, he brought along a few bottles of Italian wine and told her for the first time about the night he was wounded. He loved Italy, he said, not because he'd fought there but because it was a civilized—in other words, tolerant—country. Over time, Hadley learned to share her fiance's enthusiasm. At his suggestion, Hadley read G. K. Chesterton's account of Browning's extended stay in Italy. It became more or less settled between them that after they were married in September they would embark for la bell'Italia. A local doctor in Saint Louis warned Hadley that childbirth might be more difficult there than in the United States, because Italian doctors used anesthetics more sparingly. But never mind, Hadley decided. "If we don't take Italy now," she wrote Ernest, "when might it be shoved off to?" (186).

In the end, of course, they embarked not for Milan but for Paris, armed with letters of introduction from Sherwood Anderson to American expatriates such as Gertrude Stein and Ezra Pound. Living at Y. K. and Doodles Smiths' freeloving and freewheeling sort-of-salon over the summer months of 1921, Ernest met and made a favorable impression on both Anderson and the Chicago poet Carl Sandburg. Anderson in particular went out of his way to give the promising young writer a boost. Perhaps Ernest had shown him some of the novel he'd started writing about a character named Nick Adams; Hadley was "wild" about it.

In his letters from his Chicago digs to Hadley's home in Saint Louis, three hundred miles away, Ernest kept her apprised of evenings he'd spent in the company of other women. Lynn, who looked fetching "topside of a horse," for example, Frances, who provided "friendly company," the "lovely Jewess Irene" Goldstein from Petoskey (qtd. in Griffin 166), and Doodles herself, who'd made a pass at him as well as at several others. Hadley, predictably upset, warned him that it was "a sin" to have an affair "out of a sense of boredom or obligation with someone you're indifferent to" (166). For the most part, though, Ernest kept silent about his relations with Katy Smith, Hadley's girlhood friend, still her most serious rival, and—if the copulation between Wemedge (Ernest) and Butstein (Katy) in Hemingway's story "Summer People" was not invented—Ernest's lover as well.

Katy had good reason to be disturbed about the engagement of Hadley Richardson and Ernest Hemingway, for she was responsible for throwing them together. They met in October 1920 at a party in Y. K. Smith's apartment. Hadley was there at the invitation of Katy, sister to Y. K. and Bill Smith. Katy and Hadley had been classmates at Mary Institute in Saint Louis, and although Katy was far more an independent "new woman" than Hadley—she'd graduated from the University of Missouri and was pursuing a career as a journalist—they had kept in touch ever since.

Hadley's strong-willed mother treated her as a virtual invalid from childhood through adolescence and young womanhood. So when her mother died in August 1920, Hadley was ready and eager, at nearly twenty-nine, to take charge of her life. In asking her to come to Chicago, Katy may have had it in mind to help liberate her friend from an oppressive background. She could hardly have anticipated, though, how well the evening would work out for Hadley, and how badly for herself. Katy learned that night a lesson that Hadley herself was to learn several years later—the danger of involving Ernest Hemingway with an attractive friend.

Hemingway arrived at the party accompanied by Bill Smith. Ernest had known the Smiths for years, for they were neighbors during the summers that both families spent in northern Michigan. Bill was a favorite fishing companion and close friend. As for Katy, although she, like Hadley, was eight years Ernest's senior—she'd seen him grow from a callow ten-year-old to a remarkably good-looking young man—she was now in love with him. And there could be no doubt that he cut a dashing figure: handsome, with dark hair, a wide grin, flashing brown eyes, and an Italian officer's cape draped across his shoulders. Slim and tall, he bore little resemblance to the bearded and rugged Papa Hemingway of later years. In photographs from that time, he looks rather like a young T. S. Eliot.

Ernest was immediately drawn to the new young woman from Saint Louis. He liked Hadley's red hair and golden good looks and beautiful figure and the dress she'd bought for the party. He liked her for the way she was: in Gioia Diliberto's description, "unpretentious, submissive, intelligent, sexy, tough in spirit" (x). And they had a great deal in common as upper-middle-class midwesterners born to dominant mothers and deeply disturbed fathers: Ernest's father was to kill himself in 1928, just as Hadley's had done in 1905. Both were eager to free themselves from these unhealthy situations. "The world's a jail, and we're going to break it together" (Sokoloff 1), Hadley wrote him soon after they met.

Both had artistic ambitions, too: Ernest as a writer, and Hadley as a musician, but with the significant difference that once liberated from her confinement Hadley devoted herself to *his* future.

Hadley stayed on in Chicago for three weeks after the night of the party, and by the end of that time she and Ernest were beginning to talk about marriage. Katy Smith was embittered at being cast aside for her former school friend. "You have no judgment," she told Hadley when she heard of their engagement (qtd. in Sokoloff 52). The marriage couldn't last. If they did get married, Katy fantasized that she might join them in a ménage à trois. Hadley worried that she too might be discarded by her young lover. "The story of how you gyped Butstein makes me weak in the knees for my own future," she wrote Ernest. "I say it would be *unscroopulous* to work me that way" (52).

So there, confronting Hadley during her engagement, were Katy, who continued to see Ernest in Chicago, and the ghost of Agnes von Kurowsky he'd not yet exorcised, and various Chicago women, and Marjorie Bump, Irene Goldstein, and Grace Quinlan, the Petoskey girls he'd consorted with after the war, and, above all, the unusual pattern of the Hemingway family dynamics.

Ernest grew up in a household full of females. His three closest siblings were girls: Marcelline a year older, Ursula three years younger, and Madelaine (Sunny) five years his junior. Ernest and his older sister were "twinned" by their mother. She held Marcelline back so that they were in the same class in school, and dressed them alike during their early years: both wore skirts when the family was in Oak Park, and both donned boys' attire up in Michigan. (Much has been made of the psychological effects of this twinning, particularly by biographer Kenneth Lynn.) Despite or perhaps because of this process, Ernest felt closer to the two younger sisters, and closest of all to Ursula, who appears as Littless, his worshipful companion in "The Last Good Country"—another story, like "Summer People," that closely paralleled Hemingway's actual experiences in Michigan, and that he withheld from publication during his lifetime. He was used to being admired by the younger sisters as bigger, bolder, and more assertive, and coveted that kind of admiration from others as well: from Grace Quinlan, seven years younger, for example, and—later in life—from a succession of youthful women he called "Daughter."

In preparations for marriage to Hadley at Horton Bay in September 1921, Ernest insisted on inviting all of his Petoskey girlfriends and Agnes as well. Somewhat reluctantly, Katy came as a bridesmaid. The honeymoon was not auspicious. The couple stayed at Windemere, the Hemingway cottage in Michigan, where the neighbors kept telling Hadley "what a wonderful *young* man" she'd married (Diliberto 90). (He'd coached her, when meeting strangers, to say that he was thirty, not his actual twenty-two, but that fiction wouldn't work in the northern Michigan homes where he and his family were well known.) One day Ernest took Hadley to visit Marjorie Bump and Grace Quinlan so that she could meet the women he'd rejected for her. Grace seemed terribly embarrassed and, though cockeyed in love with her husband, Hadley resented this exercise of male vanity. She was beginning to understand that her husband would always want other women around.

When the newlyweds arrived in Paris in December 1921, they were able to live comfortably on the favorable exchange rates of dollars versus francs and two sources of money: Hadley's trust fund, once her mother's will had been probated, and Ernest's income as a newspaperman. Though barely of voting age, Ernest had wrangled a dream job as a foreign correspondent for the Toronto papers, both the *Daily Star* and the weekend feature-oriented *Star Weekly*. The space-rates pay for his dispatches was merely adequate, but the papers also paid salary and expenses when he was on assignment. On that basis Hemingway went to Genoa to cover the international economics conference in April 1922, to Constantinople for the end of the Greco-Turkish War in October 1922, and to Lausanne for the peace talks in November and December 1922. On these trips he met and learned from such prominent journalists as Lincoln Steffens and William Bolitho Ryall: figures as influential in establishing his worldview—his Weltanschauung—as Stein and Pound were in developing his writing.

These travels around Europe were highly educational for Ernest, but Hadley objected to trips that took him away from home for weeks at a time, resulted in some highly irregular financial practices, and, on the end-of-the-war assignment, placed him in harm's way. That led to their first serious marital dispute.

Hemingway spent nearly a month in Genoa, and mailed or cabled twenty-three articles back to Toronto. Most of these were anecdotal pieces. The young reporter was a quick study, but where issues were concerned he affected an authority he had not earned. No matter: the Toronto papers wanted color, and he supplied it. His copy was enlivened by irreverent and candid glimpses of the leading statesmen of the day. Chancellor Joseph Wirth of Germany, he wrote, looked like a tuba player in an oompahpah band. Jean-Louis Barthou, leader of the French delegation, resembled the left-hand Smith brother on the cough-drop box. Prime Minister David Lloyd George, given his youthful complexion, might have been mistaken for "a boy subaltern just out of Sandhurst" (*DT* 166).

John Bone, Ernest's boss in Toronto, was pleased with the dispatches. The paper paid him well enough to finance an extensive trip in the summer. Ernest took that opportunity to introduce Hadley to his Italy on the first of their two journeys there in 1922 and 1923. Both began from the Gangwisches' pension in Chamby-sur-Montreux, the inexpensive and friendly retreat in the Swiss Alps they'd discovered shortly after arriving overseas.

Chink Dorman-Smith joined them in Chamby for some fishing and mountain climbing, and then the three of them hiked over the Great St. Bernard Pass into Italy. It was a tough journey for Hadley, who gamely tried to keep pace despite lacking proper hiking boots for the heavy snow. On reaching Italy, she and Ernest stayed in Aosta for a few days while she recovered from swollen legs and blistered feet. Then they ventured on an Italian tour to revisit the sites of his 1918 wartime service.

Milan: the building on the Via Manzoni that served as the Red Cross hospital, the Duomo, and Biffi's restaurant. Schio: Ernest's first post in Italy he remembered as "one of the finest places on earth" and the Due Spadi hotel. Fossalta on the Piave: where he had been wounded. The Hemingways saw them all, but nothing was the same. The weather was rainy, the Due Spadi had become "a small mean inn," and in Fossalta, where thousands had died, he could find no sign of the war beyond a single rusty shell fragment.

"[D]on't ever go back," he wrote fellow volunteer Bill Horne in Chicago, "because it is all gone and Italy is all gone" (*Letters* 2: 33). Chasing yesterdays was "a bum show" (*DT* 180).

Shortly after their summer sojourn in Italy, Ernest left Hadley alone in Paris to cover the end of the war in Constantinople. Hadley did not want him to go. It would be dangerous in Turkey, with the war not quite ended, and she would be lonely in his absence. Then, too, she objected to the double-dipping deal Ernest made with Frank Mason of the International News Service to send dispatches to the INS under the name of John Hadley that closely mirrored the ones he was writing as Ernest Hemingway, supposedly on an exclusive basis, for the Toronto papers, and to be paid by both outlets. Ernest and Hadley were not on speaking terms when he left at the end of September.

But she could forgive him almost anything, and when he returned from Turkey three weeks later, weak and exhausted from malaria and dysentery, Hadley comforted and cosseted her husband back to health. By the time he left yet again in late November, this time for the peace negotiations in Lausanne, they were once more a happily married couple.

In Lausanne, Hemingway took on a daunting schedule, covering hard news for both the morning and evening Hearst news services (INS and Universal) under the same John Hadley pseudonym he'd used in Turkey. This time, though, he did not duplicate this coverage in articles for Toronto. Nothing he wrote from Switzerland appeared in the *Daily Star* or *Star Weekly* until well after the Lausanne conference had ended.

In loving letters to Hadley, Ernest complained about his heavy workload, appealing to her for the sympathy he knew she would supply and encouraging her to come to Lausanne as soon as her bout with the flu would allow. Meanwhile, in his rare moments of free time, Hemingway listened, rapt, as Ryall (who wrote for the *Manchester Guardian* as William Bolitho) discoursed on "the malady of power" (*BL* 226)—the way in which political dignitaries came to believe only in themselves and to distrust everyone else. Caustic and brilliant, Ryall had a gift for debunking those in authority that suited Hemingway's own proclivities.

Under Ryall's guidance, for example, Hemingway changed his mind about Benito Mussolini. Seven months earlier, when he and Hadley were in Milan, he had interviewed Mussolini and written a feature for the *Toronto*

Daily Star that presented the Italian leader in a favorable light. "Mussolini was a great surprise," Hemingway told his readers, not at all "the monster" he had been pictured but something of an intellectual (*DT* 173), a big brown-faced man with a slow smile who fondled the ears of a wolfhound puppy as they talked.

That piece ran on June 24, 1922. On January 27, 1923, Ernest once again featured Mussolini in the *Star*, this time as "the biggest bluff in Europe" (*DT* 255), a theatrical character of no substance. In an anecdote perhaps too good to be true, he cited the press conference Mussolini had called in Lausanne as evidence. Mussolini stayed deep in concentration, absorbed in a book, as two hundred correspondents crowded into the room. Hemingway "tiptoed over behind him" to see what he was reading: "It was a French-English dictionary—held upside down" (255). He also disparaged Mussolini's dramatic attire, as had Ryall. Hemingway wrote: "There is something wrong, even histrionically, with a man who wears white spats with a black shirt" (255). Ryall similarly observed: "We will never have Fascism in England; no Englishman will dress up, not even for a revolution."

In Lausanne, also, he told Steffens—who was then between wives—that he'd never gotten over Agnes von Kurowsky, and would probably have to abandon Hadley for her if their affair resumed. He knew that Agnes's engagement to an Italian officer had fallen through and decided to write her a letter, telling her that he was married and living in Paris, beginning to have some success as a writer and journalist, and—it may be (his letter has not survived)—proposing that they might reconnect. If so, Ernest must have been disappointed by her reply. In her letter, which Hemingway saved, Agnes congratulated him on his marriage and promising career but made a point of insisting that she had been right to break off their relationship. And she offered, in closing, only a virtual handshake.

In *The Paris Wife*, Paula McLain invented a scene in which Ernest more or less asked Hadley's permission to write to Agnes, and one of his biographers depicts Ernest telling his wife when Agnes's reply arrived. But there is no evidence that Hadley knew anything about her husband's overture, or Agnes's answer. That was Ernest's secret, something that would always lie between them.

As did the lost valise, the crucial event dividing the couple's two Italian trips and, very likely, the single occurrence most responsible for the dissolution of their marriage. A lot of misinformation has been circulated about the valise and what Ernest did when he found that the serious writing he'd been sweating over in Paris, the vignettes and stories he really cared about, had gone missing in the Gare de Lyon when Hadley—on her way to Lausanne on the evening of December 3, 1922—briefly left her suitcase and a valise containing Ernest's fiction in her compartment at the Gare de Lyon and returned to discover the suitcase still there, the valise gone.

Much of this misinformation came from Hemingway himself, in both published and unpublished material. In his writing, there is no reliable boundary between fact and fiction, and that was the way he wanted it. He was particularly annoyed by critics who accused him of simply converting his own experiences into stories and novels. "I write some stories absolutely as they happen" (*SL* 400), he told Max Perkins, while others he invented completely, and nobody could tell which was which.

What is certain is that he took the loss hard. "It was a bad time" (*MF-RE* 70), Ernest said, and for a while thereafter he did not feel he could write again. For seven long weeks after the Lausanne conference ended, back in Chamby for the winter sports and good fellowship, Ernest took his friend Chink's advice to "[n]ever discuss casualties" and kept epistolary silence. Finally, on January 23, he unburdened himself to Ezra Pound.

"I suppose you heard about the loss of my Juvenilia?" he began. "I went up to Paris last week to see what was left and found that Hadley had made the job complet[e] by including all carbons, duplicates etc. . . . You naturally would say, 'Good' etc.," Ernest went on. "But don't say it to me. I aint yet reached that mood. . . . 3 years on the damn stuff, some like that Paris 1922 [these were vignettes] I fancied" (*Letters* 2: 6). Hemingway exaggerated how much had been lost and the time he took to write it, but he was right about Pound's reaction to the news.

The loss was a good thing, "an act of Gawd" (*SL* 77n2), Ezra insisted. Besides, memory was the best critic. All Ernest had lost was the time it would take him to rewrite the parts he could remember. If the form of a story was right, one "ought to be able to reassemble it from memory. . . . If the thing wobbles and won't reform then . . . it never would have been right." All of that provided cold comfort to Hemingway. "I thank you for your advice to a young man on the occasion of the loss by stealing of his complete works," Ernest replied with exquisite sarcasm. "It is very sound. I thank you again" (*Letters* 2: 10).

Very likely Ernest and Hadley were in Chamby when John Hadley Nicanor Hemingway, called Bumby, was conceived. They had plenty of company during much of their two-month stay in the mountains. Dave and Barbara O'Neil came from Saint Louis, along with their two grown-up sons, one daughter, and a friend described as "the lovely Janet Phelan" (qtd. in Reynolds, *Paris Years*, 94). Chink Dorman-Smith was on hand through the holidays, and was replaced by Isabelle Simmons when he left early in January. Ernest had written Isabelle an enthusiastic letter urging her to come and singing the praises of Chamby. "We'll have a wonderful time," he assured her (*Letters* 1: 375). They'd go bobsledding and skiing, do a lot of reading, and enjoy good fellowship in the evenings.

Pretty and intelligent, Isabelle grew up down the block from Ernest in Oak Park, but she was a few years younger and they only became friends after he returned from the war. At Chamby, she and Hadley immediately bonded. They knitted sweaters, read the same books, and formed a three-way triad with Ernest. Actually, it was more a harem than a triad, and innocent enough. The day Izzy (as she was called) arrived, the Paris edition of the *Chicago Tribune* reported from Constantinople that "[t]here was joy in the Sultan's abandoned harem" (Reynolds, *Paris Years*, 94). It was payday, and eleven sultanas were awarded checks from the nationalist government ranging from sixty-five to ninety dollars. On the following day, Hadley, Izzy, Barbara O'Neil, and Janet Phelan started calling themselves "Hemingway's harem." It was all in good fun. Hadley was happy to share her man in such an amusing way, and Ernest welcomed the female attention.

When Izzy left to continue her European tour, Hadley wrote her how much she was missed, for now there was no one around to "express . . . things in a delightful and utterly congenial and feminine way." In line with the harem motif, she referred to Ernest as "the Moslem" and signed herself "Fatima" (qtd. in Reynolds, *Paris Years*, 98). Three years later, writing to congratulate Isabelle on her marriage to the scholar Francis R. B. (Frisco) Godolphin, Ernest told her that her place in the harem was "still open and being held open and will be held open and just let . . . anybody try and usurp it" (*Letters* 2: 426).

By mid-February the snow turned to slush and the Hemingways' winter companions all left. There were only two of them in Chamby, or rather two plus the child they now knew was on its way. Hadley thought a warm climate would be good for her pregnancy. Ernest was seeking a fresh venue to escape the writer's block that had descended with the loss of his manuscripts. Ezra Pound urged them to come to Rapallo, where he and his wife Dorothy Shakespear were living. The weather was fine, Pound said. The painter Mike Strater was in town and eager for some vigorous exercise with Ernest. They could get room and board at the Hotel Splendide for only 500 lire (twenty-five dollars) a week. Given such encouragement, Ernest and Hadley packed up and took the train to Rapallo.

Hadley was entranced by her first sight of the Ligurian coast, lush and green even in midwinter. She and Ernest kissed as their train went through a tunnel beyond Genoa. Coming out, she could see olive trees on one side and on the other the pastel houses of Rapallo and the sea below, very blue. "Why didn't you ever tell me about this before?" she asked. Ernest was less impressed with the city, which had been a favorite Italian stopping place for writers—Wordsworth and Keats among them—since the late eighteenth century. "The place ain't much," he wrote Gertrude Stein (*Letters* 2: 11). The sea looked "weak" (11), it rained a lot, and the fascist son of the hotel proprietor stared insultingly at the guests.

Besides, Mike Strater sprained his ankle and couldn't give Hemingway the competition in boxing and tennis he wanted. (Strater used some of his downtime to paint portraits of both Ernest and Hadley). And Ezra Pound took off soon after they arrived, possibly to pursue one of his frequent extramarital liaisons. Both he and Mike believed that artists needed multiple lovers to fuel their creativity.

Sexually, though, Ernest and Hadley were as active as they'd ever been. As he wrote in an unpublished sketch, "Cats love in the garden.... The big cat gets on the small cat. Sweeney gets on Mrs. Porter. Hadley and I ... are happiest in bed. There are no problems in bed" (qtd. in Reynolds, *Paris Years*, 103–4).

Out of bed, however, Ernest was in a sour mood. The lost valise still rankled, and both Strater and Pound commiserated with him. "You know, Mike," he said to Strater, "if you had those manuscripts in your [care], you would not have left them to go get something to read." Pound, more judgmental, told Robert McAlmon (another expatriate visiting Rapallo at that time) that he thought Hadley had lost the manuscripts deliberately.

Biographers and scholars have explored the depths writing about that incident, going inside the minds of both husband and wife.

Michael Reynolds in *The Paris Years*: The loss gave Ernest an inescapable advantage in the marital relationship. As he reconstructed the scene at the railway station in Lausanne, when Hadley gave him the terrible news, "[i]t was different between them now. He saw it in her face. Whatever else happened between them, he would always have this edge. As they hugged and he kissed away her tears, perhaps Hadley knew it as well" (90).

Jeffrey Meyers in *Hemingway: A Biography*:

> the loss was irrevocably connected in Hemingway's mind with sexual infidelity.... [He] now had something to hold against her—for he never forgot an injury.... The loss of his creative work when he was in Lausanne probably influenced his fictional portrayal of the loss of Catherine Barkley's baby in Montreux [in *A Farewell to Arms*]. In the novel he vicariously got rid of the unwanted infant just as Hadley (subconsciously, if not deliberately) got rid of the manuscripts that had kept them apart, day and night. (70)

Alice Sokoloff in *Hadley*: Meyers's comments were "too harsh," like those of various others who blamed Hadley's packing and losing all of her husband's manuscripts on her "busybodyness," "inexcusable negligence," "silliness," and "stupidity." As an alternative Diliberto suggested that the loss of the valise may have been caused, at least subconsciously, by Hadley's passive-aggressive personality, and cited as a parallel of her letting Ernest's unwelcome Christmas present of 1920—a second-hand beaded handbag—slip overboard into Walloon Lake "accidentally."

Was Hadley's a subversive act? "Was she trying to sabotage his career?" as readers of Paula McLain's best-selling *The Paris Wife* asked her. Not really, McLain answered, and yet:

> Well, of course she was jealous because she felt abandoned. The most important thing in the world to him was his work, and the most important thing in the world to her was him. There is no balance there, and that can be devastating. People also don't like—women don't like—the timing of the loss of the manuscripts and then her becoming pregnant.... It feels slightly manipulative, and yet a woman hearing the pounding of the biological clock, we get it. (qtd. in Sinclair 121)

It doesn't do to invest too much faith in such psychological speculations. Sometimes a cigar is just a cigar, a mistake only a mistake.

Despite the rain and the fascists, it was in Rapallo that Ernest began to recover from the blow of the missing manuscripts. The agent behind his recovery was a shy American named Edward O'Brien, compiler of an annual volume, *Best Short Stories*, who was staying as a boarder in a monastery above the city. Hemingway showed O'Brien his story "My Old Man," the only thing he had to show, for it had been in the mail and come back, rejected, from *Cosmopolitan*, and so escaped the theft at the Gare de Lyon. O'Brien was so impressed by the racetrack story, with its echoes of Sherwood Anderson, that he broke his own rules and accepted it for *Best Short Stories* on the spot, although all of the anthologized stories were supposed to have appeared initially in magazines. He also went one step further by dedicating the volume to Hemingway (or "Hemenway," as the book printed it). That kind of unstinting if misspelled support gave Ernest the boost he needed to start writing again. He was learning, as his mentor Ryall maintained, that the most important thing in life was not to capitalize on one's gains—any fool could do that—but to profit from one's losses.

When Pound returned to Rapallo, the two couples—Ernest and Hadley, Ezra and his beautiful wife Dorothy, who made no objection to her husband's serial adulteries—set off on a walking tour through the Romagna. Pound wanted to retrace the steps of Sigismondo Malatesta as research for his *Cantos*, and as they traveled past Pisa and Siena to Orbetello, Ernest contributed military commentary on the battlefield exploits of the fifteenth-century Malatesta. It was a good trip, Hadley thought, and their next stop in Italy was even better.

That was Cortina d'Ampezzo in the Dolomites north of Venice. Isabelle Simmons briefly joined the Hemingways there in her ideal triangular role of companion to Hadley and admirer of Ernest. In due course Izzy went back to the States and was succeeded by the talented pianist Renata Borgatti, a lesbian whose sexual orientation posed no threat to the Hemingways' marriage.

The bracing mountain air in Cortina recharged Ernest's creative engine. The stories that emerged reflected his emotional difficulties and may have helped to heal the wounds. He wrote "Out of Season" there, a story deriving its power from the tension between a fictional husband and wife. In the months thereafter, he produced "A Very Short Story," which in its bitter attack on Agnes ("Luz" in the story) may have released Ernest from his yearning for her. And later he fetched out the notes he had made in Rapallo to address the issue of premature fatherhood in "Cat in the Rain," a story manifestly more sympathetic to the "American wife" than to the husband who neglects her.

In mid-March 1923 Ernest left on assignment to write a series of articles for Toronto on rampant inflation in the Ruhr. Hadley stayed in Cortina for a while, its hotels mostly empty after the end of the skiing season. She and Renata hiked around town, wearing mountain boots and comparing notes on music and pregnancy. Hadley was happy to be pregnant. A baby would only strengthen the marriage, she felt sure, and Ernest gradually overcame his conviction that he was too young to be a father. Perhaps it was true as well, as Ernest observed in a passage cut from *A Moveable Feast*, that they had been "armored together" by the loss of the valise, for indeed he and Hadley got along very well for the next two years until, back in Paris, more dangerous triangles formed. Hadley was able to fight off the challenge of Duff Twysden. That of Pauline Pfeiffer was not to be denied.

Works Cited

Diliberto, Gioia. *Paris Without End: The True Story of Hemingway's First Wife*. New York: Harper Perennial, 2011.

Griffin, Peter. *Along with Youth: Hemingway, the Early Years*. New York: Oxford UP, 1985.

Hemingway, Ernest. *By-Line: Ernest Hemingway: Selected Articles and Dispatches of Four Decades*. Ed. William White. New York: Scribner, 1967.

———. *Dateline: Toronto: The Complete Toronto Star Dispatches, 1920–1924*. Ed. William White. New York: Scribner, 1985.

———. *The Letters of Ernest Hemingway*. Vol. 1, *1907–1922*. Ed. Sandra Spanier and Robert W. Trogdon. Cambridge, UK: Cambridge UP, 2011.

———. *The Letters of Ernest Hemingway*. Vol. 2, *1923–1925*. Ed. Sandra Spanier, Albert J. DeFazio III, and Robert W. Trogdon. Cambridge, UK: Cambridge UP, 2013.

———. *A Moveable Feast: The Restored Edition*. New York: Charles Scribner's Sons, 2014.

———. *Selected Letters, 1917–1961*. Ed. Carlos Baker. New York: Scribner, 1981.

Mellow, James R. *Hemingway: A Life without Consequences*. Reading, MA: Addison-Wesley, 1994.

Meyers, Jeffrey. *Hemingway: A Biography*. New York: Harper & Row, 1985.

Reynolds, Michael. *The Paris Years.* New York: Cambridge, MA: Basil Blackwell, 1989.
———. *The Young Hemingway.* New York: Norton, 1986.
Sinclair, Gail. "An Interview with Paula McLain, Author of *The Paris Wife.*" *Hemingway Review* 32.1 (Fall 2012): 119–27.
Sokoloff, Alice. *Hadley: The First Mrs. Hemingway.* New York: Dodd, Mead, 1973.

4

Views of Venice before Hemingway

SERGIO PEROSA

In this water-sieged, sun-drenched, and tourist-flooded city, now on the verge of collapse under their combined pressure, let me remind you that for more than a thousand years Venice was an independent republic that built an empire and became a world power: maritime, mercantile and commercial, military and territorial. She was the Queen of the Adriatic and the Levant, domineering the eastern Mediterranean Sea, its coasts and islands; she was the gateway to the East, thereby controlling the Silk Route.[1]

In the Middle Ages and the Renaissance, particularly in Elizabethan England, Venice came also to be seen and cherished as the center of culture and social splendor, looked at as one may look at New York today. In the age of Shakespeare, who was well aware of it, the myth of Venice was already well established and widely spread.

The main four points of this myth were summarized by David McPherson as:

1. Venice the wealthy (on account of her magnificence and flourishing trade, as anyone could see who visited her or received news of her urban splendor);
2. Venice the wise (on account of her "democratic" political constitution, which seemed to combine the virtues of a monarchical, oligarchic, and republican form of government);
3. Venice the just (thanks to her laws and her balanced juridical order in an age subject to the divine right of kings and the principles of absolutism);

4. Venice the gallant (for her sumptuous way of life, masquerades, festivals, and processions: the city of love and sex, famous for her numberless, learned, and refined courtesans—not a negligible attraction for visitors on the Grand Tour and on diplomatic, even academic, missions).

Her title, La Serenissima, seemed justified, though an oppositional, "dark legend" of Venice as a secret place of ruthless despotism, treachery and deceit, cruelty and corruption was also developing, descending from Christopher Marlowe, Roger Ascham, and Thomas Nashe to Thomas Moore in England and James Fenimore Cooper in America (as exemplified by Cooper's novel *The Bravo* [1831], which is set in a stereotypical Venice and was intended to show the ravages of absolute government).

It is clear that both characterizations, of beauty and darkness, were cultural, literary, and ideological constructs, representational practices and projections (as Stephen Greenblatt would call them), all the more rooted and influential for that.

Everything changed radically with the fall of the Republic to Napoleon at the end of the eighteenth century—after which an image of powerlessness, evanescence, and decay prevailed throughout the next century. Oxymoronic images and representations of beauty in decline and of transfiguration in death, reaching down from the Romantics to Thomas Mann and beyond, gradually constituted a literary topos, conceit, or *concetto* known from the title of Mann's novel (*Der Tod in Venedig*) as *Death in Venice*.

I speak of a *concetto* because death was feared, pursued, cherished, and enacted in the decay of splendor, in the excess and corruption of beauty, in the surplus and added value of crumbling art and compromised history. I will try to give some hints in preparation or as a background for what transpires in Hemingway as well, notably, but not exclusively, in his novel *Across the River and into the Trees*.

* * *

It all begins with early complaints on the historical Fall of Venice: "in the fall / Of Venice, think of thine," writes Byron (*Childe Harold's Pilgrimage*, 4.17.152–53). The fall would serve as a motto and eventually become a mirror or metaphor for the self, for a number of writers who follow in Byron's wake and in that fall find a suggestion, a seduction, and a premonition of doomed or easeful death.

William Wordsworth sets the tone in his well-known sonnet "On the Extinction of the Venetian Republic" (1802, published 1807):

> Once did She hold the gorgeous east in fee;
> And was the safeguard of the west: the worth
> Of Venice did not fall below her birth,
> Venice, the eldest Child of Liberty.
> She was a maiden City, bright and free. (1–5)

The city is specified to be "maiden" because it was never invaded or conquered before. But now "those glories fade, / Those titles vanish, and that strength decay" (9–10). In the following lines, emphasized by the rhymes, we have "its final day . . . even the Shade / Of that which once was great is passed away" (13–14), lines and stresses that will haunt the century.

For Byron, Venice was "the greenest island of my imagination" (qtd. in Tanner 30), but also, a "sea-Sodom" (*Marino Faliero* 5.3). The exaltation that inspires canto 4 of *Childe Harold's Pilgrimage* goes together with the enunciation of features of death. There Byron contemplates a "dying Glory"; on the Bridge of Sighs, in the famous beginning, one has "a Palace and a prison on each hand"; the sea-Cybele born of the Ocean seems to be mute, her palaces are crumbling (st. 3). Venice "sinks, like a sea-weed, unto whence she rose! / . . . / Even in Destruction's depth" (st. 13); she is "declined to dust" (st. 15)—but "perchance even dearer in her days of woe, / Than when she was a boast, a marvel, and a show" (st. 18).

Desolation attracts. For Shelley, too, the daughter of the Ocean, seen from afar as a glitter of light, turns into a "masque of death": her luminous and golden towers are, in fact, "Sepulchres" in human forms ("Lines Written among the Euganean Hills").

* * *

Strangely enough, it is the great singer of Venice, John Ruskin, who sowed the seeds and drew the outlines of the topos and the conceit, introducing the eminently literary element of Decadence—with a capital D—into the picture. He felt no romance in Venice. He had written to his father:

It is simply a heap of ruins "left for our beholding in the final period of her decline: a ghost upon the sands of the sea, so weak—so quiet,—so bereft of all but her loveliness, that we might well doubt, as we watched her faint reflection in the mirage of the lagoon, which was the City, and which was the Shadow." (Ruskin, *Stones of Venice* 1: 1)

Blight, stagnation, death, darkness, decline, and ruin mark the end of volume 1 of Ruskin's influential *The Stones of Venice* (1851–53); in volume 2, Time and Decay threaten the city's destruction; volume 3—significantly titled *The Fall*—registers a total disintegration. The rot and decay of Venice already show those traits with which the fin de siècle Decadents will endow her: excessive luxury and excessive refinement, intemperance, satiety, voluptuousness, morbid leanings, and aesthetic superfetation:

[Y]ear after year, the nation drank with deeper thirst from the fountains of forbidden pleasure, and dug for springs, hitherto unknown, in the dark places of the earth. In the ingenuity of indulgence, in the varieties of vanity, Venice surpassed the cities of Christendom, as of old she had surpassed them in fortitude and devotion. . . . That ancient curse was upon her, the curse of the Cities of the Plain, "Pride, fulness of bread, and abundance of idleness." . . . [S]he was consumed from her place among the nations; and her ashes are choking the channels of the dead, salt sea. (Ruskin, *Stones of Venice* 3: 165)

In spite of his conception of Venice as "the Paradise of cities," Ruskin presented a twilight view of her in the present, where the excess of beauty becomes a disease, unreality dismays, the labyrinth drags into the abyss. Venice confronts her pilgrims with a Medusa-like face: "Désespoir d'une beauté qui s'en va vers la mort" (as Maurice Barrès was to write in 1902 in *Amori et dolori sacrum*, in the chapter titled "La Mort de Venise": "une ville où nulle beauté est sans tare").

* * *

In Henry James's essay "The Grand Canal" (1892), the idea of Venice as sepulchre is overtly put forth:

[T]he essential present character of the most melancholy of cities resides simply in its being the most beautiful of tombs. Nowhere has the past been laid to rest with such tenderness, such a sadness of resignation and remembrance. Nowhere else is the present so alien, so discontinuous, so like a crowd in a cemetery without garlands for the graves. (314)

In *The Aspern Papers* (1888), Venice is a city of darkness, mystery, and mystification, where the past of the Misses Bordereau is buried and the protagonist is lost in the maze of conscience. In the short story "The Pupil" (1891) we have a cold, windswept Venice, with the rain lashing the lagoon; the city acquires a livid, lurid air, and is shaken by a "blast of desolation, a prophesy of disaster and disgrace" (159). This is already a prefiguration of the meteorological and symbolic climate—wind and rain—in which Milly Theale's emblematic death in Venice is enacted in *The Wings of the Dove* (1902): "It was a Venice all of evil that had broken out for them.... a Venice of cold lashing rain from a low black sky, of wicked wind raging through the narrow passes, of general arrest and interruption.... the rain was ugly, the wind wicked, the sea impossible" (415, 418).

It comes as no surprise that "the vice in the air, otherwise, was too much like the breath of fate" (418). We have a perfect coincidence of place and destiny, where, among the ghosts of vanishing life, Milly's fate of betrayal, dissolution, and death can be best achieved. This death in Venice has a cutting edge, it has nothing in common with the enervating, sirocco atmosphere prevailing in Thomas Mann.

Let me add that in that beautiful novel-confession *The Desire and Pursuit of the Whole* (ca. 1908), by Frederic Rolfe, Baron Corvo, the protagonist's quest in Venice has all the traits of a prolonged, pre-Mannian courtship of death; but in this exasperated daydream in the midst of the miseries of Venice we are surprisingly given a happy ending and a final transfiguration, a reversal of that streak of dissolution that so strongly runs through most of its narration.

* * *

I have elsewhere proposed a possible reason or explanation for these tendencies and attitudes in the nineteenth century, but here I can only suggest that the nature/culture oxymoron prevailing in Venice might be heavily responsible for them.

Venice is an island characterized by an imposing series of historical, cultural, and artistic incrustations, sedimentations, and superfetations over the lagoon that preexisted the island: a conglomeration created by man.

On the one hand, as many writers have observed, in Venice we have a naturalization of architecture: her palaces appear as coral reefs, and such like natural concretions. "Reefs of palaces," Herman Melville called them; Proust, too, echoing Ruskin, in *Du côté de chez Swann* (part 3, "Noms de pays: Le nom") writes of "those rocks of amethyst, like a reef in the Indian ocean" (1: 426), and in *Albertine disparue* of the rows of palaces as "a chain of marble cliffs" ("une chaîne de falaises de marbre"; 3: 644). Throughout *The Cantos*, Ezra Pound plays on the glimmering perception of palaces as forests of marble, or petrified forests.

On the other hand, in Venice nature has been subjected to a drastic form of culturalization as we can see simply by looking out of the window. The stratifications of history and art were made one with the islands; they make a splendid conglomerate and incrustation of it—as well as a deadly oxymoron.

Ruskin likens Venice to a wilderness of brick and a petrified sea, writing that the branches of forests have physically turned into marble. In a well-known, long passage he expands on the idea that her "whole architecture is architecture of incrustation" (*Complete Works* 9: 323). Both Proust and Pound would use the same word—incrustation—to define the inner nature of Venice. Proust specifies that the marble cliffs "made one think of objects of nature, but of a nature which seemed to have created its works with a human imagination" (Proust, *Fugitive* 852).

Finally, the heaviest, obsessive, suffocating conglomeration is that of past and present, on which both James and Proust wrote beautiful, suspended pages. In *On Re-Reading Ruskin*, again, Proust has an intense page on the Piazzetta, where between the pink columns he has the impression of seeing "inserted in the present actual hour, a little of the past":

> [T]he days we are living, circulate, rush buzzing around the columns, but suddenly stop there, flee like repelled bees; for those high and slender enclaves of the past are not in the present, but in another time where the present is forbidden to penetrate.... the days of the present crowd and buzz. But, interposed between them, the columns push

them aside, reserving with all their splendid impenetrability the Past; of the past familiarly risen in the midst of the present. (128)

The overall effect is uncanny, disquieting, disturbing. These images of the organic turning into the inorganic are in themselves felt as a threat. Where styles endlessly superimpose, one runs the risk of a loss of identity (Chateaubriand had called Venice an unnatural city, "une cité contre nature"; Rilke would call her "a stone fable"). The city is basically an artifact, and an artifice; a hybrid. One is beyond all measure in Venice, constantly on the brink of rupture and dissolution, confronted by an excess of contrasts, tensions, oxymora. An extreme kind of what Freud called *das Unheimliche* is at work here. Venice appears as a dangling, suspended city, a city more on the other side than on this side. There is no better place and cradle of death—a place where literary deaths are bound to happen, haunting and hovering over writers and artists.

This "quest" for a death in Venice, however, is a projection mostly from the outside: the city acts as a disquieting mirror of conditions of displacement, dismay, uncertainty, between the natural and the unnatural, the organic and the inorganic, vegetation and history, past and present, one piled uncannily on top of the other.

With a final note: this seems to involve more outsiders than insiders, visitors rather than those living there, sojourners rather than inhabitants. The Venetians may wearily become accustomed and adjusted to the lingering fall of the city; coming from outside, the force of the oxymoron is more forcefully felt. Most proponents (as well as victims) of literary deaths in Venice are foreigners, *foresti*, from Ruskin to James, from Hofmannsthal to Mann, from Milly Theale to Aschenbach (I mingle authors and characters advisedly).

In conclusion, besides the so-called Stendhal syndrome—a dismay and unease felt in front of an excess of art for which we were not prepared—one may postulate a Ruskin or an Aschenbach syndrome: when facing or entering too much art and history, nature and culture, past and present, stratified and compressed in the confines of an island, not only does the heart misgive and the mind feel at a loss, but the overwhelming force of the oxymoron arouses and compels feelings of or yearnings for death.

The culmination of all this, for our purposes, is in Thomas Mann's *Der*

Tod in Venedig (1908), which is ostensibly played and enacted on an oxymoron: the Apollonian, ethereal, perfect beauty of Tadzio set against the perturbation of an aging soul and the mephitic miasma of a diseased city. In this novel, idea and setting are thematized: beauty and sickness and death are at work in a stifling, sirocco atmosphere. The "putrid odor of the lagoon" invades the soul (22), and the inner malaise of the protagonist is a reflection of the city itself, her final, conquering blast of disaster.

This, I repeat, has much to do with the feelings and atmospheres of Decadence and fin de siècle Decadentism. After the Fall, however, so many literary deaths in Venice seem forcibly to testify to the deadly force of the oxymoron. But let us be assured: it is a condition or a proneness in all sense literary, and of the "alien." These are paper deaths, fantasies of annihilation—just like so many transfigurations and resurrections in Venice are daydreams, mirages, and wish fulfillment.

* * *

Where there is death, there is also Transfiguration. Against the deadly force of the oxymoron, writers in English who identify Venice as the place for transfigurations and resurrections were notably Robert Browning, Baron Corvo, and Pound. Opening the way to Pound's *Cantos*, in *Sordello* (1840, bk. 3) Browning muses on the steps of a Venetian palace; in the dream sequence or reverie of *Fifine at the Fair* (1872), the carnival in Venice viewed from the Campanile in Saint Mark's proves a positive experience of humanity and fullness of life; in spite of the crumbling palaces (st. 106), Venice is a topos of Life (st. 108); against all stereotypes, she brings us down to, not away from, reality: "from such pinnacled pre-eminence, I found / Somehow the proper goal for wisdom was the ground / And not the sky" (st. 103).

Mutability turns to permanence in Venice: "Mutation was at end" (st. 107), "I perceived arrest / O' the change all round about / ... / unity in the place / Of temple, tower" (st. 120). Saint Mark's is the realm of unity and wholeness for Proust, too, in *Albertine disparue*. For Baron Corvo in *The Desire and Pursuit of the Whole*, Venice is the place where, in true Platonic terms, a split self can be made whole, where wholeness can be achieved in spite of dire separations.

Finally, Venice is dealt with and evoked as the ultimate place of life, as the image of light, rescue, and salvation in Pound's poetry, and extensively in *The Cantos*: "Venice seems a type / Of Life, 'twixt blue and blue extends

/ ... / 'Tis Venice, and 'tis Life" ("Ur-Canto" 1). Against Ruskin, Pound (together with Browning) views the Renaissance as the culmination of Venice (cantos 25, 26), whose epitomes are the Tempio Malatestiano in Rimini and the church of Santa Maria dei Miracoli in Venice (cantos 72–73).

In the *Pisan Cantos*, Venice acts as sentimental recollection and elegiac appearance, as an image of appeasement and consolation in the midst of historical ruins and personal dejection, especially through the evocation of places ("the Squero where Ogni Santi / meets San Trovaso" (canto 76); "Will I ever see the Giudecca again?" (canto 83). In *Section: Rock-Drill 85–95 de los cantares*, Venice is projected in flashes of fragmentary but luminous heavenly presence, as a *terzo cielo*, while into the final *Drafts and Fragments* are woven references to her crystalline, almost miraculous essence ("granite next sea wave / is for clarity," canto 106; "The marble form in the pine wood," canto 110; "A nice quiet paradise," canto 111, where Venice becomes an epitome of serenity, the conclusion of the world: "Soul melts into air / anima into aura, / Serenitas"). Elsewhere Venice is Demeter and Aphrodite, an image of light, rebirth, and almost divine unity, leading to endless transfigurations.

* * *

All this stands or moves behind Hemingway, who was probably unaware of it, and enjoyed the city and her mountains, Harry's Bar, hunting, and drinking. What a relief from so much gloominess and exaltation! But Venice—which is presented or evoked in cool, close-up, masterly scenes in *Across the River and into the Trees*—also mellowed, matured, and even saddened him, I believe. He may not have been aware of the streak of decay and death haunting the city, her visitors, and above all her writers, but he surely felt and expressed in that novel a sensation and a premonition of incoming, hovering, and approaching death.

Note

1. For readers interested in the themes I introduce in this essay, I would encourage them to refer to my previous work on these themes: *Browning e Venezia* (Firenze: Olshki, 1991); "Dalla caduta di Venezia alle morti a Venezia," in *Venezia nella sua storia: Morti e rinascite*, ed. C. Ossola, 125–47 (Venezia: Marsilio, 2003); "The Fiction of Fr. Rolfe, Baron Corvo," *Mosaic* 4.3 (1971): 111–23; *Hemingway e*

Venezia (Firenze: Olschki, 1988); *Henry James e Venezia* (Firenze: Olschki, 1987); "Literary Deaths in Venice," in *Venetian Views, Venetian Blinds: English Fantasies of Venice*, ed. M. Pfister and B. Schaff, 115–28 (Amsterdam: Rodopi, 1999); "Romanzieri americani a Venezia," in *Italia e Stati Uniti nell'età del Risorgimento e della Guerra Civile*, 379–401 (Firenze: La Nuova Italia, 1969); *Ruskin e Venezia: La bellezza in declino* (Firenze: Olschki, 2001); "Morti a Venezia," chapter 13 in *Transitabilità: Arti, paesi, scrittori* (Palermo: Sellerio, 2005); and "Venezia, immagine e mito nella letteratura dell'Otto-Novecento," in *Venezia, immagine, futuro, realtà e problemi*, 29–47 (Venezia: Istituto Veneto di Scienze Lettere ed Arti, 2011).

Works Cited

Byron, George Gordon, Lord. *Childe Harold's Pilgrimage. The Poetical Words of Lord Byron*. London: Oxford UP, 1930. 174–244.

———. *Marino Faliero: Doge of Venice. The Poetical Works of Lord Byron*. London: Oxford UP, 1930. 397–443.

Cosgrove, Denis. "The Myth and the Stones of Venice." *Journal of Historical Geography* 8.2 (1987): 145–69.

Crouzet-Pavan, Élisabeth. *Venise triumphante: Les horizons d'un mythe*. Paris: Albin Michel, 1999.

James, Henry. *Collected Travel Writings: The Continent*. New York: Library of America, 1993.

———. "The Pupil." *Tales of Henry James*. New York: Norton, 2003. 133–71.

———. *The Wings of the Dove*. 1902. New York: Penguin, 2003.

Mamoli Zorzi, Rosella, ed. *Ezra Pound a Venezia*. Firenze: Olschki, 1985.

Mann, Thomas. *Death in Venice*. 1912. New York: Dover, 1995.

McPherson, David. *Shakespeare, Jonson, and the Myth of Venice*. Newark: Delaware UP, 1990.

Melville, Herman. "Venice." *The Poems of Herman Melville*. Ed. Douglas Roubillard. Kent, OH: Kent State UP, 2000.

Proust, Marcel. *The Captive and The Fugitive*. Vol. 5 of *In Search of Lost Time*. Trans. C. K. S. Moncrieff and T. Kilmartin. Revised by D. J. Enright. New York: Modern Library, 1993.

———. *On Re-Reading Ruskin*. Trans. and ed. J. Autret, W. Burford, and P. J. Wolfe. New Haven: Yale UP, 1987.

———. *Remembrance of Things Past*. 3 vols. Trans. C. K. S. Moncrieff and T. Kilmartin. Harmondsworth, UK: Penguin, 1984.

Ruskin, John. *Complete Works*. Ed. Edward T. Cook and A. Wedderburn. Oxford: George Allen, 1903–12.

———. *The Stones of Venicei*. Vol. 3, *The Fall*. New York: Cosimo Classics, 2007.
Shelley, Percy Bysshe. "Lines Written among the Euganean Hills." *The Major Works*. Oxford: Oxford UP, 2003. 198–207.
Tanner, Tony. *Venice Desired*. Oxford: Blackwell, 1992.
Tuttleton, James W., and Agostino Lombardo, eds. *The Sweetest Impression of Life: The James Family and Italy*. New York: New York UP, 1990.
Venezia da stato a mito. Catalogue of the exhibition. Venezia: Marsilio, 1997.

5

Torcello

From John Ruskin and Henry James to Ernest Hemingway

ROSELLA MAMOLI ZORZI

On November 4, 1948, Hemingway moved to the Locanda Cipriani at Torcello[1] from the Gritti Hotel in Venice, where he was staying after a period spent in the mountains of Cortina. For almost two months he found a haven of peace and quiet on the island, where he could write in total solitude, but where he also kept up his correspondence, for instance with his Italian translator, Fernanda Pivano,[2] whom he had met in October 1948 in Cortina, or with Italian writer Elio Vittorini, who offered to go to Torcello in January 1949 as Hemingway had volunteered to write an introduction to Vittorini's novel *In Sicily*.[3] He also went duck hunting in the surrounding lagoon, as he did when he went duck hunting in the Valle San Gaetano near Caorle, as documented by many photos.[4]

Hemingway wrote no comment on the decay of the island, certainly at the time not as touristy as it is today. However, he was fully aware of the history of Torcello, as shown in Colonel Cantwell's words in chapter 4 of *Across the River and into the Trees*, when the Colonel and his driver see the lagoon and Torcello from the mainland:

> The Colonel and the driver walked over to the Venice side of the road and looked across the lagoon that was whipped by the strong, cold wind from the mountains that sharpened all the outlines of the buildings so that they were geometrically clear.
>
> "That's Torcello directly opposite us," the Colonel pointed. "That's where the people lived that were driven off the mainland by the Vi-

sigoths. They built that church you see there with the square tower. There were thirty thousand people lived there once and they built that church to honor their Lord and to worship him. Then, after they built it, the mouth of the Sile River silted up or a big flood changed it, and all that land we came through just now got flooded and started to breed mosquitoes and malaria hit them. They all started to die, so the elders got together and decided they should pull out to a healthy place that would be defensible with boats, and where the Visigoths and the Lombards and the other bandits couldn't get at them, because these bandits had no sea-power. The Torcello boys were all great boatmen. So they took the stones of all their houses in barges, like that one we just saw, and they built Venice." (20–21)[5]

When one reads previous descriptions of Torcello and its lagoon, for instance those of John Ruskin and Henry James, one feels these offer views that are very different from Hemingway's. But we will see that there are in fact some quite unexpected connections.

Ruskin wrote on Torcello in the second volume of *The Stones of Venice* (1851–53). The preceding chapter was a description of the lagoon as a place of desolation, the very desolation that the future Venetians found, coming from the mainland, fleeing from the hordes of Attila (chap. 1). As Jeanne Clegg writes, Ruskin presents the lagoon as "a landscape of creation without light, heat or sound" (107). He was preparing his reader to see the Torcello lagoon exactly as the inhabitants fleeing from Altino had seen it. The lagoon is a "melancholy plain" (Ruskin 8):

> [T]he black desert of their [the waters] shore lies in its nakedness beneath the night, pathless, comfortless, infirm, lost in dark languor and fearful silence, except when the salt runlets plash into the tideless pools, or the sea-birds flit from their margins with a questioning cry; and he will be enabled to enter in some sort into the horror of heart with which this solitude was anciently chosen by man as his habitation. (8–9)

The description of this "sorrowful wilderness" prepares the reader for the description of Torcello (chapter 2). Ruskin continues in his desolate description of the island and the lagoon, as seen from the top of the "rude brick campanile" (which has no guardians: "and there are none to hinder us, the door of its ruinous staircase swinging idly on its hinges"; 11). The description matches the one in chapter 1: "a waste of wild sea moor, of a lurid ashen grey ... lifeless, the colour of sackcloth, with the corrupted seawater soaking through the roots of its acrid weeds, and gleaming hither and thither through its snaky channels" (11). Ruskin sets the stage—the desolate stage—where "[t]hirteen hundred years ago" the people sought refuge from Altino (12). From the top of the campanile, the eye of Ruskin catches the presence of the island buildings, just as desolate, and starts examining the Cathedral, the Palazzo Pu[b]blico (13), and the octagonal church of Santa Fosca.

It is only at this point that Ruskin can praise the church—and its interior—also in its details (the capitals and the pulpit) as the expression of a people who "sought for comfort in their religion" (18), emphasizing two moments of their faith, that is "the present mercy of Christ to his Church" (19), represented by the Virgin portrayed in the apse mosaic, and Christ's "future coming to judge the world," represented in the mosaic of the Day of Doom:

> [T]he two solemn mosaics of the eastern and western extremities—one representing the Last Judgement, the other the Madonna, her tears falling as her hands are raised to bless,—and the noble range of pillars which enclose the space between ... are expressive at once of the deep sorrow and the sacred courage of men who had no home left upon earth. (14)

Torcello is a place where men of faith managed to build a home, waiting for their real, eternal home. A home, the church, that is appreciated by Ruskin *as the material artifact of a people full of faith.*

One should underline at this point that—independent of his theories—Ruskin saw Torcello at the peak of its decay, that is, after the 1806 and 1810 dissolutions of monasteries had erased most of the churches from the island. A map published in Lorenzetti shows the nine churches that existed in Torcello: Santa Margherita, abandoned in 1521 (80); Santa Andrea; Santa Zuane (or San Giovanni Evangelista, suppressed in 1810; 46); Santa Anzolo de Zampenigo (demolished after 1668; 84); and Santa Antonio Abate (suppressed in 1806; 82–83), which had paintings of the life of Santa Cristina by Veronese (partly in the museum; see Zorzi 2: 434–37); Santa Giovanni Evangelista (also suppressed in 1810; Zorzi 2: 439); and the great San Tomaso dei Borgognoni, which was near the present boat stop (abandoned in 1806, and then demolished; *Monasteri benedettini* 67).[6]

An etching from the *Forestier illuminato* (302–3) shows clearly that there were many churches as late as the eighteenth century.

Surely Ruskin's description of the lagoon is geared toward preparing the reader to see the island in its uninhabited state, and not a bit of admiration of the lagoon is to be found in this description, as one might expect from someone who admired the Romantic landscape of the ragged Alps, even if in the description of his approach to Murano there is some admiration for the Alps crowning the lagoon to the north (sections 3, 28).

However, Ruskin celebrated the "strength of heart" of the people who had fled to and had founded Torcello; he appreciated their work, even if he saw it in its decay and desolation.

Of course Ruskin was in Torcello *before* any work of restoration was started; *The Stones of Venice* came out in 1851–53 and some work of restoration was carried out only between 1854 and 1858.[7]

It would take almost a century before the Locanda Cipriani would open in 1934, as a simple wine shop.

In the nineteenth century the desolation of the island was total, as mentioned also by previous writers who influenced Ruskin in *The Stones of Venice*: William S. Rose, for instance, had found the island "depressing rather than picturesque" (qtd. in Hewison 18). "Dilapidation and decay" is also what William Dean Howells noticed, in spite of his joyful picnic shared with the dirty and poor inhabitants of the island (235).

In general, the impression of the island was that of a depressed and very poor place. It was so for James, who wrote on Torcello in the essays *Venice: An Early Impression* (1872) and *Venice* (1882). In 1872, James was still very much influenced by Ruskin, as his letters show. In Torcello James saw, just like Ruskin: "a ruinous church of the eleventh century. It is impossible to imagine a more penetrating case of unheeded collapse. Torcello was the mother-city of Venice, and she lies there now, a mere mouldering vestige, like a group of *weather-bleached parental bones left impiously unburied*" (emphasis added; *Venice* 1872, 53).

Later on in the essay James dwelt upon the buildings, writing:

> The church, admirably primitive and curious, reminded me of the two or three oldest churches of Rome—St. Clement and St. Agnes.

> The interior is rich in grimly mystical mosaics of the twelfth century and the patchwork of precious fragments in the pavement is not inferior to that of St. Mark's. But the terribly distinct Apostles are ranged against their dead gold backgrounds as stiffly as grenadiers presenting arms—intensely personal sentinels of a personal Deity. (54)

Before describing the island and the cathedral, however, James wrote a long passage in which he celebrated the beauty of the lagoon and its light, a "magician" that can transform anything it touches upon, including "slimy brick, marble battered and befouled, rags, dirt, decay" (52). The lagoon is where

> [s]ea and sky seem to meet half-way, to blend their tones into a soft iridescence, a lustrous compound of wave and cloud and a hundred nameless local reflections.... You may see these elements at work anywhere, but to see them in their intensity you should choose the finest day in the month and have yourself rowed far away across the lagoon to Torcello. (52–53)

Thanks to the light, which makes the lagoon so appealing, a ruinous landscape can have charm, as James annotated regarding the square in front of the cathedral at Torcello:

> The charm of certain vacant grassy spaces, in Italy, overfrowned by masses of brickwork that are honey-combed by the suns of centuries, is something that I hereby renounce once for all the attempt to express; but you may be sure that whenever I mention such a spot enchantment lurks in it. (53)

The feeling of depression has given way to a feeling of appreciation of *the picturesque.*

James continued his description, dwelling on the "delicious stillness" covering the "little campo at Torcello," and proceeding to praise the "brilliant air" (53).

He then dwells on a group of children, representative of James's view of the Italian poor people. These "little brats" in their nakedness are compared to savage "infant cannibals," but their grinning transforms them into "cherubs." These children suggest "forcibly that the best assurance of happiness in this world is to be found in the maximum of innocence and the minimum of wealth" (53).

One child in particular has "a smile to make Correggio sigh in his grave" (54), and these children cannot be forgotten, contrary to what may happen on seeing "an infant citizen of our own republic, straight-haired, pale-eyed and freckled, duly darned and catechised, marching into a New England schoolhouse" (54), an annotation not lacking irony.

In his later 1882 essay, James found Torcello "improved," which meant

> the deeply interesting little cathedral of the eighth century, which stood there on the edge of the sea, as the bleached bones of a human skeleton washed ashore by the tide, has now been restored and made cheerful, and the charm of the place, its strange and suggestive desolation, has well-nigh departed. (*Venice* 1882, 29)

James takes up the simile of the *bleached bones*, only to underline the loss of the picturesque due to restoration.[8]

In Ruskin we find a religious-aesthetic approach to the island; in James a purely aesthetic approach; if Ruskin does not praise the lagoon in the approach to Torcello, and James does, surely neither Ruskin nor James ever thought of *staying* in Torcello. Hemingway appreciated the very solitude of the island, without its desolation, as the comforting Locanda provided good fare and wine;[9] he appreciated also the beauty of the lagoon, but he was also interested in the art of Torcello, as several photos document. We see him in front of Santa Fosca, in front of sculptures, with the parish priest, but the main attraction of Torcello for Hemingway was the daytime silence and peace in which he could write, and the lagoon for duck hunting.[10] He was also enchanted by the nights at Torcello: "Waking up in the night in front of a fireplace, one can hear the shots of the hunters on the lagoon, and moving to the window one can see the lagoon in the mist with the moon, and the skyline of Venice in the background" (see "Torcello Piece" on page xi of this volume).

This passage belongs to a typescript in the John F. Kennedy Library called "Torcello Piece," a fragment that this volume publishes for the first time. In this text there is a passage that seems to show Hemingway not only as a duck hunter, writer, and appreciator of the wine and food provided by the Locanda Cipriani, but also as possibly influenced by Ruskin.

In the "Torcello Piece" Hemingway shows his appreciation for the three monuments on Torcello, that is, the basilica, the church of Santa Fosca, and the baptistery. He writes that these were built by men who believed in

God, and in Torcello. So was the mosaic in the apse of the church, where there seems to be "no doubt" ("There is no doubt in the one mosaic of Our Lady"), but as regards the other mosaic, the huge Day of Doom, on the inside wall of the facade, "doubt" seems to be there; the young men from Caorle who made this mosaic did not believe in God, "did not know whether they cared for it [the product] or not" (see "Torcello Piece" on page xi of this volume).

Now, this linking of an art product to the faith of the artisan—sculptor, painter, mosaicist—is a fundamental and well-known tenet in Ruskin's aesthetics. It is well known that Ruskin placed a date, 1418, to mark the decline of Venice, and, more specifically of her art, built with faith until then, and then ugly because faith was lacking. Art—basically Ruskin's beloved Gothic—was beautiful and successful *because* it was created by people who believed in God, while the art that followed, defined as that of the "grotesque renaissance," was made by people who no longer believed in God (of course, with such notable exceptions as Tintoretto, absolutely adored by Ruskin).

In this declaration linking art and faith, Hemingway seems to be influenced by Ruskin, even if for Ruskin and for James Torcello was only a place of ruin, while for Hemingway it was a place of beauty and peace where he could create.

Did Hemingway read Ruskin?[11] No Ruskin seems to have been included in Hemingway's library, and Ruskin is not named among the writers who wrote on Venice mentioned by Colonel Cantwell in *Across the River*. The writers who are mentioned in the novel are Byron, Browning, Shakespeare, and D'Annunzio. However, in the recording of Hemingway's "In Harry's Bar in Venice," Ruskin is mentioned as one of the writers who wrote on Venice, together with Sinclair Lewis and Robert Browning:[12]

> The book came to me in a sort of a haze in Harry's Bar in Venice. Harry's Bar is a small place, but it is, in effect, a microcosm of all of that great and beautiful city which has been so well described by those writers Ruskin, Sinclair Lewis, Byron, and others. (qtd. in Cirino 210)[13]

Perhaps Hemingway *was aware* of Ruskin's theories, whether he had read Ruskin's *The Stones of Venice* or not. In spite of the different views of Torcello expressed by Ruskin and James, a thin line unites Hemingway to his predecessors.

Notes

1. Zorzi and Moriani 22. See Moriani for the Torcello photos.

2. From the Gritti and from Torcello, Hemingway kept up a correspondence with Pivano, who had translated *Death in the Afternoon.* Two letters from Torcello, dated November 11 and November 22, 1948, discuss Pivano's work on Hemingway and her translations, and the concepts of war and death. The November 11 letter has an odd slip of the pen, as the place is marked as "Torcello (Prov. Belluno)," the Province of Belluno referring to Cortina, and obviously not to Torcello. Hemingway also wrote to "Nanda" about his missing Mary in Torcello: "I miss her terribly. She owns my heart and when she goes away she takes it with her just as she takes the car;" typescript letter of November 22, 1948, from Torcello to Pivano, signed "Mister Papa, Fondo Pivano, Milano" (Fondazione Benetton). In her autobiography Mary remembered that at Torcello Ernest told her many of his boyhood memories; see Mary Welsh Hemingway, *How It Was,* 226–28.

3. See Gronda 382. Hemingway did write an introduction to Vittorini's *In Sicily,* dated "Cortina d'Ampezzo 1949," which was published in the American edition by New Directions in November 1949.

4. See these photos in Moriani 107–10.

5. The Colonel's history lesson continues for another paragraph, regarding the history of Venice and the arrival of Saint Mark's body in the city.

6. See also Zorzi 1: 52.

7. See the article by Treadgold on the different viewpoints of *ingeniero* Giacomo Peri and director Giovanni Battista Meduna regarding the restorations. Meduna did not agree with the director of the works, Peri, on various issues regarding the restoration, or on the dating of the cathedral, which was founded in the fifth century according to Peri, and in 1008 according to Meduna. See Treadgold 89. In a document published by Treadgold, Meduna wrote, "[R]iguardo al disfacimento di una parte del mosaico . . . fu disposto perché il mosaicista sig. Moro consegni il materiale alla Fabbriceria di Torcello." Treadgold 122, document of December 7, 1848, signed by Meduna.

8. On this point, we might recall Cantwell's remarks upon seeing the boats as he enters Venice: "It's not that they are picturesque. The hell with picturesque. They are just damned beautiful" (*ARIT* 40).

9. See photos in Moriani 116–18.

10. Other photos of Torcello show the turkeys (Moriani 114), which apparently you could call by whistling—at least according to what Hemingway wrote. For the duck hunting photos, see 111–15.

11. I was not able to find out if Hemingway had read Ruskin. See James D. Brasch and Joseph Sigman's *Hemingway's Library*, and Michael Reynolds's *Hemingway's Reading, 1910–1940*, Princeton: Princeton UP, 1981.

12. In a letter of May 29, 1949, to Dos Passos, where Hemingway complains about the presence of Sinclair Lewis in Venice, he writes: "The Venetians liked Mr. Byron better [than Sinclair Lewis] and I think this did not please Mr. Lewis too much. The Venetians, however, did not like Mr. Browning, either, nor his wife, nor their dog. Mr. Byron is their writer. He really was pretty good there and I will tell you about it sometime." Ernest Hemingway Personal Papers, "Letters," John F. Kennedy Library Hemingway Collection.

13. The book mentioned is, of course, *Across the River and into the Trees*.

Works Cited

Cirino, Mark. *Reading Hemingway's* Across the River and into the Trees. Kent, OH: Kent State UP, 2016.

Clegg, Jeanne. *Ruskin and Venice*. London: Junction Books, 1981.

Forestier illuminato. Venezia: Albrizzi, 1765.

Gronda, Giovanna, ed. *Per conoscere Vittorini*. Milano, Mondadori, 1979.

Hemingway, Ernest. *Across the River and into the Trees*. London: Arrow Books, 1994.

———. "In Harry's Bar in Venice." *The Ernest Hemingway Audio Collection*. New York: HarperCollins, 2001. CD.

———. "Torcello Piece." Unpublished Manuscripts. John F. Kennedy Library #773.

Hemingway, Mary Welsh. *How It Was*. London: Weidenfeld and Nicolson, 1977.

Hewison, Robert. *Ruskin on Venice: "The Paradise of Cities."* New Haven: Yale UP, 2009.

Howells, William Dean. *Venetian Life*. 1867. Boston: Houghton, 1895.

James, Henry. *Italian Hours*. Ed. John Auchard. Pennsylvania: Pennsylvania State UP, 1992.

———. "Venice." 1882. In James, *Italian Hours*.

———. "Venice: An Early Impression." 1872. In James, *Italian Hours*.

Lorenzetti, Giulio. *Torcello: La sua storia, i suoi monumenti*. Venezia: Carlo Ferrari, 1939.

Merkel, Ettore. "Contributo archivistico al restauro del 'Giudizio Universale' di Torcello." *Quaderni della Sovrintendenza ai Beni Artistici e Storici di Venezia* 7 (1978): 54.

Monasteri benedettini nella laguna di Venezia, a cura di Gabriele Mazzucco. Venezia: Arsenale Editrice, 1983.

Moriani, Gianni. *Il Veneto di Hemingway / Hemingway's Veneto*. Crocetta del Montello: Antiga, 2011.

Ruskin, John. *The Stones of Venice*. Vol. 2. London: Allen & Unwin, 1925.

Treadgold, Irina Andreescu. "Modifiche alla cattedrale di Torcello nel restauro del 1854–58." *Bollettino d'Arte del Ministero per i Beni Culturali e Ambientali*, no. 25 (May/June 1984): 89–122.

Zorzi, Alvise. *Venezia scomparsa*. 2 vols. Milano: Electa, 1971.

Zorzi, Rosella Mamoli, Gianni Moriani, and Arrigo Cipriani. *In Venice and in the Veneto with Ernest Hemingway*. Venezia: Supernova, 2011.

6

Hemingway at Lignano Sabbiadoro and in Friuli-Venezia Giulia

DAVIDE LORIGLIOLA

TRANSLATED BY NICHOLAS STANGHERLIN

The beach resort of Lignano Sabbiadoro has utilized Ernest Hemingway as its most prestigious promoter for the last sixty years. Both a public park (in 1984) and a journalistic literary prize (May 1985) have been dedicated in his name. In particular, he is often quoted as having said when he first saw the city "but this is the Italian Florida." This useful piece of advertising, combined with the documented presence of Hemingway in Lignano, has reinforced the positive image of the city.

In 2004 the city of Lignano Sabbiadoro, and in particular the municipal library, decided to add to an open-air photographic exhibition in Hemingway park titled *Gli sguardi di Hemingway* (Hemingway's glances), a contribution that would reconstruct the presence of Hemingway in Lignano and situate it in the general context of the writer's relationship with the people and places of the Veneto and Friuli regions, in particular with the Kechler family. The task was assigned to me, who was once again asked by the city (in 2008) to embark on a definitive and conclusive study of the question and both the exhibition and the catalogue, *Amore e gratitudine: Il Friuli di Hemingway* (Love and gratitude: The Friuli of Hemingway), began as a result of this research. From 2008 to the present, thanks to various works on Hemingway's relationship with the places he visited and thanks to new discoveries made by the Kechler family, I have been able to validate or to refute some of the details that were part of previous reconstructions. I can now present a more precise account of Hemingway's presence in Friuli and Lignano.

On September 21, 1948, Hemingway and his wife Mary Welsh arrive at Genoa from Havana. Ernest wants to show Mary the area of Italy he got to know thirty years before during his voluntary service in the First World War. For this reason Hemingway brings his blue Buick, which he assigns to an Italian driver. In October, after having traveled along the plains of north Italy, the couple arrives at Cortina d'Ampezzo, where Hemingway had taken up skiing with his first wife Hadley in 1923. The Hemingways stay at the Concordia Hotel with the intention of setting out for Venice soon. Ernest wishes to take advantage of his stay by going trout fishing in the nearby streams. He asks Luigi Zambelli, who is the owner of the famous sporting goods store Olympia Sport, for advice and is directed toward a Friuli nobleman who is an expert on the matter. It is Count Federico Kechler, whom Hemingway meets at the bar of the Post Hotel. A great friendship is immediately formed. Kechler (1901–1970), a former naval officer during the Second World War, speaks perfect English and is a true fishing expert: these are all characteristics that Hemingway appreciates and in conversation with Aaron Hotchner he says of Kechler, "What a damn classy gent he is" (91).

The Kechler dynasty has its roots in the mountainous regions of the Black Forest. After having been Hapsburgic vassals, they moved first to Prague, then to Lubiana and Fiume, and finally to Udine. Carlo Kechler, Federico's grandfather, distinguished himself as the business administrator of Pietro Antivari, who was the largest silk merchant of the province. After having married Antivari's niece, Angiola Chiozza, in 1854, Carlo Kechler was responsible for some of the great enterprises in the history of Friuli's economy, such as the Contonificio (cotton mill) Udinese, the excavation of the Ledra-Tagliamento canal, and the founding of the Bank of Udine. His son, Roberto, who had a passion for horses and hunting and founded the Friuli Fox Hunting Society, married Costanza dei Conti Crotti di Costigliole and had four sons: Federico, Carlo, Alberto (known as "Titi"), and Mario.

That autumn, in 1948, Federico takes Ernest to his fishing reserve in the Anterselva Valley and they practice the technique of fly-fishing. Federico accommodates Hemingway in his villa and introduces him to his wife Maria Luisa, his brother Alberto, and his brother's wife Costanza de Asarta. On October 24—as documented by an autographed inscription in the guest book—Ernest and Mary are in Friuli for the first time, as guests of Alberto at his villa in Fraforeano (in the province of Udine) for a "lovely visit and a good shoot." After having gone back to Cortina, the Hemingways leave for Venice, where they arrive on October 30. In Venice, Ernest once again meets his friend Federico Kechler, who introduces him to the young Baron Nanyuki Franchetti. Ernest is invited by the third Kechler brother, Carlo, to stay in his villa in San Martino di Codroipo for a day of partridge shooting on December 10.

At dawn the next day, the writer's blue Buick exits the villa, driven by the Kechler's chauffer Adamo De Simon, in the direction of San Gaetano di Caorle, where Baron Franchetti has invited Ernest for a weekend of duck hunting in barrels. Carlo Kechler is also with Hemingway. They stop for breakfast in Alberto Kechler's villa at Fraforeano and Ernest discusses war at length. They arrive an hour late at an appointment in Latisana that Carlo had made with Adriana Ivancich, an eighteen-year-old Venetian aristocrat who lived between Venice and San Michele al Tagliamento.

Hemingway falls in love with her almost immediately and is reciprocated only platonically. He will transfigure her into Renata in *Across the River and into the Trees*. She too is invited by Franchetti to the weekend of hunting in the lagoon, and they proceed to San Gaetano di Caorle. After having seen Adriana again in Venice, Ernest leaves for Cortina, where he spends Christmas with his wife. In the winter of 1948–49 Hemingway was reading two books, Irwin Shaw's *The Young Lions* and Elio Vittorini's *Conversazione in Sicilia* (Conversation in Sicily). There exists a copy of *The Young Lions* (a Random House 1948 first edition) full of autographed notes on the text by Hemingway that are everything but benevolent. On the title page there is an inscription dedicated to his friend Carlo Kechler that reads: "For Carlo from Ernesto" with two different dates, written with two different pencils: 2nd March 1949 and 22nd January 1950, and the same place, San Martino di Codroipo. A 1948 American edition of *A Farewell to Arms* bears the inscription "1949, San Martino di Codroipo" dedicated to Costanza Kechler. These documents and the recollections of Roberta Kechler, daughter of Federico, confirm the presence of the writer in Friuli on at least one occasion before mid-March of 1949, when Ernest contracts erysipelas, a serious eye infection, in Venice and—after being hospitalized in Padua—is forced to a period of rest.

The Hemingways leave Venice on April 30, 1949, for Genoa and embark for Havana. Hemingway later returns to Europe with Mary, arriving at Le Havre on November 25 and then in Venice during the first week of January 1950, where he reencounters Baron Nanyuki Franchetti and Adriana Ivancich. Ernest and Mary are Carlo Kechler's guests for two days on January 22 (as per the inscription in *The Young Lions* mentioned above) in his villa in San Martino di Codroipo. Carlos Baker writes that "Carlo had sold his Alfa Romeo and many horses in order to buy a 'really excellent Goya' and a 'better than fair El Greco.' Ernest had brought a tin of gray caviar and two bottles of Gordon's Gin, and they all sat before a fire of mulberry roots drinking gin and Campari" (481).

Halfway through May, Ernest and Mary left for Paris, where Ernest meets Adriana once again and declares his love for her but at the same time admitting the impossibility of it. Adriana is on the quay of Le Havre on March 22nd to say goodbye to the Hemingways, who are leaving for New York. Hemingway's last trip to Friuli—and to Italy—is in 1954. On the 23rd and 25th of January Ernest and Mary miraculously survive two plane crashes at the end of a safari in West Africa. Ernest in particular has sustained serious injuries to his intestines, kidneys, and head, and to his hearing. From Mombasa, at the end of March, the Hemingways set off for Venice, where Ernest wishes to spend some time resting at the Gritti Hotel.

Hemingway receives various visitors in his room, among them Federico Kechler, who invites him to his family villa in Percoto (Udine) for a few days. He also meets Sergio Maldini, a young reporter for the local newspaper *Il Messaggero Veneto* who had won the Mondadori Hemingway Award with his first novel, *I sognatori* (The dreamers). On April 9, Federico Kechler sends his driver De Simon and his brother Carlo to pick up the Hemingways from the Gritti. De Simon makes an impromptu deviation to the north, at Udine, at the restaurant of the Friuli Hotel in Piazza XX Settembre, which is the haunt of the artists and intellectuals of Udine in the 1950s. There are various youngsters present all eager to meet the writer, among them Carlo Scarsini, journalist for the local *Gazzettino*, who had convinced De Simon to make that detour that Hemingway enthusiastically accepted. The encounter between Hemingway and the youngsters is documented in a series of photos by the most famous photojournalist of the city—Tino da Udine—and in reports that are published two days later in

Il Gazzettino and *Il Messaggero Veneto*. Among the youngsters Hemingway meets there are those who will later become famous, such as Loris Fortuna (the father of the Italian law on divorce), the journalist Isi Benini, and the architects Gino Valle and Aldo Bernardis.

Ernest and Mary's stay in Villa Kechler in Percoto is characterized by absolute rest on Hemingway's part, as he is still recovering from his injuries. Roberta Kechler, daughter of Federico, recalls passing under the writer's window on a horse with her twin sister Carla in the morning and receiving a "buongiorno" from him. Of the few trips that Ernest made in this period, only the one to Torviscosa, the city "inaugurated" in 1940 by Benito Mussolini, is documented. On this occasion Hemingway casually meets Gianfranco D'Aronco, a university professor and an important figure of the autonomy-for-Friuli movement, and Chino Ermacora, a famous writer and journalist. They exchange a few words in English and a handshake.

On the morning of Thursday, April 15, Ernest leaves Villa Kechler in Percoto. Before departing, he leaves an inscription that is a tribute both to his hosts and to Friuli: "With much love and gratitude," signed "Mr. Papà—Ernesto Kechler Hemingway." In the Kechler's Lancia Aurelia B21, apart from the driver Adamo De Simon, there are also Maria Luisa Kechler and Count Federico. It is Count Federico who decides to make a small detour toward Lignano Pineta before bringing the Hemingways back to Venice. Federico's daughters, Carla and Roberta, are also part of the group; together with his brother Mario and Carlo's wife, Ornella, and their children Caesar, Fiamma, and Roberto.

They stop at the Kechler villa of San Martino of Codroipo in order to visit the Kechler's sick mother Costanza dei Conti Crotti di Costigliole (who will die a few days later and to whom Ernest will dedicate a mass in Venice). Afterward, Hemingway has breakfast in a restaurant in Latisana, La Bella Venezia, which is famous also outside Friuli for the game and fish dishes prepared by the cook Onelia Mondolo. As Costanza's daughter Maria remembers, "He had already had the occasion of appreciating the sea bass with some Brolio del Chianti, brought specially from Udine."

In the late morning Hemingway and the Kechlers arrive at Lignano Pineta. Alberto Kechler started the construction of the new beach resort in 1953, and to draw up the master plan of the city the then young architect Marcello D'Olivo (1921–1991) was called. He would later go on to become one of the most important representatives of organic architecture in Italy.

The inward spiral scheme he designed for Lignano Pineta—studied as a balanced intertwining of green and concrete, trees and houses—is very famous. It is after having passed through the pine trees to the sandy seaside that Hemingway pronounced the famous sentence "But this is Florida, or better, it's the Italian Florida!" A Florida that the writer, who had lived in Key West from 1931 to 1939, identified mainly with the savage mixture of green vegetation and the Everglades' waters, to which the Lignano Pineta of the time might have looked similar.

At a certain point of their stay, Federico Kechler gives Hemingway the map of the Pineta designed by D'Olivo, asking him to put his signature on a portion of land that the family was offering to him as a gift so he could build his own house in Friuli, a house that was never built. Hemingway signs with a smile on his face and gets back into Kechler's car to return to Venice. He would never return to Friuli or to Lignano, where he had spent a little more than two hours.

In Venice on May 5 an American-style dinner is organized at Ivancich Palace. Ernest and Mary are invited, and this dinner is followed by a goodbye party in Ernest's apartment at the Gritti Hotel: that was the last time Hemingway would see Adriana in Venice. On May 6, the Hemingways leave Venice, heading toward Genova. The last, indirect contact Hemingway has with Friuli is through the journalist from Udine, Mario Casamassima, a friend of Adriana's brother Gianfranco. On the September 8, 1956, Casamassima leaves Udine on a Lancia Aurelia B21, hired from the famous dealership Ferri, in the direction of Le Havre, where Ernest and Mary Hemingway are waiting for him: during the next two months he will accompany the couple in a long tour of the Spanish corridas, as an RAI reporter. In August 1959 Casamassima buys a Lancia Flaminia from Ferri on Hemingway's behalf and gives it to Hemingway in Madrid.

Works Cited

20. premio Ernest Hemingway—"Lignano per la cultura" 2004: Gli sguardi di Hemingway. Lignano Sabbiadoro: Comune di Lignano Sabbiadoro, 2004.
Amore e gratitudine: Il Friuli di Hemingway—Mostra fotografica open air—Parco Hemingway. Lignano Sabbiadoro: Comune di Lignano Sabbiadoro, 2008.
Baker, Carlos. *Ernest Hemingway: A Life Story.* New York: Scribner, 1976.
D'Aronco, G. "Hemingway torna in Friuli (Pittana, 9.5.1978)." *Ce fastu?* 62 (1986): 1.

Gaberscek, Carlo. "Hemingway e il Friuli," *La Cineteca del Friuli*, http://www.cinetecadelfriuli.org/cdf/produzioni_tv/hemingway_friuli.html (accessed June 11, 2014).

"Hemingway dispensa sorrisi e autografi." *Il Messaggero Veneto*, April 11, 1954, 5.

Hotchner, A. E. *Papa Hemingway*. New York: Random House, 1966.

Ivancich, Adriana. *La torre bianca*. Milano: Mondadori, 1980.

Kert, Bernice. *The Hemingway Women*. New York: Norton, 1999.

Knigge, Jobst C. *Hemingway's Venetian Muse: Adriana Ivancich*. Berlin: Humboldt U, 2012.

Maldini, Sergio. "Incontro a Venezia con Hemingway." *Il Messaggero Veneto*, April 3, 1954.

Moriani, Gianni. *Il Veneto di Hemingway*. Cornuda: Antiga, 2011.

Moriani, Gianni, and Rosella Mamoli Zorzi. *A Venezia e nel Veneto con Ernest Hemingway*. Venezia: Supernova, 2011.

Pivano, Fernanda. *Diari, 1917–1973*. Milano: Bompiani, 2008.

———. *Hemingway*. Milano: Tascabili Bompiani (ebook), 2009.

Procaccioli, C. *Generosità di un fotoreporter di provincia: A proposito di Tino da Udine*. Tavagnacco: Dindi, 2008.

Ritorno al Tagliamento sul set di "Addio alle armi." Udine: Grafiche Filacorda, 2006.

C. S. [Carlo Scarsini]. "Sorride felice Hemingwai [sic] fra i 'giovani turchi' di Udine." *Il Gazzettino*, Sunday, April 11, 1954.

Simoncelli, Paolo. *Sergio Maldini: Biografia della nostalgia*. Venezia, Marsilio, 2008, chapter 14.

Sindelar, Nancy W. *Influencing Hemingway: People and Places That Shaped His Life and Work*. Lanham, MD: Rowman & Littlefield, 2014.

III

A Farewell to Arms

7

The Many Faces of Defeat

Italian Ideological Contexts in Frederic Henry's Caporetto

ALBERTO LENA

From its publication in 1929, Hemingway's *A Farewell to Arms* represented a threat to Mussolini's totalitarian regime. Because the Italian defeat at Caporetto is at the very core of the novel, and this issue was a symbol of national humiliation for the Fascist regime, Hemingway's tragic work of love and war was prohibited by the Italian government and would not be translated into Italian until 1945 (Pivano xi–xv). Studies such as those of Michael Reynolds (128–59) and Linda Wagner-Martin (90–94), among others, have researched the ideological importance of the Caporetto episode in the novel analyzing the American, English, and French sources that frame Frederic Henry's discourse. In this essay, I would like to analyze Frederic's discourse from another perspective, that of the Italian ideological context of the novel. My point is that the Italian context will help us to understand Hemingway's need to communicate to his audience what happens to others when a democratic culture collapses and a whole society fades away due to the devastating effects of the Great War.

Fascism and the First World War

To begin with, I want to point out that Caporetto's defeat was one of the biggest disasters in Italian military history, an Italian Sedan, in General Luigi Cadorna's terms (Gatti 203). On October 24, 1917, the Austro-Hungarian and German forces launched an onslaught on the Italian front with the aim of reaching the Tagliamento River. The attack broke the Italian line on the Isonzo River. General Cadorna was in charge of the army during the battle and he painfully witnessed how the Italians suffered the death of nearly 12,000 soldiers, with an additional 30,000 wounded and 290,000 imprisoned. During the days following Caporetto's retreat, the sense of chaos was so huge that the whole country was on the verge of collapse. There were more than 350,000 disbanded men roaming the Veneto and Friuli countryside, causing havoc, and civilians had to pack their belongings in order to escape across the Piave River (Thompson 324). Close to the Tagliamento River, where Hemingway's novel takes place, the situation was even worse. Italian eyewitnesses, such as Lieutenant Piero Rossi, described the state of chaos, commenting that the remaining population seemed as much afraid of the disbanded Italian Army as the Austrian troops. All of a sudden, the army high commanders had seemingly vanished (283). Also, the power of the Italian state to exercise law and order had almost disappeared completely. Thus, in his war memoirs, *Giorni di Guerra* (Days of War), the poet Giovanni Comisso, then a lieutenant in the engineers, portrayed with acute detail the desolation of the Veneto cities during the aftermath of the retreat. He described how many cities across the Piave, such as Treviso, became deserted and the whole country became desolated. The middle classes and political authorities fled and only the very poor dwellers remained. Caporetto's disaster had turned Italy into a world upside-down.

Caporetto's retreat happened on November 27, 1917. In the following months, the Italian Army was able to reconstruct itself. A series of victories starting from the heroic defense of Vidor Bridge by a new generation of Italian soldiers (that of the 1899) paved the way to the following year's summer victory at the Battle of the Solstice and led to the final collapse of the Habsburg Army at Vittorio Veneto (Tazzer 37). These victories restored the confidence of the Italian people on their army. In just a few months Italy passed from being on the verge of total disintegration to becoming a victorious and unified nation that would be eager to fight for its territorial rights at international forums (Isnenghi and Rochat 482–83).

When Mussolini came to power in 1922, he boasted that he had brought to the nation the Italy of Vittorio Veneto. The war symbolized for a major part of the Italian population a new beginning, the fresh refunding of a humiliated nation. In fact, Great War history became "sacred History" and the Fascist government joyfully started to celebrate the dates of Italian intervention. Italians approached the memory of the war from a different paradigm from that of other European nations, which mourned the tragic loss of the very best of their youth. Italy, on the other hand, could still claim tangible rewards from the military butchery that rendered Italian the territories of Friuli, Trieste, the Trentino, and Alto Adige. The new territory justified for the Fascist and for many patriotic voices the 1.3 million people who had died, three times the number of Italians that would perish in the Second World War (Thompson 4–6).

No wonder that for Fascists during the 1920s the shadow of Caporetto was a heavy one hanging over the political unconscious of a new social system. This defeat represented a living nightmare, a past to be repressed. There was no room for military failure within the armed nation the Fascists artificially wanted to construct. The behavior of generals such as Cadorna tended to be defended by Fascists (Rochat 320–21). In fact, Fascists stressed that the Italian government had been mainly responsible for the defeat, thereby obliterating any of the army's responsibility. They argued that the Roman politicians had allowed Socialists and defeatists to demoralize that army after an initial tactical success of the enemy. Thus, during the 1920s, when General Gatti tried to analyze the real causes of the defeat, Mussolini sought to discourage him by saying it was a time for myths, not history. The real Italy, the Italy worth remembering, was the one emerging from the battles fought at the Piave and Vittorio Veneto, declared Mussolini (Thompson 327). From these battlefields emerged a brave new political elite who firmly intended to rewrite Italian history and regenerate a whole nation after centuries of defeat and humiliation.

Hemingway's Caporetto

When Hemingway wrote *A Farewell to Arms* in the late 1920s, he had to face the ideological background and mythical reconstruction of recent Italian history. Hemingway was aware that the myth of the war and the ideological manipulation of Italian history were not the only products of Fascism. Hemingway's juvenile literature, written back home after his World War I experiences, mirrored some of the patriotic enthusiasm of the Italian population. Immediately after the Great War, his early writings were crammed with references to Italian patriotic figures such as the flamboyant poet and warrior Gabriele D'Annunzio. Although a great artist and bold man of action, D'Annunzio embodied the ideals of Fascist Italy and was one of the main figures responsible for Italian involvement in the First World War (Comley 46–47). In fact, Hemingway expressed his enthusiasm for D'Annunzio when the Italian poet occupied Fiume, a major Adriatic seaport and industrial center that had formerly been part of the Habsburg Empire. The port was claimed by Italy against the international community that recognized the territory as part of the new kingdom of the Serbs, Croats, and Slovenes (Yugoslavia). Italy had entered the war after signing with the Allies the Treaty of London (1915) in which the Fiume's claim had been accepted. Hemingway had so deeply interiorized Italian Adriatic expansionistic discourse during the war that in a letter to his mother, Grace Hall Hemingway, on November 11, 1919, he expressed his wish of joining D'Annunzio and defending his actions, in these terms: "What do you think the 500,000 dear old wops that died think of Wilson robbing them of what they fought for? . . . Wish I were at Fiume tho" (*Letters* 1: 211).

From the early 1920s onward, after returning to Italy and working in Paris as foreign correspondent, Hemingway gradually abandoned his somewhat romantic enthusiasm for Italian patriotism. His writings became more mature as well as more politically alert. Unlike many American intellectuals, such as Samuel Putnam, Hemingway was one of the first American writers who understood the danger of Fascism not only for Italy but also for the entire international community (Cirino 41–43). Mussolini represented a totalitarian system that destroyed the very essence of democracy. In late August 1925, Hemingway wrote a letter to Ernest Walsh commenting on his complete delusion regarding the political situation in Italy. On June 10, 1924, Giacomo Matteotti, the leader of the Italian United Socialist Party, had been assassinated after denouncing in the Italian Parliament Mussolini's violent politics. Hemingway was utterly disappointed when he heard that the Senate High Court had dismissed the proceedings against the possible Matteotti murderers. The charges implicated Fascist leaders suspected of involvement in that crime. Hemingway expressed his anger and despair:

> I can't live in Italy [. . .] because the political situation makes me so furious that I'm upset and in trouble all the time. Imagine amnestying the murderers of Matteoti [sic] just one year after the crime. It was one of the most horrible crimes ever committed by any government. [. . .] I've promised myself never to go down into the country again

as long as Fascists are in power and I don't see why the hell I should. It is awfully discouraging to think that the country that produced Garibaldi should be ruled by that horrible gang. Well I suppose no country gets any better than it deserves and as soon as Italy became a united nation it was finished. Poor old Cavour. (*Letters* 2: 386–87)

After his bitter experiences in Italy during the 1920s, especially his return to Fossalta and his dramatic trip to La Spezia in 1927, Hemingway gradually changed his mind about the meaning of his military experience in Italy. When looking back at his Italian war experience, he passed from imagining that front as a place of heroic enthusiasm to that of angry bitterness: "The last war, during the years 1915, 1916, 1917, was the most colossal, murderous, mismanaged butchery that has ever taken place on earth. Any writer who said otherwise lied" (*MAW* xiii).

In *A Farewell to Arms*, Hemingway deliberately chose defeat. He avoided the new Italy born again at Vittorio Veneto. His representation of Caporetto is in fact essentially related to tragedy. In this novel Hemingway managed to show the horror of the war and its futility. To begin with, in *A Farewell to Arms*, the Italian front does not seem to be a singular chapter in European history, an isolated episode in the First World War, but the beginning of a chain of related events leading to the destruction of a nation. Because of his intimate knowledge of recent Italian history, Hemingway saw the front as the embryo of a new society, and when writing *A Farewell to Arms* he was not only looking backward in time but also looking forward. The mere fact of talking about Caporetto in the late 1920s is a direct challenge to the Italian reputation. Mussolini's government had complete control over every aspect of the lives of the citizens and passed censorship on Great War memoirs. Works such as Curzio Malaparte's *Viva Caporetto!* (1921) were forbidden by the regime. Popular books such as Attilio Frescura's *Diario di un imboscato* (1919) relating the horrors of the front had suffered severe censorship (Rigoni Stern 5–9). The unpleasant dimension of the war, as related to Italy's humiliation, was systematically obliterated. Whether Hemingway liked it or not, his representation of the front was destined to damage the public image of the Fascist regime in the United States. He was showing Italy as a nation on the brink of chaos during the Caporetto retreat, as well as the dark side of a war that many Fascists and interventionists celebrated as a mirror of national unity and political regeneration.

Realism against Defeatism

General Cadorna's tactics, especially those employed during the battle to conquer Mount San Gabriele, had generated continuous discontent among the troops. Cadorna's tactical blindness fostered a permanent state of anxiety and defeatism, as appeared in the diaries of contemporary eyewitness such as General Gatti (194). The troops and the high military staff were longing for a quick peace with the Austrians. They were exhausted and beaten up after that brutal battle (218–19). The Italian soldiers truly believed that the Austrian army was as much exhausted as they were. Yet, in Hemingway's novel, Frederic does not believe in Austrian defeatism. Quite the contrary, in his conversation with the priest, Father Galli, there emerges a pessimistic view not only of the continuity of the war but also of human nature:

> "Who won the fighting this summer?"
> "No one."
> "The Austrians won," I said. "They kept them from taking San Gabriele. They've won. They won't stop fighting."
> "If they feel as we feel they may stop. They have gone through the same thing."
> "No one ever stopped when they were winning."
> "You discourage me."
> "I can only say what I think."
> "Then you think it will go on and on? Nothing will ever happen?"
> "I don't know. I only think the Austrians will not stop when they have won a victory. It is in defeat that we become Christian."
> [...] He said nothing.
> "We are all gentler now because we are beaten. How would Our Lord have been if Peter had rescued him in the Garden?" (*FTA* 178)

Frederic's opinions must be placed within the context of the 1920s and should be addressed to understand contemporary European events. Frederic, very much like Hemingway, believed that to be defeated in a war would only help to make matters worse. Frederic saw the war in terms of realpolitik, as he stated to the priest regarding the final outcome of it: "No one ever stopped when they were winning." This opinion mirrors Hemingway's view of European politics after assisting at Genoa and Lausanne conferences and observing the Greco-Turkish War. The First World War represented the beginning of unending international greed among the nations as Hemingway shows in his poem "They All Made Peace—What Is Peace?" (*CP* 63).

In the days previous to the disaster of Caporetto, Frederic thinks that a nation has to be defeated in order to understand the moral meaning of any war. Frederic expresses this belief during his conversation with the priest: "I don't believe in defeat. Though it may be better" (*FTA* 179). This statement also serves to understand the nature of Italian foreign politics right after the war. For Italian Prime Minister Vittorio Orlando, who was in charge of negotiating peace for the Italian nation, the war had been fought to achieve the completion of Italian national unity and the security of Italian borders on land and sea. The war was indeed a national affair: the Italians did not fight to end all the wars of the world but to fulfill some of the national expectations of nineteenth-century Italian history elaborated during the Risorgimento (Thompson 381). No wonder that by 1919 politicians and popular leaders such as the poet D'Annunzio felt that the conditions of peace put forward by the international community were not good enough for Italy. D'Annunzio ventured into Fiume in order to fulfill Italian geopolitical expectations that would be followed by the Fascist regime during the 1920s at the Genoa and Lausanne conferences (Isnenghi and Rochat 229–32). These issues created an enormous political controversy and represented a dangerous precedent that would be fatally copied by Hitler during the 1930s (Ferguson 428, 440).

Therefore, Frederic's discourse is far-reaching. For his 1920s audience, his comments implied that the Italian unlimited expansionism and militarism after the war were the ideological products of the final victories. Italians wanted more than other nations because they simply thought of themselves as victorious. Like Frederic Henry, Hemingway would think about the international consequences of the First World War and its impact on the morale of the nations. He would express the importance of national defeat in understanding the subsequent development of European politics: "France was not beaten in 1940. France was beaten in 1917. Singapore was not really lost in 1942. It was lost at Gallipoli and the Somme and in the mud of Passchendaele [. . .] Austria was destroyed in the battle of Vittorio-Veneto at the end of October in 1918" (*MAW* xx–xxi).

A Doomed Army

In the days before the Caporetto retreat, Frederic's discourse foreshadows the Italian disaster in terms of national history. He did not believe in the Italian Army as a real army capable of defeating the Central Powers because "[t]hey were beaten to start with. They were beaten when they took them from their farms and put them in the army. That is why the peasant has wisdom, because he is defeated from the start. Put him in power and see how wise he is" (*FTA* 179).

Frederic portrays the Italian soldiers merely as peasants, too fatalistic and too interested in their own private affairs to understand the whole meaning of the human sacrifice that represented the war. His negative comments on the Italian soldiers are similar to those of the French General Foch after Caporetto (Gatti 241–42). Frederic seems to forget that during the early Battles of the Isonzo, this kind of peasant army managed to stop the Habsburg forces and prevented the Central Powers from sending forces into the French front (Thompson 283). The Italian people had made a great sacrifice not only for their own country but also by extension for the whole of democratic Europe. Indeed, Hemingway came back to America after the First World War with a great opinion of the Italian Army (*Letters* 1: 118). During the 1930s, Hemingway would stick, however, to Frederic's negative view of the Italian Army when Mussolini sent forces to participate in the Spanish Civil War. Mussolini struggled to militarize the Italian people, something that Hemingway found somewhat odd and unnatural, as he would state in his article "The Time Now, The Place Spain," published in Arnold Gingrich's *Ken* on April 7, 1938:

> Mussolini has forged a people into a war machine. Some of them are good fighters, and he has some excellent troops. His Alpine troops are as good as any in the world. But he needs those good troops to defend his frontiers [. . .] Mussolini, to make war, as soon as he has used up his elite, has to depend on the ordinary run of the mine conscripts. The average Italian conscript is only a passable soldier, even if he is exceptionally well-led, and there never have been enough brave, cool, non-panicky Italians in Italy, not even in Caesar's time, to officer an army of the size Mussolini has built.

The Italian peasantry are a sound, solid, hard working, peaceful, very wise and excellent people. [...] But the sum of this people does not add up as soldiers.

Fascism in Italy is the bluff of a bully playing at soldier. (*Literary Reference* 205)

In many respects, in *A Farewell to Arms* Frederic's negative opinions of the Italian Army are closer to those of General Cadorna and General Leonida Bissolati. The generals pointed out that a kind of national degeneration was the first cause of the Italian defeat at Caporetto (Gatti 229). Other writers, such as D'Annunzio and Filippo Tommaso Marinetti, mentioned the general degeneration of Italian society and expected that the war could change the average Italian (Bonadeo 83). Yet Frederic's discourse corrects conservative and militaristic ideologies. On the one hand, the Italian generals could not understand that the Italian people were fed up with the abuses of the elite. If they wanted to be soldiers, they should be firstly free citizens. On the other hand, Marinetti and D'Annunzio were unable to understand the importance of the people, their wisdom. Frederic could not hide that state politics, and not so much the people, was the womb in which the Italian war was developed. As Alfredo Bonadeo remarks:

> A recent study of documents on public opinion compiled by the civil governors of the provinces shows that in April 1915 the Italian people "did not want war," that the peasants, the largest part of the lower class, "wanted peace," and that even the bourgeoisie, which included most of the interventionists, had "a very limited desire" to go to war to annex Trento, Trieste, and territories on the Adriatic coast. (72)

Frederic's comments on the lack of power of the Italian peasant imply that the hidden ambitions of a minority of people were the embryo for a mass war that made thousands and thousands of unknown soldiers crash against Austrian artillery in a confined alpine space. Two men, Prime Minister Antonio Salandra and Foreign Minister Sidney Sonnino, managed to win King Emmanuelle II's support for entering the war. As Mark Thompson points out, "The constitution gave the monarch overarching power. [...] He could issue decrees with the force of law, and declare war without consulting parliament" (19). Although apparently a liberal democracy, Italy was in fact an absolutist regime, technically speaking (Gentile 11–15). Moreover, the Great War would only serve to uphold a small elite of entrepreneurs and politicians who wanted to control the totality of the Adriatic Sea (Rusconi 27–133).

Frederic Henry's statements regarding the importance of the people and of democracy mirror those that would develop in Hemingway from the 1930s onward. He could only see this lack of democracy as a constant threat to the world, as in the end Fascist power proved more potent when it was imitated by Hitler and Franco just a few years later. In the early 1940s, when looking back at the world emerging after the First World War and branching into a new world war, Hemingway vehemently expressed that "there will be no lasting peace, nor any possibility of a just peace, until *all lands* where the people are ruled, exploited and governed by any government whatsoever against their consent are given their freedom" (*MAW* xxi). Hemingway realized that in the modern geopolitical paradigm emerging from the world wars, no nation could be totally immune from disaster, for the bells toll for everybody sooner or later.

A Tragic Front

Book 3 of *A Farewell to Arms* represents a complex meditation on the nature of the First World War using the disaster of Caporetto as a case in point. At the very beginning of the section, as soon as he returns to the Italian front in the autumn of 1917 after his convalescence in Milan, Frederic approaches the front from a different perspective than that of a mere soldier following the orders of his superiors. He analyzes with Gino the nature of the Italian front in these terms:

> [...] I thought a ridge that flattened out on top and had a little depth would be easier and more practical to hold than a succession of small mountains. It was no harder to attack up a mountain than on the level, I argued.
>
> [...] I did not believe in a war in mountains. I had thought about it a lot, I said. You pinched off one mountain and they pinched off another but when something really started every one had to get down off the mountains.

> [. . . I]n the old days the Austrians were always whipped in the quadrilateral around Verona. They let them come down onto the plain and whipped them there. (*FTA* 183)

Frederic implicitly criticizes the very core of the military tactics of his superiors. In fact, General Cadorna was convinced that frontal attack was always profitable even against mountainous positions that might seem at first glance "impregnable." In his book *Attacco frontale e ammaestramento tattico* (Frontal attack and tactical training) published in 1915, the general stated that in the mountains dead ground allowed advance under cover and deployment toward the flanks unseen by the enemy. Unfortunately for Cadorna, the Italian military campaigns on the Isonzo and the Carso had contradicted his theory. As Mark Thompson points out: "Where was the dead ground at the foot of Carso escarpments? What would the Habsburg forces not see from their trenches on the summit ridges? Even if the enemy had to retreat, how would their difficulties compare with those of the Italians, attacking uphill all the way?" (54). Rather, in *A Farewell to Arms*, Frederic's comments on army tactics evoke recent military history, especially the Napoleonic Wars (Reynolds 153–58). The French General had shown that the only way to beat an enemy in an environment such as that of the north of Italy was to wage a defensive war on the Venetian plateau. Cadorna never understood, as did Napoleon, the importance of waging a defensive war in order to beat the Austrians. Like a modern version of General Braddock, Cadorna blindly followed the paradigm of French generals such as Joffre, Foch, and Nivelle, who defended the concept of *offensive à outrance* (Bonadeo 77–78). Before the Caporetto's defeat, Frederic has come to understand that this kind of offensive could only be destructive for the Italian Army in the long run and implicitly finds an explanation for the lack of morale of the troops.

A Sacred War

Before Italy's entrance into the war, interventionist writers such as Giuseppe De Robertis celebrated the opportunity of joining the Allies in a common cause by stressing that common people "should be thankful for the opportunity to fight and die on the battlefield. Death conferred upon them some dignity, which they lacked entirely before the war" (qtd. in Bonadeo 125). When returning to Bainsizza Plateau, the place where he had been wounded, Frederic Henry's discourse undermines patriotic convictions such as those of De Robertis. While talking with another patriot, Gino, Frederic gradually unearths the obscure truth hidden underneath the bombastic rhetoric on the Italian front. Thus, when he asks Gino if he likes the Bainsizza Plateau, the driver's answer reveals the huge gap separating patriotic rhetoric from sheer reality:

> "The soil is sacred," he said. "But I wish it grew more potatoes. You know when we came here we found fields of potatoes the Austrians had planted."
> "Has the food really been short?"
> "I myself have never had enough to eat but I am a big eater and I have not starved. The mess is average. The regiments in the line get pretty good food but those in support don't get so much. Something is wrong somewhere. There should be plenty of food." (*FTA* 184)

In a grotesque fashion, like a modern Sancho Panza, Gino realizes the difference between idealism and reality, between the sacred soil and the need of "growing more potatoes." He notices the ugly reality of the front: how the high commanders, such as Cadorna, can force exhausted troops to a miserable death in such a deadly ground as the Bainsizza Plateau, while simultaneously forgetting to provide the army's basic needs. Moreover, unconsciously, in mentioning that the soil "is sacred," Gino is also mocking a peculiar aspect of Italian front ideology, that of the mystification of the front. For, before the arrival of the Fascist regime, extremely popular poets such as Vittorio Locchi introduced in their war poetry religious motifs "to induce awe and deference" (Thompson 182). In 1917 Locchi published *La sagra di Santa Gorizia* (Sabbath of holy Gorizia) after the ninth Battle of the Isonzo, on November 18, 1916. Mixing up D'Annunzio's sadism and popular religious feeling, his popular piece recreated the horror of war as a ritual of blood as much as of mystic transformation (Isnenghi 288–89):

> all the bayonets
> yield like ensigns
> on the altars of the mountains,
> on the sacred carnage of our dead. (translated in Thompson 182)

Vittorio Locchi's poetical piece, with his "altars" and "sacred carnage," epitomizes what Emilio Gentile describes as the progressive transference of the sacred from the domain of established religions to that of politics. Political movements appropriated religious discourses and began to occupy the ground left by the sacred from the French Revolution onward. In Italy, this issue had started in the post-Risorgimento liturgy of the State, continued during the war front, and would be entirely developed by the Fascist regime (Burdett 2–3). In *A Farewell to Arms*, Frederic challenges this ideology as he watches the desolate image of the front from the Bainsizza Plateau:

> I was always embarrassed by the words sacred, glorious, and sacrifice and the expression in vain [. . .] I had seen nothing sacred, and the things that were glorious had no glory and the sacrifices were like the stockyards at Chicago if nothing was done with meat except to bury it. (*FTA* 184–85)

In destroying the mystifying ideology of the front, Frederic also appropriates D'Annunzio's rhetoric of death and then modifies it thoroughly. In *Notturno* (Nocturne), a book that deeply influenced Hemingway, the Italian poet faces the death of his friends as a case in point of how modern war had reduced death to animal degradation (Comley 48). Thus, D'Annunzio describes his feelings when evoking the image of a fallen friend, Giuseppe Miraglia: "My grief is full of blood. My dreams are full of blood. Every thought of mine is soaked with blood. Sometimes my past repulses me and bleeds like a slaughterhouse filled with quartered beasts hanging from the walls" (D'Annunzio 166–67; translated in Bonadeo 132). D'Annunzio also describes how the corpse of another dead friend, Giovanni Federico, a twenty-year-old sailor of Abruzzi, "is laid out like one of those animals that the butcher has quartered on the slaughterhouse's chopping block. His soul is divine in proportion as his body is brutish" (D'Annunzio 166; translated in Bonadeo 131). D'Annunzio finds a transcendental sense in patriotism that can redeem the brutality of the Great War. Yet, unlike D'Annunzio's sadistic heroism (the belief that blood and death can put a soldier in a state of grace and make brutal war something divine), Frederic Henry's view of the front as a Chicago stockyard is realistic and material. Modern war has shown Hemingway's hero that there is no room for patriotic transcendence, only for brutish and degrading death.

The Laws of Unnatural Selection

In 1915 nationalists such as D'Annunzio welcomed Italy's entrance into the war as the first true collective national experience of the nation, and then during the Fascist regime Mussolini struggled to offer a positive myth of the conflict. The veterans were the aristocracy of "new men" bound to regenerate the nation. War was commemorated in cities, towns, and villages. The common Italian soldier was represented as the *umile fante*—energetic, aggressive patriots, "meeting death with a song and a smile" (Burdett 3–4; Thompson 390). Frederic's account of Caporetto's retreat undermines the ideology of national unity as well as the concept of *umile fante* embedded in Fascist and nationalist cultures. Through Frederic, Hemingway succeeds in debunking patriotic ideology by illustrating how degenerated Italian soldiers in the war can become. He shows how the military men are unable to follow the prescription of their duty. Thus, one of the sergeants who has joined Frederic's group tries to steal a clock from an abandoned farmhouse. Later, another sergeant is shot after disobeying Frederic's demand for authority.

The war was also an occasion to vent political resentment and created a hellish landscape of social disintegration. Socialist Bonello seizes the opportunity to legally kill their class superiors following Frederic's orders (208). Bonello cannot hide a sense of accomplishment: "[A]ll my life I've wanted to kill a sergeant" (207). That evening Bonello deserts from the group because he was afraid to die. Implicitly, Bonello questions the legality of Frederic's execution order. As Linda Wagner-Martin states, "[H]aving witnessed—been part of—the killing of the sergeant surely made Bonello tentative about his own desertion. Who could be sure that Frederic Henry would not draw on him?" (95). As the group approaches the Tagliamento River, Frederic observes how some of the soldiers throw away the arms and shout, "*A basso gli ufficiali!*" (*FTA* 219). The atmosphere of chaos escalates when Aymo dies because of friendly fire. In Frederic's narrative, the war is not a collective experience of national unity but rather an instrument of chaos, cowardice, and degeneration. Certainly, neither Aymo nor the sergeant met death "with a song and a smile" in Hemingway's novel, nor did they embody the ideals of the trench aristocracy bound to regenerate the Italian nation.

Frederic soon discovers, however, that political and military chaos degenerates into a new kind of order when he approaches the bridge over the Tagliamento. An order from General Cadorna, on October 31, 1917, authorized officers to shoot any soldier who happened to be separated from his unit or offered the least resistance. As Mark Thompson points out, this order "made a target of ten divisions of the Second Army. The worst abuses occurred near the northern bridges over the Tagliamento, where commanders who had abandoned their men days earlier saw a chance to redeem themselves" (319). When arriving at a bridge over the Tagliamento, Frederic describes how the military police, with the excuse of enforcing military order, took the occasion to wipe out many war veterans. As he observes: "[T]he questioners had all the efficiency, coldness and command of themselves of Italians who are firing and are not being fired on" (*FTA* 223).

Frederic describes how a new bureaucracy was seizing power in Italy at the rear of the front. The final aim is a state machine stamping out an old generation of exhausted combatants such as the fat gray-haired little lieutenant colonel executed by the *carabinieri*. Hemingway portrayed the dignity of these veteran soldiers facing ignominious death in the rain. These soldiers represented the best of the Italian Army; they represented wisdom and dignity, and the new generation was trying to take their posts by wiping them out miserably. This efficient behavior as embodied in the noncombatant *carabinieri* is very similar to that of the Fascist forces of which Hemingway reported for the *Toronto Star* during his return to Milan in the early 1920s: the Fascist thugs "had a taste of killing under police protection and they liked it" (*DT* 175). At the Tagliamento River bridge, the *carabinieri* also embodied the "greatest Italian sense" of "self-preservation" of the Fascist hitchhiker that Hemingway had come across in 1927 when he traveled to La Spezia (*CSS* 224).

Indeed, the episode narrated by Frederic might have infuriated Fascist authorities. On November 2, 1917, Cadorna gave General Andrea Graziani the task of restoring discipline among the troops retreating from Caporetto. Graziani was a brutal officer who would shoot nineteen men in the back for minor offenses on the morning of November 16. After the war, Graziani became an enthusiastic Fascist, rising to the highest level of the military (De Simone 251). *A Farewell to Arms* brilliantly suggests how potentially Fascist killers (of the Graziani type) managed to wipe out, under the protection of General Cadorna's authoritarian law, a whole generation of exhausted soldiers. Whereas the narrator of the contemporaneously published novel by Erich Maria Remarque, *All Quiet on the Western Front*, analyzes the key to German disaster during the war in terms of a battle between an old generation that embodied authority and deception, and a new generation lacking any kind of practical patriarchal guide, Frederic views the war in totally different terms (Remarque 19–20). Frederic appreciates the wisdom and the courage of the former generation of Italian officers who fought on the Carso, the Alps, and the Bainsizza Plateau. This generation dramatically perished at Caporetto, not only physically but also morally, and would be symbolically obliterated from Italian memory by Fascist ideology.

Moreover, in Hemingway's novel the fact that sheltered noncombatants exercised power over worn-out combatants casts doubt on Mussolini, who had managed to escape the harsh reality of the front (*DT* 255–56). In fact, ever since his meeting with Mussolini in Lausanne, Hemingway started to cast doubt on the real identity of Il Duce and by extension on the Fascist movement. From 1925 onward, for Hemingway Mussolini was only a pretender, not a real warrior. Hemingway would comment on Il Duce:

> Mussolini himself was wounded superficially in the legs and backside by the premature explosion of an Italian trench mortar in the early years of the war and never returned to the front. I have often thought that all his martial bombast and desire for military glory was a defense mechanism formed against his knowledge of how frightened he had been in the world war and the ignominious exit he had made from it. (*MAW* xviii)

Very much like Berthold Brecht's view of Nazism in *The Resistible Rise of Arturo Ui*, written in 1941, Hemingway saw the elite governing Italy as a group of pretenders and killers who tried to shelter themselves under the umbrella of law in order to commit murder. For Frederic, the war is not only a personal tragedy but also a collective tragedy, for the military debauchery deprived Italy of a whole generation of brave men who could exercise leadership in postwar Italy. They were executed by incompetent military policemen. Quoting war theorist Carl von Clausewitz, policemen ignored the fact that "everything is very simple in war, but the simplest thing is difficult. These difficulties accumulate and produce a friction which no man can imagine exactly who has not seen war" (qtd. in *MAW* 640).

Against D'Annunzio's sacred heroism and Fascism's national regeneration rhetoric, Frederic could see the Italian Front only as representing a real hell in which an unnatural selection of the brave was taking place. War became the very region of chance. Caporetto's defeat provides the reader with a tragic image of modern warfare in which "[t]he coward dies a thousand deaths, the brave but one" (*FTA* 139). The courageous ones, the best ones, the very brave, were the first to die in that kind of war. The survivors were not really the powerful and the brave but only the fake creators of myth epitomized by the rising of Fascism into power after the First World War. Frederic could endorse another Italian front's witness terminology, that of Giuseppe Tomasi di Lampedusa, who was taken prisoner by the Austrian army in November 1917 (Gilmour 42–43). Like the Sicilian author, Frederic could also see current Italian history as the triumph of "the little jackals, hyenas" (di Lampedusa 183).

Conclusion

First, Frederic's discourse sheds light on how greedy politicians, sadistic military tactics, and a rhetoric of blind patriotism and mystic brutality managed to bring a whole nation to the verge of chaos after Caporetto's defeat. Secondly, Frederic's account portrays how Socialist and defeatist ideologies contributed to increase the front's chaos but were unable to articulate a practical political solution to stop the war and the systematic slaughter of the Italian people—a people without a real political voice before and after the conflict. Then, through Frederic's account of the Tagliamento executions, there emerges a representation of a powerful and authoritarian bureaucratic system that the Fascist regime would be in charge of perpetuating and improving after the conflict.

Finally, Frederic's words represent a tragic memory of a lost Italian generation: that of Gino, Bonello, Aymo, Passini, and Piani, among thousands and thousands of soldiers, a generation doomed to fight an impossible offensive war in rugged mountain terrain. The endurance and courage of that generation is worth remembering.

Works Cited

Bonadeo, Alfredo. *Mark of the Beast: Death and Degradation in the Literature of the Great War*. Lexington: UP of Kentucky, 1989.

Burdett, Charles. *Journeys through Fascism: Italian Travel Writing between the Wars*. New York: Berghahn Books, 2007.

Cirino, Mark. "The Nasty Mess: Hemingway, Italian Fascism, and the *New Review* Controversy of 1932." *Hemingway Review* 33.2 (Spring 2014): 30–47.

Comisso, Giovanni. *Opere*. Ed. Ronaldo Damiani and Nico Naldi. Milano: Mondadori, 2002.

Comley, Nancy R. "The Italian Education of Ernest Hemingway." *Hemingway's Italy: New Perspectives*. Ed. Rena Sanderson. Baton Rouge: Louisiana State UP, 2006. 41–50.

D'Annunzio, Gabriele. *Notturno*. Ed. Elisa Maria Bertinotti. Milano: Mursia, 1995.

De Simone, Cesare. *L'Isonzo mormora: Fanti e generali a Caporetto*. Milano: Mursia, 1995.

Di Lampedusa, Giuseppe. *The Leopard*. Trans. Guido Waldman. New York: Pantheon Books, 2007.

Ferguson, Niall. *The War of the World*. London: Allen Lane, 2006.

Fortunati, Vita. "Hemingway, the Embodiment of the American Myth, and Italian Leftist Writers." *Hemingway's Italy: New Perspectives*. Ed. Rena Sanderson. Baton Rouge: Louisiana State UP, 2006. 225–31.

Gatti, Angelo. *Caporetto: Diario di guerra (maggio–dicembre 1917)*. Ed. Alberto Monticone. Bologna: Il Mulino, 1997.

Gentile, Emilio. *Il culto del littorio*. Bari: Laterza, 2001.

Gilmour, David. *The Last Leopard: A Life of Giuseppe Tomasi di Lampedusa*. London: Eland Publishing, 2007.

Hemingway, Ernest. *A Farewell to Arms*. New York: Simon and Schuster, 1995.

———. *The Complete Poems*. Ed. Nicolas Gerogiannis. Lincoln: U of Nebraska P, 1992.

———. *The Complete Short Stories: The Finca Vigía Edition*. New York: Scribner's, 1998.

———. *Dateline: Toronto: The Complete Toronto Star Dispatches, 1920–1924*. Ed. William White. New York: Charles Scribner's Sons, 1985.

———. *The Letters of Ernest Hemingway*. Vol. 1, *1907–1922*. Ed. Sandra Spanier and Robert W. Trogdon. Cambridge, UK: Cambridge UP, 2011.

———. *The Letters of Ernest Hemingway*. Vol. 2, *1923–1925*. Ed. Sandra Spanier, Albert J. DeFazio III, and Robert W. Trogdon. Cambridge, UK: Cambridge UP, 2013.

———. *A Literary Reference*. Ed. Robert W. Trogdon. New York: Carroll & Graf, 1999.

———, ed. *Men at War: The Best War Stories of All Time*. New York: Crown, 1942.
Isnenghi, Mario. "La Grande Guerra." *I luoghi della memoria: Strutture ed eventi dell'Italia unita*. Ed. Mario Isnenghi. Bari: Laterza, 1997. 273–309.
Isnenghi, Mario, and Giorgio Rochat. *La Grande Guerra, 1914–1918*. Bologna: Il Mulino, 2008.
Pivano, Fernanda. "Introduzione." *Addio alle armi*. Milano: Mondadori, 1965. i–xv.
Remarque, Erich Maria. *All Quiet on the Western Front*. Trans. Brian Murdoch. London: CRW, 2012.
Reynolds, Michael. *Hemingway's First War: The Making of "A Farewell to Arms."* Princeton: Princeton UP, 1976.
Rigoni Stern, Mario. "Prefazione." *Diario di un imboscato*. Milano: Mursia, 1999.
Rochat, Giorgio. *L'esercito italiano da Vittorio Veneto a Mussolini, 1919–1925*. Bari: Laterza, 2006.
Rossi, Pio. *La prima guerra mondiale: Diario inedito*. Pordenone: Edizioni Biblioteca dell'Immagine, 2014.
Rusconi, Gian Enrico. *L'azzardo del 1915: Come l'Italia decide la sua guerra*. Bologna: Il Mulino, 2009.
Sanderson, Rena, ed. *Hemingway's Italy: New Perspectives*. Baton Rouge: Louisiana State UP, 2006.
Tazzer, Sergio. *Ragazzi del Novantanove*. Vittorio Veneto, Treviso: Kellermann Editore, 2012.
Thompson, Mark. *The White War: Life and Death on the Italian Front, 1915–1919*. London: Faber and Faber, 2008.
Wagner-Martin, Linda. *Ernest Hemingway's "A Farewell to Arms": A Reference Guide*. Westport, CT: Greenwood Press, 2003.

8

Reading and Not Reading *The Black Pig* in *A Farewell to Arms*

MIRIAM B. MANDEL

In chapter 2 of *A Farewell to Arms*, we come across the following dialogue:

> "Did you ever read the 'Black Pig'?" asked the lieutenant. "I will get you a copy. It was that which shook my faith."
>
> "It is a filthy and vile book," said the priest. "You do not really like it."
>
> "It is very valuable," said the lieutenant. "It tells you about those priests. You will like it," he said to me. I smiled at the priest and he smiled back across the candle-light. "Don't you read it," he said.
>
> "I will get it for you," said the lieutenant. (7–8)

This short passage lets us know several things: that *Black Pig* is a book; that it probably presents a strong anti-Christian or anti-Church argument; that Lieutenant Rinaldi, like most Italians of his generation, was brought up as a believing Catholic; and that he reads, or knows about, Church dogma and books about the Church. The priest's denunciation of *Black Pig* indicates that he too is familiar with the book, or at least with its reputation, which further suggests that it might have been a fairly well known item in the Italy of World War I. And Frederic Henry's inclusion of this reference in his retrospective narrative indicates that, whether or not he himself reads, discussions about literary texts stay in his memory.

We all know that authors can tell their readers a lot about their characters by supplying details about their intellectual furniture, most directly by having the characters make literary or artistic references in speech. In *A Farewell to Arms*, Hemingway avails himself of this technique to show us, in general, the lack of intellectual curiosity of his two main characters. Frederic Henry and Catherine Barkley show familiarity with well-known painters (Mantegna, Rubens, Titian) and with canonic authors (Shakespeare, Marvell), but their current reading is sparse, practical, and not literary: Catherine reads the *Almanac* and Frederic reads magazines and newspapers (mostly out of date). The priest, when he visits Frederic in the hospital, brings him that scandalous weekly tabloid, *News of the World*, figuring that this is the sort of thing that Frederic will enjoy reading. The most intellectually sophisticated and up-to-date reader in the novel is probably its oldest character, Count Greffi, who recommends contemporary novels by Henri Barbusse (*Le Feu*) and H. G. Wells (*Mr. Britling Sees It Through*), both published in 1916. Frederic has read and disagrees with Wells's patriotic British best seller, which he dismisses as not "any good" (*FTA* 261), but he has not read Barbusse's famous antiwar novel (it won the prestigious Prix Goncourt in 1916), even though it had already been translated into English at the time of the action. And in spite of Count Greffi's warm recommendation, Frederic did not seek to obtain this book, just as he does not seem to have obtained, from Rinaldi or anyone else, a copy of *The Black Pig*.

Although not listed in the *Index Librorum Prohibitorum*, *The Black Pig* has been remarkably difficult to locate. Looking for it in the late 1980s and early 1990s, I corresponded by letter and by fax with several American and Italian academics and institutions, but with no success. And so, when my book of annotations—*Reading Hemingway: The Facts in the Fictions* (1995)—came out, it presented an embarrassingly blank space where that annotation ought to have been. Soon after, however, Professor Gianfranca Balestra of the Università Cattolica del Sacro Cuore (Milan) not only located the book but took the extraordinary trouble of having the whole thing xeroxed for me. Finally, in late 1995, I had the 288 pages of *Il maiale nero: Rivelazioni e documenti* in my hands.

Hemingway scholarship has displayed surprisingly little curiosity about *The Black Pig*. To date, no articles have been written about it, and no one has translated it into English. But in 2004, a new reader, Antoine Blanche, brought it up in an Internet discussion group:

I've just (in the past hour) read the first five chapters of Hemingway's *A Farewell to Arms*. Very early on, Lieutenant Rinaldi taunts the priest with *The Black Pig*: a very unholy book if the priest's reaction is anything to go by. Is *The Black Pig* a genuine work of literature or merely from the depths of Hemingway's imagination? I can't find a reference to it anywhere (Wikipedia, Britannica, Amazon, etc.), not even when the title is translated to Italian.

This elicited a number of responses, among them an incorrect identification, complete with Internet abbreviations and decorations: "AFAIK, it's a genuine piece of English poetry. :-) William Butler Yeats: 'In the Valley of the Black Pig'" (Paolo Pizzi). Blanche rightly rejected this answer:

Of course, I came across that during my research but that's not it. Thanks for the response though. :)

It's definitely a real work of Italian literature; a book and not a poem. Doubtfully published in English at all. Definitely not by Yeats. A very anti-Church and anti-Priest book.

The puzzle was partially solved by Enzo Michelangeli:

"Il Maiale Nero" is a novel written by Umberto Notari in the early 20th Century. His most famous book is the first he published in 1904, "Quelle signore" ("Those ladies"), about the world of prostitution: it earned him a prosecution for obscenity resulting in a fine, but the book was reprinted and by 1920 had sold more than half million copies.

Eventually Notari ended up as a fascist, founding the Milanese newspaper "L'Ambrosiano" in 1922, and was appointed to the very institutional "Accademia d'Italia": just like another firebrand-turned-reactionary, the initiator of the Italian Futuristic movement Filippo Tommaso Marinetti, who, as a young, used to call for burning academies down... [signed] Enzo.

Umberto Notari was also identified as the author in a Chinese forum under the title "Critical Analysis of Hemingway's *A Farewell to Arms*." Here, an unidentified person writes:

Some think war is about right and wrong, but through the dialogue between the priest and the soldiers we learn that values are not always so clear cut. The uniform they wear makes them very proud. It is almost sacrilege for the man of fighting age not to be fighting. They are hypocritical. Hemingway shows the Pity and irony in this story when one of the Italian lieutenants tells Henry and the priest that he likes a book called "The Black Pig" written by Umberto Notari.

The Black Pig is not a novel, as Enzo claims, but an energetic, apparently learned, vitriolic attack on the precepts and clergy of the Catholic Church. It was first published in 1907 under the title *Il maiale nero: Rivelazioni e documenti* (Sesto S. Giovanni, Milano: A. Barion). A later edition carried the title *Dio contro Dio* on the first title page and at the top of every page, with the previous title presented as subtitle on the second title page.

In 1907, Notari (1878–1950) was already a best-selling journalist, polemicist, biographer, novelist, and dramatist. All told, he would write more than thirty books, in six of which he examines the position of women in society, most notably with a 1903 exegesis of prostitution in high and low places called *Signore sole: Interviste con le più belle e le più celebri artiste* (Single women: Interviews with the most beautiful and famous artists) that sold 21,000 copies and was denounced as immoral and obscene and taken to court, which inevitably increased its readership. It was followed by *Quelle signore: Scene di una grande città moderna* (Those women: Scenes of a great modern city; ca. 1904), which was set in a house of prostitution and whose main character, Ellere, was recognizably based on Notari's good friend Filippo Tommaso Marinetti (1876–1944), an Egyptian-born Italian poet, editor, firebrand, and founder of the Futurist movement. Notari's novel sold 80,000 copies in six months and sales only increased when it was accused of offending public morality; it and its author were acquitted, with Marinetti serving as witness for the defense. "It was Notari's good fortune," one scholar writes, "to be accused of obscenity by a court in Parma. . . . Marinetti, who attended and clearly relished the trial, wrote a detailed account of it for Parisian readers . . . and then translated his account into Italian, appending a brief, self-congratulatory introduction" (Adamson 97). Marinetti bragged that the trial "gave an extraordinary boost to the book's sales such that, today, one finds it in all the elegant parlors, in all the bedrooms, under the virginal bedlinens of all the convent-school girls and inside the prayer benches of all the new brides" (qtd. in Adamson 97–98). Notari quickly produced a sequel, *Femmina: Scene di una grande capitale* (1906), which also became a best seller before it too was seized and banned. Notari proudly listed these three books' sales figures and legal histories in the front matter of his next book, *The Black Pig* (1907).

By this time, Notari, born into a poor family, had become quite well-to-do. In 1901 he had married a rich widow, bought an estate, and established a literary salon; in 1910, he launched a publishing house, Società Anonima Notari, through which he later published classical editions, musical scores, and some of his own work, including the first few of what would become a long list of journals devoted to a variety of topics that interested him: sports, theater, medicine, finance, the culinary arts, and, of course, politics. He supported universal suffrage and divorce and argued strongly for expelling the Vatican from Italy. Some twenty years after the publication of *The Black Pig*, he retook the "woman question" with *La donna "tipo tre"* (The type-three woman; 1929), about the woman who is financially, socially, and otherwise independent. The year 1930 saw two more titles on the topic of women: *Le ragazze allarmanti* (The alarming girls) and *La donna negli affari* (The woman in business).

The Black Pig's front matter also mentions two earlier publications that reveal Notari's anticlerical bias: *Carducci Intimo* (1903), a biography of Giosuè Carducci (1835–1907), the Italian poet, professor, classicist, translator, freethinker, fierce opponent of the Catholic Church, and author of "Hymn to Satan," who would be awarded the 1906 Nobel Prize in Literature; and *Il Papa alla porta! Inchiesta e conclusioni per l'abolizione del Papato* (Throw the Pope out! An inquest and conclusions for the abolition of the Papacy), aimed at the recently elected and very conservative Pope Pius X. Notari's anticlericalism is also visible in his dedication of *The Black Pig*: "A due invitti rinnovatori di un Italia pagana e virile, dedico questo libro di demolizione di una Italia chiercuta e bazzotta" (To two indomitable revivers of a pagan and virile Italy, I dedicate this book aimed at the destruction of a tonsured and limp Italy).

These paratexts are followed by an address to the reader, decrying the contemporary Church's attempt to regulate behavior by means of what Notari called "the Society in Defense of Public Morality." This exordium introduces the reader to Notari's strong, personal style: his use of the first-person point of view, his direct address to the audience, his tone (variously sarcastic, incredulous, and outraged), his penchant for using repetition and rhetorical questions to emphasize a point, and his reliance on footnotes, not just to document his sources but also and mainly to offer quotes from holy books as a sarcastic counterpoint to his exposé of that same matter on the page itself. This continuous dialogue between text and paratext underscores his thesis: that the Church is hypocritical and its clergymen despicable.

Notari does not offer a table of contents, so I created one:

Table of Contents for *Il maiale nero* (1907 edition)

Cap. I	L'origine del "Maiale nero"	19
Cap. II	Primi grugniti	45
Cap. III	Il Maiale grufola	67
Cap. IV	Satanismo e stregoneria	111
Cap. V	La messa nera	157
Cap. VI	In pieno brago	178
Cap. VII	Il "maiale nero" assassino	205
Cap. VIII	Il "maiale nero" ladro	221
Cap. IX	Il "maiale nero" papa	241
Cap. X	Perorazione a Sua Santità Pio X	277
	Fonti principali di quest'opera	287

The chapter titles faithfully reflect the book's thesis:

Chap. I	The Origins of the "Black Pig"
Chap. II	First or Early Grunts [first oinks]
Chap. III	The Pig Roots About
Chap. IV	Satanism and Witchcraft
Chap. V	The Black Mass
Chap. VI	Right in the Mire
Chap. VII	The "Black Pig" Assassin
Chap. VIII	The "Black Pig" Thief
Chap. IX	The "Black Pig" Pope
Chap. X	Peroration to His Holiness Pope Pius X
	Principal Sources for This Work

Chapter I explains that the term *maiale nero* (black pig) is a common appellation for priests, and then proceeds to attack the texts, ceremonies, and precepts of the Catholic Church, finding them to be not divine revelation but plagiarized from other cultures and religions. Moses, for example, is simply a version of Bacchus, the Roman god of wine and intoxication, of drunken revelries and orgies. Notari supports his claim with a long list of similarities between Bacchus and Moses, to whose validity I cannot attest. The Christian myth of creation is also derivative, based on Phoenician, Chaldean, and Indian myths, which in turn derive from *gambahar* or Zoroastrian creation myth, adopted by the Persians. Adam, the first man, is none other than Adimo of the ancient Brahmin book of *Ezourveidam*; the Garden of Eden derives from Saana in Arabia, the serpent from an Indian myth, and Noah was saved from the flood just as Deucalion and Pyrrha were saved from a great deluge in the Greek myths. Elijah and his fiery chariot derive from Apollo. The only difference, says Notari, is that the pagan imagination was more graceful. Notari also traces pagan origins for Abraham's sacrifice of his son and Samson's victory over the Philistines; the Immaculate Conception, he argues, derives from Asian idols such as the Chinese Foe and the Indian Vishnu, as well as Xaca, Brahma, Sammonocodom, and so on. The angels, the devil, the resurrection, the Trinity, baptism, holy water, confession, heaven and hell, mortification of the flesh—all these concepts exist in earlier cultures and are not original or unique to Catholicism. Even the Eucharist, Notari says, was prefigured in Roman sources: "Mankind have attempted all the frightful insane things of which they are capable: they have just to take one more step and that is to eat the God they adore" (34).

Chapter II, "First or Early Grunts," focuses on martyrs and saints, starting with those who earned their sainthood by inflicting violence on others and consequently being beaten, flayed, or sentenced to death (i.e., martyred) for their earlier "pious" deeds; that is, they became martyrs when what they had done to others was done to them. Notari also deconstructs hagiographies in terms of history, finding, for example, that one early Christian was martyred by having to swallow needles long before needles were invented in the nineteenth century. He also rails against the sanctification of unsanitary behaviors, such as refusing to bathe or to undress in order to wash one's clothes; he sees these excesses of purity, abstinence, and modesty as pathological expressions of sexual repression. Citing Professor Ermete Rossi's *Psicopatia cristiana* (1892), Notari argues that teaching stories that extol filth, violence, torture, self-flagellation, starvation, and other activities performed by or inflicted upon martyred and sainted Christians does great damage to children. And he claims to be puzzled by the fact that, according to the Chronicles of the Church, three or four thousand sanctified women see themselves as married to Christ: does this mean that the

Church approves of bigamy? A mixture of obscure stories and acid deconstruction defines this chapter.

Chapter III, "The Pig Roots About," and Chapter IV, "Satanism and Witchcraft," are the book's longest (forty-four and forty-six pages, respectively). The first deals with sects and gnostic heresies that developed within early Christianity, each one claiming to possess the "vera essenza della nuova religione" (true essence of the new religion) and the path to salvation (67). Notari begins with *agape* (love) in the name of which some sects practiced free love. He mentions the Carpocratians, who insisted that salvation comes only when everything, including all forms of love and lust, has been experienced, thus allowing the soul to stop migrating from body to body and to rest in peace; the Stercorari, who sacramentally ingested human excrement, semen, and menstrual blood in the name of love; the followers of Éon de l'Étoile, who accepted him as the Final Judge; the followers of Wilhelmina of Bohemia, who accepted her as the female embodiment of the Holy Spirit; the Dulcinians, who sought salvation by sleeping in cribs, obtaining nourishment from wet nurses, and holding all their possessions, including their wives, jointly; and a number of other sects and beliefs that led to salvation through *agape*. Notari then devotes some thirteen pages to the Christian versions of the Roman cult of Priapus, discussing a number of phallic saints (e.g., Saint Priapus, Saint Foutin or Faustin, Saint Guerlichon or Greluchon, Saint Giles of Britain, Saint Renatus of Angers, Saint Guignolé of Brest, Saint Anthony of Zaragoza, Saints Cosmas and Damien, etc.) who offered miracles of fertility, virility, health, and salvation. Priests and worshippers were drawn to these sects, Notari insists, as a reaction to the sexual repression that the emerging Church advocated.

The medieval Church empowered priests to regulate the sexual behavior of its congregants, particularly women, and priestly intervention in matters such as proving virginity, dissolving or annulling marriages, proving and punishing frigidity or adultery, and even priestly participation in the custom of *droit du seigneur*, led husbands and fathers to keep their wives and daughters (via nuns, duennas, and even chastity belts) from the very priests who, under the guise of preaching purity and performing other priestly duties, corrupted their congregants. Sexual activity among priests was so widespread, Notari says, that William VII, duke of Aquitaine, and Joanna I, queen of Naples, established brothels disguised as abbeys, nunneries, or convents to keep priests from preying on the faithful, on the one hand,

and to raise money for themselves and for the Church, on the other. Notari spends the final sixteen pages of this long chapter on art and literature: depictions of depraved behaviors presented to worshippers in Church-approved illustrations of manuscripts, in paintings and icons of saints, and on stained glass windows, he argues, promulgate corruption. He mentions that lascivious poems (too filthy for him to translate into Italian) and other such literary documents were sometimes incorporated into sermons, and he summarizes the activities of the annual Feast of Fools, a carnivalesque mass and debauch held in churches. He remarks sarcastically that no "Society in Defense of Public Morality" has ever objected to any of this, because everything that priests do is declared to be holy and above reproach.

Chapter IV discusses satanism and witchcraft, explaining the role of the priests in encouraging visions and apparitions as expressions of the divine, and then, later, when the Church was sated with saints, as expressions of the satanic, the work of witches whom the priests had to identify (an easy task, as the least accusation would suffice to brand a person as a witch, and torture would cause the accused to confess), examine, try, and then neutralize, whether by exorcism, banishment, or death. The chapter details two complicated cases of satanic possession, one featuring Maria di Nogaredo that oddly enough involved a priest named Rinaldo Rinaldi (115–21), and the other focusing on Catherine Cadière and her confessor/seducer Girard, which involved a conflict between Jansenists and Jesuits (123–56).

In the next chapter, "The Black Mass," Notari explains that priests whose ambitions were thwarted or disappointed, or whose prayers to God went unanswered, all too often switched allegiances from God to Satan and performed parodies of the mass that gave free rein to the sexuality that had formerly been repressed, resulting in perversions such as the use of naked women as altars, the corruption of the Host in a variety of obscene ways, and even human sacrifice. Notari describes one of a series of such masses reportedly performed by the Abbé Étienne Guibourg on behalf of Madame de Montespan, the mistress of King Louis XIV (158–63), and then discusses other such manifestations in the nineteenth century, both in Europe and in the Americas, where, so Notari claims, Longfellow was involved (165–66). The chapter ends by translating the description of the black mass (166–77) from Joris-Karl Huysmans's cult novel *Là-bas* (1891).

Chapter VI, "Right in the Mire," focuses on Biblical and other "holy" texts that the Church prescribes for its faithful, thus exposing them to the lascivious, adulterous, and incestuous matter that is presented the Song of Songs, the books of Ezekiel and Hosea, and the story of Lot's incestuous relations with his daughters. Notari concludes that by rewarding Sara (with a child) for having procured Hagar to her husband, God in fact approves of pandering and concubinage. *Manual of Confession*, Notari continues, offers a question-and-answer presentation for defining the various degrees of sin involved in conjugal and extraconjugal relations, including sodomy, prostitution, homosexuality, polygamy, and customs such as *droit du seignor* (often by churchmen). These detailed Church-generated and -approved texts actually serve to stimulate the imaginations of both the confessors and their priests, a situation that puts the Church in the position of inspiring sexual behaviors that it hypocritically pretends to forbid and punish.

Notari begins Chapter VII, "The 'Black Pig' Assassin," by claiming that, throughout history, the ministers of God have, in the name of Christian dogma, dedicated themselves to "tre cardini fondamentali: corrompere, ucciere, rubare" (three fundamental principles: to corrupt, to kill, to rob; 205). Having already demonstrated how the priests corrupt the citizenry in the preceding chapters, Notari now turns to how they murder, listing some twenty-one historical events, starting with the conflicting claims of Cornelius and Novatian to the Papacy in 251 CE, which claimed two hundred of their followers as victims. The largest numbers emerge from the "horrible folly" of the Crusades (one million persons killed), the 150 years of religious wars in Europe spanning the reigns of Pope Leon X to Clement IX (two million people), and the Spanish conquest of America (five million indigenous people killed by missionaries and conquerors). All told, Notari's catalogue (208–12) totals up 9,723,500 people killed in the name of Christ. To this Notari adds a three-and-a-half-page list of religiously motivated political murders, ending with the stabbing, in 1847, of Pellegrino Rossi by a Jesuit.

The next chapter, "The 'Black Pig' Thief," details some of the Church's financial misdeeds against its faithful and against the State, sometimes in collusion with the State or with certain branches of the State. Notari mentions the sale of indulgences, quoting prices established by the fourteenth-century Pope John XXII and approved by the Court of France in 1691; he also quotes from "La Secreta Monita," a secret document (which actually seems to have been a forgery), purportedly sent by the Jesuit leadership to local priests, instructing them in careful detail how to handle the wealthy, and especially rich widows, so as to extract the most profit from them.

Chapter IX, "The 'Black Pig' Pope," reviews the scandalous behaviors of Popes through history, including stories about Pope Joan (a putative female pope); Pope Sergio III and his affair with Marozia (which yielded a son who also became Pope); Pope John XIX, who sold absolutions; and Pope Benedict IX, who sold his throne to Pope John XX, who in turn sold it to Pope Sylvester III, whereupon they all three trafficked it to Pope Gregory VI. Notari also debunks Popes Gregory VII, declared a martyr by the Church; Innocent III, declared a hero; Innocent IV, declared a philanthropist; and Boniface VIII, whom Dante placed in the Inferno while the Church consigns him to heaven. Notari claims that if the law were to be applied equally to all men, twenty-five of the last forty-eight Popes would have been indicted for the crimes of murder, poisoning, homicide, fraud, rape, armed assault, etc., and that at least eight of them would have been deported (he names them; 257). He names another ten allegedly guilty of rape, incest, violation, and necrophilia (257) and finishes the chapter with several short biographies detailing the malfeasance of individual Popes, cardinals, papal secretaries, and other Church officials. In short, this chapter exposes the sins and crimes of scores of those who occupy the highest positions possible within the Church. Logically enough, in the next chapter, "Peroration to His Holiness Pope Pius X," Notari addresses the current pope, Pious X, enjoining him to leave Italy and go away, perhaps to New York, before he's thrown out. Finally, in his short and incomplete "Principal Sources for This Work," Notari claims that he relied so heavily on his sources (identified within the chapters) that if this book were to cause him to be indicted, his sources, which include the Old and New Testament, would have to be indicted with him.

Indeed, as Rinaldi claims, *The Black Pig* "tells you about those priests" (*FTA* 8). And it is easy enough to see why the priest thought it "a filthy and vile book." But Rinaldi's complaint, that it "shook my faith" (7), needs to be read in the context of everything else we know of this character. If Rinaldi is a real believer—which I doubt—he would disdain Notari's book, which, although heavily documented, is dripping with scorn, irony, and bias. But if his faith is automatic and largely irrelevant, or if it has already been shaken, he might have read on, attracted by Notari's wide reading, his witty, strong prose, and his relentlessly rationalist logic, sometimes reminiscent of Mark Twain. Rinaldi is well educated both in religion (he quotes Saint Paul, 171, 173) and in medicine; he studies English, and we twice see him reading and studying (17, 27). Knowing a little more about his intellectual furniture will help us read this complicated, sometimes contradictory character who connects so importantly to all the other main characters (the priest, the main female character, and the protagonist-narrator himself) in this carefully structured novel.

Works Cited

Adamson, Walter L. "Futurism, Mass Culture, and Women: The Reshaping of the Artistic Vocation, 1909–1920." *Modernism/Modernity* 4.1 (1997): 89–114.

Blanche, Antoine. "The Black Pig." *Mombu*. Online forum. 2004. Accessed October 21, 2016. http://www.mombu.com/culture/t-the-black-pig-1219334.html.

Brasch, James Daniel, and Joseph Sigman. *Hemingway's Library: A Composite Record*. New York: Garland, 1981.

Caccia, Patrizia, ed. *Editori a Milano (1900–1945): Repertorio*. Milan: Franco Angeli, 2013.

Hemingway, Ernest. *A Farewell to Arms*. 1929. New York: Scribners, 1957.

Hertzog, Dagmar. Email communication, August 11, 2014.

———. *Sexuality in Europe: A Twentieth-Century History*. Cambridge: Cambridge UP, 2011.

Mandel, Miriam B. *Reading Hemingway: The Facts in the Fictions*. Metuchen, NJ: Scarecrow Press, 1995.

Michelangeli, Enzo. "Re: The Black Pig." *Mombu*. Online forum. 2004. Accessed October 21, 2016. http://www.mombu.com/culture/t-the-black-pig-1219334.html.

"Notari, Umberto." Appendice 1 (1938): 900. *Enciclopedia Italiana*, edizione 1949. Rome: Istituto della Enciclopedia Italiana, 1950.

Notari, Umberto. *Il maiale nero: Rivelazioni e documenti*. Sesto S. Giovanni (Milan): A. Barion, [1907].

Pizzi, Paolo. "Re: The Black Pig." *Mombu*. Online forum. 2004. Accessed October 21, 2016. http://www.mombu.com/culture/t-the-black-pig-1219334.html.

9

"What If You Are Not Built That Way?"

H. G. Wells and the Conflict of Science and Faith in *A Farewell to Arms*

MICHAEL KIM ROOS

Hemingway leaves little doubt that the clash of science and faith is preeminent among his concerns in *A Farewell to Arms*. He plunges us full force into the hot cauldron of the topic almost immediately, in the novel's very first conversation, as a group of Italian officers winefully bait the blushing priest over his lack of a sex life. The jocular mood quickly turns dark when the major brazenly declares himself an atheist and the lieutenant (whom we know later as Rinaldi) recommends that the American Frederic Henry, the novel's protagonist, should read a very salacious book on the Catholic Church called *The Black Pig*.[1] "It was that which shook my faith," the lieutenant declares. "It is a filthy and vile book," the priest enjoins Frederic. "Don't you read it." The Italian lieutenant, however, promises to get the book for Frederic, and the major flatly insists, "All thinking men are atheists" (*FTA-HL* 7).

Neutral by all appearances, Frederic attempts to change the subject, but the debate merely shifts to whether he should spend his upcoming leave pursuing carnal delights in places like Rome and Naples, as the lewd officers suggest, or maintaining his spiritual health in the purified atmosphere of the Abruzzi, as the priest recommends. Although he and the priest exchange smiles, Frederic leaves no indication whether he will read *The Black Pig* or not or whether he will spend his leave in the cities of sin or in the Abruzzi, although it is noteworthy that when the conversation ends he heads off to the bawdy house with the officers. Thus, the gauntlet of the novel has been laid down. With this contentious point-counterpoint Hemingway establishes the overriding conflict between science and faith that pervades the entire novel, a conflict that neither Frederic nor Ernest Hemingway ever seem willing or able to resolve. And while many commentators have remarked upon the book's contrapuntal arrangement of science and faith, no one till now has fully recognized the impact of the writings of H. G. Wells in moving Hemingway to make science and faith central to the theme of his great war novel.[2]

A Farewell to Arms ought to be read as the quest of one man—whether you wish to call that man Frederic Henry or Ernest Hemingway—to discover the way to wisdom and happiness. The question of whether it is better to pursue happiness through faith or through science is perhaps best expressed in a passage Hemingway wrote for the beginning of chapter 40 and later excised:

> [I]f happiness is an end sought by the wise it is no less an end if it comes without wisdom.... To seek it through the kingdom of heaven is a fine thing but you must give up this life first and if this life is all you have you might have remorse after giving it up and the kingdom of heaven might be a cold place in which to live with remorse. (*FTA-HL* 301)

Although the passage is part of a very revealing segment that Hemingway apparently felt too explicitly revealed the theme of his book, removing it in no way alters the novel's essential focus. Implicit on virtually every page is this question of whether it is better to follow the path of "this life," the path of earthly, material existence and experience (the way of the surgeon Rinaldi and science) or to follow a path "through the kingdom of heaven" (the way of the priest and religion). Through the first half of the novel, Rinaldi and the priest are each carefully given equal time with Frederic, arguing for their neatly divergent points of view, with neither, however, at any point gaining a clear upper hand in Frederic's preferences. Although some commentators wish us to think that Frederic steadily moves away from Rinaldi toward the priest, strictly speaking this never happens. It is true that Frederic learns to love Catherine Barkley in something akin to the priest's definition—"When you love you wish to do things for. You wish to sacrifice for. You wish to serve" (62)—but he never learns what the priest knows (in spite of what some commentators wish us to believe)—the way to love God. Although Frederic never renounces his faith to become an atheist, his faith never grows beyond something he experiences only at night, as expressed early in the novel with the priest (62) and late in the novel with Count Greffi (226). At the end, after all the horrific suffering he has witnessed firsthand, his attitude toward God seems only to harden (again exemplified in a continuation of the excised passage from the beginning of chapter 40):

> I am afraid of God at night but I would have admired him more if he would have stopped the war or never have let it start. Maybe he did stop it but whoever stopped it did not do it prettily. And if it is the Lord that giveth and the Lord that taketh away I do not admire him for taking Catherine away. He may have given me Catherine but who gave Rinaldi the syphilis at about the same time? The only thing I know is that I do not know anything about it. I see the wisdom of the priest at our mess who has always loved God and so is happy and I am sure that nothing will ever take God away from him. But how much is wisdom, and how much is luck to be born that way? And what if you are not built that way? (302)

Even though the novel seems to offer some hope for resolution of the conflict between science and faith through Frederic's relationship with the atheistic yet spiritual Catherine, in the end, Frederic cannot reconcile what experience has shown him about the true nature of the world and what he has been taught to believe about a loving deity. The best conclusion he can come up with is that he does "not know anything about it."

Indeed, we might regard the three words "I don't know" as Frederic Henry's motto or catchphrase. It and other derivations of "not knowing" are used ninety-two times in *A Farewell to Arms*, an average of about once every four pages. In other words, we are almost constantly being reminded of how little Frederic truly knows—how little he sees through things. And therein lies evidence of the influence of H. G. Wells. For, in introducing Wells's 1916 war novel, inaccurately but tellingly presented by Count Greffi in book 4 as *Mr. Britling Sees Through It*, Hemingway is demonstrating his skepticism not only that Mr. Britling could see through to the truth of things but that anyone can. Unlike Mr. Britling, who believes that he has come to see some kind of positive spiritual message in the slaughter of World War I, Frederic

Henry finally must admit that he "does not know anything about it." Unlike Mr. Britling, he is never able to see through to an ultimate meaning of things, never able to translate his earthly secular love into a satisfying divine love, never able to bridge the gap between a scientific/rationalist understanding of the way of the world and a nourishing faith in any kind of a loving God.

Given how little H. G. Wells is read these days, outside of his well-known and influential science fiction novels, it is easy to overlook how important he was as a writer and a thinker in Hemingway's world in the 1920s. For example, in a 1934 essay, Malcolm Cowley insisted that by the time Wells was forty (in 1906), his influence was "wider than any other living English writer" (22), and I believe that Wells's ideas, particularly those contained in Mr. Britling and his 1921 magnum opus of nonfiction, *The Outline of History*, were a driving force behind Hemingway's writing of *A Farewell to Arms*. In the 1920s, Wells was one of several important writers who documented a real crisis of belief and disenchantment in the modern world, a combination of the effects of modern scientific discoveries, most importantly those of Charles Darwin, and the disillusionment in the aftermath of the Great War. Indications are that, for Hemingway, Wells was the most influential of these commentators.[3] We already know that by the time Hemingway composed his major works of the 1920s he had certainly been exposed to major doses of Darwinian perspective from a variety of sources, including his high school zoology text,[4] as well as assorted writings of Jack London, Theodore Roosevelt, Havelock Ellis, Carl Akeley, and W. H. Hudson. Now we can add H. G. Wells to this list of luminaries.[5]

Wells's two-volume *The Outline of History* was published in 1921, the year before Hemingway's arrival in Paris, and, in spite of its length (nearly 1,000 pages in its two initial volumes), it was almost instantly an enormous bestseller. The book sold over 500,000 copies in its first year and two million by the end of the decade (Smith 259; Sherborne 252).[6] In other words, by 1930, nearly every literate, well-read English-speaking person, including Hemingway, owned a copy of the book. And the book remains in print even today. The fact that Hemingway still possessed a copy of the book at the end of his life attests to the respect he held for it.[7]

Hemingway almost certainly read *The Outline of History* for the first time within a year after his arrival in Europe early in 1922, at a point when the book was still a hot topic of conversation among the literati he was meeting almost daily. Evidence exists in the fact that, years before including Wells in *A Farewell to Arms*, Hemingway made two other prominent references to him in print. The first occurred in March 1923, in a review of Gertrude Stein's *Geography and Plays*, which he wrote for the Paris edition of the *Chicago Tribune*. In thrall to his literary mentor, the young Hemingway wrote:

> Gertrude Stein is probably the most first rate intelligence employed in writing today. If you are tired of Mr. D. H. Lawrence who writes extremely well with the intelligence of a head waiter or Mr. Wells who is believed to be intelligent because of a capacity for sustained marathon thinking or the unbelievably stupid but thoroughly conscientious young men who compile the Dial you ought to read Gertrude Stein. ("Review"[8])

Given that none of the other works by Wells that Hemingway might have read by this point was longer than 525 pages, reference to Wells's "capacity for sustained marathon thinking" undoubtedly refers to the nearly 1,000 pages of *The Outline of History*, and the mocking tone of the passage conveys the distinct impression that Wells has been disturbing Hemingway's thinking in some way.

Wells appears again in the text of *The Torrents of Spring*, also in a somewhat mocking and ambiguous light, where Hemingway, with tongue firmly in cheek, imagines the need to defend his satirical and somewhat farcical work against an entirely fictionalized criticism from Wells:

> Mr. H. G. Wells, who has been visiting at our home (we're getting along in the literary game, eh, reader?) asked us the other day if perhaps our reader, that's you, reader—just think of it, H. G. Wells talking about you right in our home. Anyway, H. G. Wells asked us if perhaps our reader would not think too much of this story was autobiographical. Please, reader, just get that idea out of your head. We have lived in Petoskey, Mich., it is true, and naturally many of the characters are drawn from life as we lived it then. But they are other people, not the author. (68–69)[9]

These two references demonstrate the degree to which the famous English novelist occupied Hemingway's mind throughout the decade. At the very least, Wells was a writer with whom Hemingway would have felt competitive, but the passages also betray a grudging respect. After all, Hemingway could little deny Wells's astonishing panoramic achievement in *The Outline of History*, for all its "sustained marathon thinking." There is much in the work with which Hemingway in all likelihood agreed, particularly the book's astute analyses of military and political battlefields. But the way Wells proposed a resolution of the conflict between science and religion must have stirred Hemingway's thinking deeply and moved him to test the hypothesis in his own work.

Published in the same decade as the Scopes Trial, *The Outline of History* is unabashedly founded on the facts of Darwinian science: the opening chapters tell a grand story of evolution—beginning with the origin of space, time, the solar system, and life on earth, through eons of evolutionary history, before it settles into a grand synthesis of the development of human civilization in all its manifestations across the globe, admirably avoiding Eurocentrism and racism in the process. The book is breathtaking in its sweep and comprehensiveness, leaving out no significant human development, whether it occurred in Europe, Asia, Africa, or the Americas. Later, in discussing developments in the nineteenth century, the book includes a particularly pointed chapter titled "How Darwinism Affected Religious and Political Ideas," describing in some detail the modern world's crisis of faith. Numerous recent books by writers such as Richard Dawkins, Daniel Dennett, Jerry Coyne, and Steve Stewart-Williams have demonstrated how serious comprehension of Darwinian evolution is "a universal acid," which dissolves all that it contacts (Dennett 63) and does "major violence to . . . religious beliefs" (Stewart-Williams 64). None of these books, however, has been nearly as popular as Wells's book was in the 1920s. If Hemingway had not thought this through for himself, reading Wells would have made it plain for him. Regarding the evidence of the geological record and Darwin's writings, Wells comments:

> If the animals and man had been evolved in this ascendant manner, then there had been no first parents, no Eden, and no fall. And if there had been no fall, then the entire historical fabric of Christianity . . . collapsed like a house of cards.
>
> It was with something like horror, therefore, that great numbers of honest and religious-spirited men followed the work of the English naturalist Charles Darwin. (*Outline of History* 543–44)

As Wells indicates, for most people, the realization of these implications was profoundly unsettling and demoralizing.

However, unlike Dawkins, Dennett, Coyne, and Stewart-Williams, who wish to eradicate religious sentiment wherever they find it, Wells bemoans the disastrous effects of Darwinian science on religion, while never denying the truth of Darwinism. He most assuredly does not wish to retreat into atheism. Indeed, much earlier in the book, during his analysis of the true message of Jesus, whom he sees as a profoundly evolutionary figure, Wells makes the following startling assertion:

> And though much has been written foolishly about the antagonism of science and religion, there is indeed *no such antagonism*. What all these world religions declare by inspiration and insight, history as it grows clearer and science as its range extends display, as a reasonable and demonstrable fact, that men form one universal brotherhood, that they spring from one common origin, that their individual lives, their nations and races, interbreed and blend and go on to merge again at last in one common human destiny upon this little planet amidst the stars. (*Outline of History* 291; emphasis added)

He further insists that the religious crisis of the modern world is, in his view, based upon a misconception of Darwinian science. "In the end," he asserts, "men may discover that religion shines all the brighter for the loss of its doctrinal wrappings, but to the young it seemed as if indeed there had been a conflict of science and religion, and that in that conflict science had won.... The true gold of religion was thrown away with the worn-out purse that had contained it for so long, and it was not recovered" (545). As one of the young to whom Wells refers, reading these compelling passages, Hemingway may have stumbled upon the theme for *A Farewell to Arms*.

Significantly, Wells is more comfortable with what he regards as the true message of Jesus to be found in the gospels, a message consistent with the universal love found in all the world's great religions, than he is with the version of Christianity established by Saint Paul, whom he blames for a host of problems. "What Jesus preached," Wells writes, "was a new birth of the human soul; what Paul preached was the ancient religion of priest and altar and propitiatory bloodshed" (*Outline of History* 293). Similarly, in *A Farewell to Arms*, Rinaldi declares, in very Wellsian fashion, "That Saint Paul.... He's the one who makes all the trouble.... He was a rounder and a chaser and then when he was no longer hot he said it was no good. When he was finished he made the rules for us who are still hot" (151).

By the end of the big tome, following an insightful analysis of the causes and consequences of the Great War, Wells offers a lyrical vision of humankind's future that insists on the elevation of science, rationalism, democracy, and universal peace to the level of religious fervor in order to bring about the unification of all the peoples of the earth. Admittedly, he wants to discard the trappings of traditional religions, yet he wishes to unite everyone under one universal religion in the service of one God, following universal moral truths that he finds common among all the world's great religions. Seeking a balance between the rationalist scientific perspective and faith, Wells declares:

> The overriding powers that hitherto in the individual soul and in the community have struggled and prevailed against the ferocious, base, and individual impulses that divide us from one another, have been the powers of religion and education. Religion and education, those closely interwoven influences, have made possible the greater human societies whose growth we have traced in this Outline, they have been the chief synthetic forces throughout this great story of enlarging human co-operations that we have traced from its beginnings. (*Outline of History* 622–23)

Ultimately, Wells wishes to unify religion and education (i.e., science). If the gap is not bridged, he plainly fears for the future of the species.

There are indeed numerous indications in the text of *A Farewell to Arms* that Hemingway was attempting to test out Wells's hypothesis that science and religion could be reconciled. The careful balancing of Rinaldi's science and the priest's religion is the most obvious. As noted earlier, Catherine seems to strike a balance between science and religion that Wells and Frederic seek—the hypothesis that Hemingway is testing. Though Catherine insists that nothing exists beyond death and spurns Frederic's suggestion that they pray in the Milan Duomo, she does give Frederic the Saint Anthony medal for possible protection, participates with him in experiments in thought transference, and clairvoyantly fears the rain because she sees herself dead in it. Most important, she makes Frederic her religion, and her love for him exemplifies in human terms the kind of love the priest defines early on.

The way she balances science and religion becomes clearer as the novel proceeds. In Stresa, after Frederic is reunited with Catherine, they spend a happy night together, and Frederic meditates on the supreme quality of their love:

> I know that the night is not the same as the day: that all things are different, that the things of the night cannot be explained in the day, because they do not then exist, and the night can be a dreadful time for lonely people once their loneliness has started. But with Catherine there was almost no difference in the night except that it was an even better time. (216)

The night, the realm of the spirit, the realm of the supernatural, the realm of faith, contrasts with the daylight of reason and science, where the things of the night don't exist. Early on, Frederic tells the priest that he fears God at night, and later he tells Count Greffi that he is *croyant*, a believer, only at night. However, with Catherine, the conflicts between day and night disappear. In other words, through her, science and faith seem to be reconciled. Sadly, however, any sense of reconciliation seems to end with her death.

The stay in Stresa is also noteworthy for Frederic's encounter with his old friend Count Greffi, who, as one of Hemingway's exemplars of wisdom and in keeping with the general theme of the book, weighs in on the conflict between science and faith. Although the ideas of H. G. Wells have been just below the visible portion of the iceberg throughout the novel, Frederic's encounter with the Count provides Hemingway an opportunity to bring Wells explicitly into the light. Their conversation begins with the Count's asking Frederic what he has been reading. "Nothing," Frederic replies. "What is there written in war-time?" The Count suggests *Le Feu*, by Frenchman Henri Barbusse, and *Mr. Britling Sees It Through*, H. G. Wells's very popular 1916 war novel, although Count Greffi presents the title as *Mr. Britling Sees Through It*. As James Hinkle has noted, the Count has probably read the French translation, freshly published in 1917, which was titled *Mr. Britling commence à voir clair*, literally "Mr. Britling begins to see clearly." The French title, however, could be reasonably translated as "Mr. Britling sees through it." When Frederic responds, "No, he doesn't" (225), we understand him to mean, first of all, that he has, in fact, read the book and, secondly, that Mr. Britling, as well as, by extension, H. G. Wells, doesn't "see through" to the truth of things. Wells's biographer David C. Smith comments that "Mr.

Britling Sees Through It" is a "good title for the inner meaning of the book" (224), even though, as Wells's other biographer, Michael Sherborne, has indicated, the garbled French translation celebrates Britling's "perspicacity rather than his perseverance" (236), as the actual English title does.

Perspicacity, however, suits Hemingway's purpose here perfectly. While Frederic seems to be disparaging Wells's novel and perspicacity, there's much more to this reference than meets the eye. The attempt to "see through" to the truth of things is, of course, what I suggest lies at the heart of Hemingway's novel—determining what is knowable and what is unknowable. The Count, whose viewpoint we have no reason to disrespect, does rebut Frederic's view with a defense of the novel, calling it "a very good study of the English middle-class soul" (226). In response, Frederic seems to retreat somewhat, implying that his disparagement may well be the result of a deficiency of his own: "I don't know about the soul," he says, relying upon his favorite catchphrase. "Poor boy," the Count replies sympathetically, underscoring once again the theme of the book. "We none of us know about the soul" (226).

On close inspection, *Mr. Britling* is, in fact, a very religious book, though not, as we would expect, given Wells's comments on traditional religion in *The Outline of History*, religious in any standardized Christian sense. In fact, Hemingway may well have gotten the idea to treat love as a religion from reading Wells's novel. Just as Catherine and Frederic regard their love as their religion, an idea underscored and blessed by Count Greffi, Wells insists through one of his chief characters, Mr. Direck, that love "is nothing more nor less than Religion—I don't mean this Religion or that Religion but just Religion itself, a Big, Solemn, Comprehensive Idea that holds you and me and all the world together in one great, grand universal scheme" (*Mr. Britling* 122–23).

Further on, Mr. Britling's meditation on the existence of evil in the world, when he learns that his beloved son has been killed in World War I, echoes some of Frederic Henry's broodings in books 4 and 5 of *A Farewell to Arms*:

> His [Mr. Britling's] mind drifted back once more to those ancient heresies of the Gnostics and the Manichaeans which saw the God of the World as altogether evil.... Is the whole scheme of nature evil? Is life in its essence cruel? Is man stretched quivering upon the table of the

> eternal vivisector for no end—and without pity? . . . He thought of certain instances of boyish cruelty that had horrified him in his own boyhood, and it was clear to him that indeed it was not cruelty, it was curiosity, dense textured, thick skinned, so that it could not feel even the anguish of a blinded cat. (236–37)

After reading this passage, Hemingway may well have been moved to compose Frederic's boyhood memory of the ants on the flaming log, an instance in which, in the role of God or potential Messiah, he passively allows the ants to suffer needlessly when he could easily remove the log from the fire and eliminate their suffering.

Although Wells certainly acknowledged the violent impact modern science had had on traditional religious belief, he was, as I have noted before, no atheist, and therein may lie one explanation, at least, of why Hemingway might have found him intriguing, if not convincing, as a writer. Amazingly enough, Wells was somehow able to retain and even celebrate a belief in a loving God. As Michael Sherborne has surmised, Wells was "peculiarly well equipped to build a bridge between science and religion. From early on his writings show not only an engagement with scientific understanding but a recurrent sense of being part of a greater consciousness and intuition that a perfect world is as latent in the structure of things as mathematics or music" (Sherborne 239). Near the end of *Mr. Britling Sees It Through*, Mr. Britling, clearly based on Wells himself, experiences a profound epiphany: "I have suddenly found it and seen it plain," he declares. "It is, you see, so easy to understand that there is a God and how complex and wonderful and brotherly He is, when one thinks of those dear boys who by the thousand, by the hundred thousand, have laid down their lives" (322–23). Finally, to share what he has learned with the world, Mr. Britling writes a treatise, which seems to convey the culminating message of the novel:

> Religion is the first thing and the last thing, and until a man has found God and been found by God, he begins at no beginning, he works to no end. He may have his friendships, his partial loyalties, his scraps of honour. But all these things fall into place and life falls into place only with God. Only with God. God, who fights through men against Blind Force and Night and Non-Existence; who is the end, who is the meaning. (349)

Passages like these are undoubtedly why *Mr. Britling Sees It Through* was for a time required reading in many of Britain's chaplain schools (Smith 234). Indeed, Hemingway's priest would very likely approve of the tenor of these passages.

But what of Frederic? What of Hemingway himself? When we examine the evidence in *A Farewell to Arms*, we have to conclude that one reason Frederic states that Mr. Britling does not see through it is that Frederic's state of mind in the final segment of the novel is far different from Mr. Britling's. There is no evidence that Frederic can believe in a God who "fights through men against Blind Force and Night and Non-Existence." In fact, everything about his experience in the world suggests the opposite to Frederic, and it is likely that it is this very perspective that Frederic is rejecting when he states that Mr. Britling does not see through it. Mr. Britling's facile belief that the Great War will be the "War to End All Wars" does ally him to Hemingway's characters like Gino and the priest, with both of whom Frederic profoundly disagrees on the direction of the war. By the late 1920s, as Hemingway was writing *A Farewell to Arms*, there were already many signs in Italy and Germany that the world had not seen the last of horrific warfare. Writing twelve years later than Wells, Hemingway could provide his protagonist with enough critical foresight and perspicacity to recognize cynically that much more suffering was ahead for the world. In general, throughout the final half of the book, Frederic consistently rejects Wells's and the priest's notion of a benevolent, loving creator and the progression of humans toward a peaceful, higher state of being.[10] In fact, Hemingway was probably prescient in rejecting Wells's and Mr. Britling's religiosity. As Michael Sherborne suggests, the religious ending that contributed to the novel's popularity in wartime Britain may be one of the chief reasons so few people read the book today (240).

At the very least, in their conversation, neither Frederic nor Count Greffi professes to a profound and satisfactory faith. The Count confides in Frederic that he had thought he would become more devout as he grew older. "[B]ut somehow I haven't," he confesses (226). Count Greffi has apparently been one of the lucky ones in this world, relatively untouched by suffering. (Remember that Frederic tells the priest that it is "in defeat that we become Christian"; 156.) "This life is very pleasant," the Count says. "I would like to live forever" (226). With his apparent lack of certainty in a next world, the

Count provides support for what Frederic has come to value the most—secular love, which the Count, in agreement with Catherine and H. G. Wells, counts as a religious feeling. However, in spite of his lack of religious feelings, the Count is apparently not ready to cast his lot completely with atheism. He asks Frederic to pray for him if he ever becomes devout after the Count is dead. Although Frederic asserts that he "might become very devout" and promises to pray for the Count, he concludes this ambivalent discussion of faith by repeating his claim that his own religious feeling "comes only at night" (227). Thus, the chapter reaches its conclusion without a ringing endorsement for either faith or reason.

All of this provides context for the suffering and death of Catherine and the child at the end of the novel. Frederic frames our thoughts and feelings on what happens through a series of meditations that attempt to rationalize the existence of suffering in this world. The first is the famous "the world breaks everyone" passage, a continuation of the passage previously quoted, where Frederic declares that with Catherine there was almost no difference between the night and the day. However, from this lofty romantic lyricism he immediately descends into bitterness over the inexplicable cruelties of the world:

> If people bring so much courage to this world the world has to kill them to break them, so of course it kills them. The world breaks every one and afterward many are strong at the broken places. But those that will not break it kills. It kills the very good and the very gentle and the very brave impartially. If you are none of these you can be sure it will kill you too but there will be no special hurry. (216)

This darker-than-Manichean observation from Frederic—in all its bitterness over what he sees as not just indifference from the universe but absolute malevolence—surely, with its present-tense verbs, comes from his present state of mind as he writes the story, however many years after the events he recounts.[11] The anger and bitterness are what grab. If Frederic were to do a scientific study of the suffering and death of humans across the globe, he would likely discover that the brave, except perhaps those in battle, are not killed any sooner than are the nonbrave. Yet, in his grief over Catherine's death, this must be how it appears to him, and his anger is visceral. The excised passage from the beginning of chapter 40, as previously noted, seems to have been intended as a continuation of this tenor, yet it makes obvious that, in spite of his anger, Frederic never descends into atheism. He clings to a tortured faith in a God whose ways are mysterious and unknowable. Still the meditation goes nowhere, ending only in some kind of resignation, though certainly not a peaceful one. "And it doesn't do any good to talk about it either," Frederic concludes. "Nor to think about it" (302). In other words, it is all unknowable. He has given up trying to "see through it." In the final analysis, neither science nor faith can provide any satisfying answers to the problem of human suffering. As Steve Stewart-Williams comments,

> The apparent clash between the nature of God and the existence of evil leaves the thoughtful theist with a number of options, none of which is particularly appealing. One is to concede that God is powerless to prevent evil. Another is to concede that God is not all-good. Maybe God is evil! Or maybe God is indifferent rather than evil. . . . A final option is that we were wrong about God all along—that we've been making a terrible mistake for the last few thousand years and that there is no God. (105)

As a thoughtful theist, Frederic (and Hemingway) have presumably considered all of these options, but there remains no evidence in the novel that either has reached the final conclusion—that there is no God. It seems that the existence of God is a given. However, if God exists, then any rational, scientific observation of the universe, with all its evil and suffering, can lead only to a conclusion that God is impotent, indifferent, or evil.

The sense of a malevolent or at least an indifferent deity is further reinforced after Frederic learns that his infant son has died, apparently strangled in utero by his umbilical cord. The death triggers the following tirade:

> That was what you did. You died. You did not know what it was about. You never had time to learn. They threw you in and told you the rules and the first time they caught you off base they killed you. Or they killed you gratuitously like Aymo. Or gave you the syphilis like Rinaldi. But they killed you in the end. You could count on that. Stay around and they would kill you. (279–80)

The use of this indefinite "they" doesn't disguise the fact that he is talking about God. This is immediately followed by the memory from his youth of watching ants on a burning log. There is no mistaking the point of this either, particularly in this context. The predicament of the ants is intended to parallel our own predicament as humans, and Frederic places himself in the role of God. In his own refusal to play messiah and save the ants from suffering by removing the log from the fire—indeed perhaps making it worse by emptying his cup on them and steaming them—he is comparing God's inaction to his own. He obviously does not admire this in himself, and this is certainly tantamount to the God that he says he cannot admire. Frederic might find more peace in this world, the kind of peace that Catherine seems to have, if he were able to give up his belief in God. But just as he admits to not being built like the priest, neither is he built like Catherine. As a result he is left to boil in his own bitterness. As Catherine lies dying, Frederic resorts to desperate pleading and bargaining with his God, promising, "I'll do anything for you if you won't let her die" (282). There is no answer of course. Catherine dies, and if there is any hint of redemption in the final farewell to her, I fail to see it. There aren't many colder endings in all of literature: "But after I had got them out and shut the door and turned off the light it wasn't any good. It was like saying good-by to a statue. After a while I went out and left the hospital and walked back to the hotel in the rain" (284).

Although religiously inclined critics want us to believe that the novel teaches Frederic and us the redemptive power of suffering, there is simply no real evidence to reach that conclusion.[12] No assertion that the act of writing the novel is redemptive can overcome the weight of what Hemingway actually wrote, what is present in the text—which ultimately amounts to Frederic's anger with and inability to love God. However, Frederic never stops believing in this God he refuses to admire. Even when he says, following the death of the child, that he "had no religion," he still insists that the child should have been baptized. "Poor boy," as Count Greffi would say. The conflict between science and faith never reaches a resolution in the novel, and that lack of resolution seems exactly the point Hemingway wanted to make. In the end, Frederic Henry remains deeply unsettled in his thinking and unable to accept the assertion of H. G. Wells that reconciliation between science and faith is possible. The ambiguity and ambivalence that prevail throughout the novel constitute all he has to say on the matter. In the end, he still does not know anything; he still does not "see through it."

Notes

1. Some commentators have speculated that *The Black Pig* was not an actual book but merely a creation of Hemingway's for the purposes of his novel; however, in a presentation at the 2014 Hemingway Conference in Venice, Italy, Miriam Mandel convincingly identified the source as *Dio contro Dio: (Il maiale nero)*, by Umberto Notari, published in Milan in 1908. The title in translation is *God against God (The Black Pig)*. According to Mandel, it is every bit as salacious as the discussion in *A Farewell to Arms* implies. However, no English translation of the book exists; therefore, it is doubtful that Hemingway actually read the book. See Mandel's chapter in this volume.

2. Only James Hinkle and H. R. Stoneback have commented briefly on the reference to *Mr. Britling Sees It Through* in Frederic Henry's discussion with Count Greffi, but neither attempted an exploration of the larger significance of Wells's writings to Hemingway's novel.

3. Max Weber and Joseph Krutch were two other prominent voices. For a Darwinian counterview to this disenchantment, see George Levine's excellent *Darwin Loves You*.

4. See Roos.

5. A measure of the esteem in which Hemingway held these writers is their significant representation on the shelves at the Finca Vigía. The library included Roosevelt's *African Game Trails* and two other works (Brasch and Sigman 318); the four volumes of Ellis's *The Psychology of Sex*, plus two other Ellis works (113); no less than sixteen books by Hudson (180–81); and eight different works by Wells (394), including the very Darwinian *Outline of History*, as discussed here. (See also Reynolds, *Hemingway's Reading*.)

6. In fact, during the 1920s, it spawned a number of imitators, both serious and comic, such as Hemingway pal Donald Ogden Stewart's *A Parody Outline of History*.

7. However, although he undoubtedly read Wells's war novel, *Mr. Britling Sees It Through*, that book was not among the eight by Wells that Hemingway possessed at the end of his life. Books by Wells in the Finca, and likely read by Hemingway prior to the writing of *A Farewell to Arms*, included *The World Set Free* (1914), a novel in which Wells predicts the development of nuclear weapons and includes a peace conference in the Swiss town of Brissago (where Frederic and Catherine first step foot in Switzerland); the feminist novel *The Wife of Sir Isaac Harmon* (1914); the satirical novels *Bealby* (1915) and *Boon* (1915); and the nonfictional *The Outline of History* (1920). The Finca library also included three

later works by Wells: *The Bulpington of Blup* (1933), *World Brain* (1938), and *You Can't Be Too Careful* (1942).

8. Thanks to John Beall for locating Hemingway's review of Stein's *Geography and Plays*.

9. There is no evidence, by the way, that H. G. Wells ever actually visited Hemingway's home or that they ever met at all prior to their only known meeting, arranged by Martha Gellhorn at Wells's request, in a New York hotel room in 1940 (Baker 355). Late in life Hemingway made a final reference to Wells in *A Moveable Feast*, where, in the midst of a disparaging discussion of Ford Madox Ford, he mentions Wells as one of Ford's defenders, a fact he rationalizes by explaining that Wells knew Ford during a "good epoque," while he (Hemingway) did not (*MF* 199).

10. H. R. Stoneback insists that the real meaning of Frederic's statement "I don't know about the soul" is that H. G. Wells "knows nothing about the soul, for how could a scientific materialist whose vision was a pastiche of watered-down Darwinian and quasi-Marxist thought, a positivistic bio-social world planner enamored of the myth of progress—how could such a writer know anything about the soul?" (40). But this surely says more about Stoneback's point of view than it does about Hemingway's or Frederic Henry's. Count Greffi takes Frederic at his word, and we should as well. I contend that Frederic's (and Hemingway's) problem with Wells's book is that it attempts to reconcile science and religion, and Frederic has not found any way to achieve such a reconciliation. Ultimately, I have to agree with Frederic that *Mr. Britling* is not a very good book, but not for the reasons listed by Stoneback, which generally distort what Wells was about anyway. In fairness to Wells, by the time he wrote *The Outline of History* two years after the war, he was not at all sanguine about the prospects for universal peace. And by the time he wrote his *Experiment in Autobiography* (1934), he was essentially disavowing his earlier religious fervor and was much closer to what we would term as atheism. But that was well after the writing of *A Farewell to Arms*.

11. It is not really significant whether Frederic is writing the novel three, four, five, or ten years after the events recounted. Nothing in the telling of the story indicates that his thinking has become any clearer, that he has achieved any substantial insights into the meaning of suffering, or become any more (or any less) confirmed in his Catholic faith. He still, to put it simply, does not "know about the soul."

12. For religious interpretations of the novel, see Nickel, and Stoneback.

Works Cited

Akeley, Carl. *In Brightest Africa*. Garden City, NY: Garden City Publishing, 1920.

Baker, Carlos. *Ernest Hemingway: A Life Story*. New York: Scribners, 1969.

Beall, John. "Stein, Joyce, and Hemingway's Construction of *In Our Time*." Conference presentation. *Hemingway Society XVI Biennial International Conference*. June 27, 2014, Venice.

Brasch, James D., and Joseph Sigman. *Hemingway's Library: A Composite Record*. New York: Garland, 1981.

Cowley, Malcolm. "Outline of Wells's History." *New Republic* 81.1041 (November 14, 1934): 22–23.

Coyne, Jerry. *Why Evolution Is True*. New York: Viking, 2009.

Darwin, Charles. *On the Origin of Species: A Facsimile of the First Edition*. Cambridge, MA: Harvard UP, 1964.

Dawkins, Richard. *The Blind Watchmaker: Why the Evidence of Evolution Reveals a Universe without Design*. New York: Norton, 1996.

Dennett, Daniel. *Darwin's Dangerous Idea*. New York: Simon and Schuster, 1995.

Ellis, Havelock. *Studies in the Psychology of Sex*. Philadelphia: F. A. Davis, 1914.

Hemingway, Ernest. *The Complete Short Stories: The Finca Vigía Edition*. New York: Charles Scribner's Sons, 1987.

———. *A Farewell to Arms: The Hemingway Library Edition*. New York: Charles Scribner's Sons, 2012.

———. *A Moveable Feast: The Restored Edition*. New York: Charles Scribner's Sons, 2014.

———. "Review: Geography and Plays, by Gertrude Stein." *Chicago Tribune*. Paris edition, March 5, 1923: 2.

———. *The Sun Also Rises*. New York: Charles Scribner's Sons, 1926.

———. *The Torrents of Spring*. New York: Charles Scribner's Sons, 1926.

Hinkle, James. "Seeing Through It in *A Farewell to Arms*." *Hemingway Review* 2.1 (1982): 94–95.

Hudson, W. H. *Far Away and Long Ago*. New York: E. P. Dutton, 1918.

Krutch, Joseph Wood. *The Modern Temper: A Study and a Confession*. New York: Harcourt Brace, 1929.

Levine, George. *Darwin Loves You: Natural Selection and the Re-enchantment of the World*. Princeton: Princeton UP, 2006.

Linville, Henry R., and Henry A. Kelly. *A Text-Book in General Zoology*. Boston: Ginn & Co., 1906.

London, Jack. *The Call of the Wild*. New York: Grosset & Dunlap, 1903.

Mandel, Miriam B. "Two Mysteries: Reading and Writing in *A Farewell to Arms*." Conference presentation. *Hemingway Society XVI Biennial International Conference*. June 24, 2014, Venice.

Nickel, Matthew C. *Hemingway's Dark Night: Catholic Influences and Intertextualities in the Work of Ernest Hemingway*. Wickford, RI: New Street Communications, LLC, 2013.

Reynolds, Michael. *Hemingway's First War*. Princeton: Princeton UP, 1976.

———. *Hemingway's Reading, 1910–1940: An Inventory*. Princeton: Princeton UP, 1981.

———. *The Young Hemingway*. New York: Norton, 1986.

Roos, Michael. "Agassiz or Darwin: The Trap of Science and Faith in Hemingway's High School Zoology Class." *Hemingway Review* 32:2 (Spring 2013): 7–27.

Roosevelt, Theodore. *African Game Trails: An Account of the African Wanderings of an American Hunter-Naturalist*. New York: Syndicate Publishing, 1910.

Ross, William T. *H. G. Wells's World Reborn: The Outline of History and Its Companions*. Selinsgrove, PA: Susquehanna UP, 2002.

Sherborne, Michael. *H. G. Wells: Another Kind of Life*. London: Peter Owen, 2010.

Smith, David C. *H. G. Wells: Desperately Mortal: A Biography*. New Haven: Yale UP, 1986.

Stewart, Donald Ogden. *A Parody Outline of History*. Kindle eBook edition. 2012.

Stewart-Williams, Steve. *Darwin, God, and the Meaning of Life: How Evolutionary Theory Undermines Everything You Thought You Knew*. Cambridge: Cambridge UP, 2010.

Stoneback, H. R. "In the Nominal Country of the Bogus: Hemingway's Catholicism and Biographies." *Hemingway: Essays of Reassessment*. Ed. Frank Scafella. New York: Oxford UP, 1991. 105–40.

———. "'Lovers' Sonnets Turn'd to Holy Psalms': The Soul's Song of Providence, the Scandal of Suffering, and Love in *A Farewell to Arms*." *Hemingway Review* 9.1 (Fall 1989): 33–76.

Weber, Max. *From Max Weber: Essays in Sociology*. Ed. and trans. H. H. Gerth and C. Wright Mills. New York: Oxford UP, 1958.

Wells, H. G. *Bealby: A Holiday*. New York: MacMillan, 1915.

———. *Boon, The Mind of the Race, The Wild Asses of the Devil, and The Last Trump: Prepared for Publication by Reginald Bliss, with an Ambiguous Introduction by H. G. Wells*. New York: George H. Doran, 1915.

———. *Experiment in Autobiography*. New York: MacMillan, 1934.

———. *Mr. Britling commence à voir clair*. Trans. M. Butts. Paris: Payot, 1917.

———. *Mr. Britling Sees It Through*. New York: MacMillan, 1916.

———. *The Outline of History: Being a Plain History of Life and Mankind*. New York: MacMillan, 1921.

———. *The Wife of Sir Isaac Harmon*. London: MacMillan, 1914.

———. *The World Set Free: A Story of Mankind*. New York: E. P. Dutton, 1914.

10

"I Was in Italy . . . and I Spoke Italian"

The Cosmopolitan Battlefield of *A Farewell to Arms*

JOHN D. SCHWETMAN

Frederic Henry gets frequent quizzical looks from other characters in *A Farewell to Arms* because he is an American in an Italian soldier's uniform, and the suspicions of these observers are justified because a noncitizen in an Italian military uniform is a walking transgression of established codes governing national identity and allegiance. This mismatch between Henry's nationality and his uniform sends various signals, some of which might be quite threatening. The misfit soldier could, for example, be a spy or a mercenary. That is, the uniform could be a disguise veiling the soldier's actual agenda. Or, the non-Italian could be a traitor to his own nation of origin, a status that calls into question the fixity of his current loyalty to the Italian nation. While these more alarmist readings of the uniform-clad protagonist of *A Farewell to Arms* would be perplexing to Henry himself, who is, in his own mind, just there to help, this tension nonetheless drives the narrative toward the events of the retreat from Caporetto in which Henry's uniform makes him a target of Italy's *carabinieri* for being a deserter, that is, for failing to live up to the promise offered by his uniform. In this chapter, I will argue that his situation results from a larger cultural shift from local, place-based group affiliations to an ethos of cosmopolitanism that, like Frederic Henry's uniform, destabilizes the nationalist dichotomy that serves as the basis for World War I.

In her essay "Internal Structures: The Conservatism of *A Farewell to Arms*," Miriam Mandel produces a persuasive reading of the novel based on the characters' statuses as members of discreet groups, and her approach constitutes a helpful starting point for my line of inquiry into Frederic Henry's membership in his various circles of community. Mandel concludes in her essay that the various group dynamics depicted in the novel compel an interpretation of it that contrasts sharply with a common assertion that the novel is, at its root, subversive. As the title of Mandel's essay suggests, the various group identities come together to give the novel a very conservative orientation toward "a post-war longing for structured village life—redefined, of course, but still identifiably a village, a gang, a group, a tribe, a system that works for some or most of those who are in it" (183). Mandel points out that "the individuals seek comfort in a small group" (183), and this article explores this individual connection to small and larger groups that all produce a notion of ethnic and national affiliation. Mandel concludes her article by considering the alternatives that Frederic Henry encounters in the figures of the secular, individualistic Lieutenant Rinaldi and the religious, community-oriented priest from Abruzzi, and, in her reading, "the priest's generosity . . . and his altruistic, oft-quoted definition of love . . . gain authority" (182) over Rinaldi's individualist secularism. Her claim for the novel's conservatism is in this sense quite persuasive.

As Hemingway's own postwar life was to demonstrate, the new small tribes to which he was to attach himself consisted of fellow exiles, people like him who had proudly detached themselves from territorial connections of the sort embraced by their parents' generation. As Michael Reynolds points out in *The Young Hemingway*, Hemingway's hometown of Oak Park "was a world about which Hemingway never wrote a single story" (5). Indeed, the only story in Hemingway's *In Our Time* that portrays a traditional home is "Soldier's Home," and that story merely situates its main character, the returning soldier Krebs, there in order to dramatize his utter lack of connection to it. His home no longer functions as a home to him as his experiences upon returning to it demonstrate: "[N]one of it had touched him" (76–77). Carlos Baker likewise notes the spatial detachment of the characters in *A Farewell to Arms* who "seem to come from nowhere, move into the now and here, and depart again for nowhere after the elapsed time of the novels" (114). The key to understanding Hemingway's approach to community is to situate the novel in a larger movement to reject attachments to place and instead to define community in terms of shared interests or activities. This cultural shift parallels advancements in communications and transportation technology that appear to have rendered attachment to physical place obsolete, but this lingering yearning for place in Hemingway's works suggests that even he had trouble progressing beyond place-based attachments. To demonstrate this point further, it will be necessary to consider Hemingway's efforts to transcend place in the context of a larger-scale cosmopolitan turn, and my essay argues that Hemingway's *A Farewell to Arms* is an exemplar of this more widespread effort to get beyond the dictates of place attachment.

Another perspective on place and placelessness emerges in Carlos Baker's book *Hemingway: The Writer as Artist*. Like Mandel, Baker identifies a clear dichotomy separating the Abruzzese priest from Doctor Rinaldi, and he distinguishes these characters in terms of their attitude toward home based on a "natural-mythological structure" associating the mountains with structural stability and the lowlands with disordered violence:

> The Home-concept, for example, is associated with the mountains; with dry-cold weather; with peace and quiet; with love, dignity, health, happiness, and the good life; and with worship or at least the consciousness of God. The Not-Home concept is associated with low-lying plains; with rain and fog; with obscenity, indignity, disease, suffering, nervousness, war and death; and with irreligion. (102)

Baker's analysis thus provides further justification for Mandel's association of Henry's attachment to home with a conservative political orientation. Being inhospitable to farming and remote from transportation, mountains are prone to offer a haven away from concentrations of people and their resulting conflicts. Lowlands provide good farmland and access to transport that make them worth fighting over. However, the mountains are not as peaceful in *A Farewell to Arms* as Baker's analysis suggests. They are the site of Henry's grievous wounding in the Battles of the Isonzo, a territory as contested as any other in World War I. Even the homelike haven provided by the mountains near Montreux in the novel's final book offers only a false sense of home. This analytically potent binary at the core of Baker's reading is helpful as a means of understanding the novel, and Hemingway's disruption of this binary is equally noteworthy. The mountain is an image of peace away from the war, but Hemingway establishes this possibility only to unsettle it in other ways, and this is part of a larger pattern in which Hemingway defines clear geographical distinctions only to dismantle them.

One place-based community distinction that is of central importance to *A Farewell to Arms* is the line dividing the army of the Italians from the army of the Austrians in the vicinity of the city of Gorizia in the valley of a river known as the Isonzo to speakers of Italian and as the Soča to speakers of Slovenian. Of course, the features of a contested territory often have multiple names, and Hemingway consistently uses the Italian because of his position on the Italian side of the battle. Hemingway elaborates on this battle line extensively from the first page of the novel, as anyone in the proximity of the battlefield would always be sensitive to this line's exact location. This line marks the divisions that set the terms for the various Battles of the Isonzo, or Soška Fronta, that raged between Italian and Austro-Hungarian troops stationed in the hills and mountains looking down into the Isonzo Valley. Of 600,000 Italian soldiers who died in the entire war, fully half died in the Battles of the Isonzo, which began on June 23, 1915, and continued sporadically until the November 7, 1917, invasion of Italy known as the Battle of Caporetto. And, the Italians' chaotic retreat during the Caporetto invasion serves as the setting for book 3 of *A Farewell to Arms*, the section in which Henry's Italian uniform becomes such a liability to him.

The logic of World War I was nationalistic, dependent on a clear delineation of opposing sides facing off across a battle line extending across the territory. Combatants on both sides took this national identity for granted and equated it with an obligation to fight for their country in the event of war. The logic was so strong that execution struck many as a reasonable punishment for violating its terms by refusing to fight or by aiding the enemy. Hemingway has nonetheless chosen to complicate the battle line as much as possible by juxtaposing it with many other different lines that cross the novel's terrain. It might be tempting, for example, to regard the river itself as the battle line. Would it not be convenient if the political divisions separating these two warring nations had etched themselves into the landscape itself, ever visible in the twists of this river? In "Mending Wall," his influential poem on the interaction between the physical terrain and human differences, Robert Frost writes of a belief: "Good fences make good neighbors" (l. 27), that a physical mark on the land can preempt and head off conflicts over ownership. Frost offers this proposition only to contradict it when conflicting readings of the wall drive the two neighbors apart as they work together to repair it. The Isonzo River's course, like Frost's wall, likewise has the potential to serve as an arbiter for Austro-Hungarian and Italian claims to the territory. However, there is no evidence that it has ever served this function. Even now, the national boundary between Italy and Slovenia disregards the course of the Isonzo, currently intersecting the Isonzo in Gorizia, a town that is itself divided by the border between Italy and Slovenia.

The opening paragraph of chapter 2 of *A Farewell to Arms* anticipates this discord between river and political boundary when it provides Frederic Henry's perspective on the river from his vantage in the city of Gorizia, recently invaded by the Italian troops with whom he is stationed: "The town was very nice and our house was very fine. The river ran *behind us* and the town had been captured very handsomely but the mountains beyond it could not be taken" (5; emphasis added). Hemingway's use of the preposition "behind" subtly reinforces the primacy of the battle line as the reference point for both sides, the line that is ahead of the combatants. Unlike the river, which changes course rarely as a result of geological shifts, the battle line's location is quite unstable, and the potential for future shifts of this line shapes the battle strategies of the Austrians in the hills. As Henry notes: "I was very glad the Austrians seemed to want to come back to the town some time, if the war should end, because they did not bombard it to destroy it but only a little in a military way" (5). A map is typically itself an argument for permanence, and few who look at maps can resist the temptation to at least tacitly acknowledge this reality on the ground. Or, as Denis Wood argues in *Rethinking the Power of Maps*, naturalizing the map by accepting it as an accurate representation of a place on the earth "has the effect of *universalizing* it, and this helps explain the map's origins in the rise of the state" (19; emphasis in original). However, the battlefield of the Isonzo is a place of radical contestation of the boundaries of the state and is thus violently in flux. Hemingway, very much aware of this, creates maps in his narrative that correspond with and challenge the nationalist arguments legitimating such maps.

Another line dividing the territory is the sight line of the Austrian gunners in the hills. Sight lines play a significant role in determining the placement of Italian guns in Gorizia, as Henry learns:

"Do they ever shell that battery?" I asked one of the mechanics.

"No, Signor Tenente. It is protected by the little hill." (15)

While within Italian control, Gorizia is thus divided into various regions depending on what the gunners in the hills can see, and every experienced soldier maintains a continually shifting, uncharted "map" of these sight lines in his head in order to survive life under the shadow of Austrian artillery barrages. More lines join this jumble of conflicting boundary markers as Frederic Henry approaches the key moment in book 1 of *A Farewell to Arms*, the moment of his severe injury beneath the blast of an Austrian trench mortar. As he drives up the river toward Plava, the lines multiply. The road he drives on, for example, is yet another line:

> Beyond the mule train the road was empty and we climbed through the hills and then went down over the shoulder of a long hill into a river-valley. There were trees along both sides of the road and through the right line of trees I saw the river, the water clear, fast and shallow. The river was low and there were stretches of sand and pebbles with a narrow channel of water and sometimes the water spread like a sheen over the pebbly bed. (44)

Hemingway depicts this road as an element that partly defines the landscape around Frederic Henry and the valley itself. The builders of this road, conscious of its function as a component of the landscape, have planted trees along it, making it visible from a distance and offering drivers a constant reminder of where the edges are. Henry's drive continues into an ever more jumbled multiplicity of lines:

> I could look down through the woods and see, far below, with the sun on it, the line of the river that separated the two armies. We went along the rough new military road that followed the crest of the ridge and I looked to the north at the two ranges of mountains, green and dark to the snow-line and then white and lovely in the sun. Then, as the road mounted along the ridge, I saw a third range of mountains, higher snow mountains, that looked chalky white and furrowed, with strange planes, and then there were mountains far off beyond all of these that you could hardly tell if you really saw. (45)

In examining the same passage, Carlos Baker finds a reinforcement for his mountain/lowland dichotomy: "[T]he mountain-image has developed associations; with the man of God and his homeland, with clear dry cold and snow, with polite and kindly people, with hospitality, and with natural beauty" (103). However, Henry looks at the "clear dry cold and snow" of the mountains and sees this multitude of lines. These are not blurry lines, but, in their crisp clarity, they fail to provide the needed distinction because of their excessive number. Through this endless accretion of different lines—the road, the snow line, the ridge line, the river—Hemingway takes a simple boundary between two sides in a war and turns it into a confounding, seemingly infinite regression into a chaos of lines "that you could hardly tell if you really saw," and this is the landscape of Henry's violent encounter with the trench mortar near Plava. It is almost as though this line-destroying trench mortar, rather than being lobbed over Henry by Austrian gunners, had rather been summoned into the scene by the entropic array of lines itself. The trench mortar is, in its own way, the "[s]omething there is," to return to Robert Frost's "Mending Wall," "that doesn't love a wall" (l. 36), or, in this case, a clear battle line, and Frederic Henry becomes a victim of its destructive argument.

This map of curving, overlapping lines between adversaries in the Battles of the Isonzo presents readers with a strong symbol of erratic inconsistencies within the armies on each side. Their internal composition has become as jumbled as the lines that separate them and, thus, it counteracts any effort to produce a simplistic, nationalistic map of the war. The Austrian army, after all, consists of soldiers from a large variety of ethnic, linguistic, and religious backgrounds all joined together somewhat arbitrarily by the rule of the Hapsburg family. At one point much later in the novel, Hemingway refers to the Croatians who "came over across the mountain meadows and through patches of woods and into the front line" (186). At another point, he addresses the much-anticipated and dreaded arrival of "fifteen divisions of Germans" in aid of their Austrian allies. German military strength seems to guarantee the Italian Army's collapse in the retreat from Caporetto (187). A study of the already hyphenated Austro-Hungarian army might also reveal Hungarians, Czechs, Slovaks, and, of course, the Slovenian fighters who actually lived the closest to this contested border with Italy. The Italian side is composed more uniformly of Italian soldiers. But, of course, as Hemingway's narrative reminds readers repeatedly, Italy, too, consists of numerous competing subcultures within a nation that is not nearly as unified as proponents of the Italian national identity might wish. Modern Italy only unified as one country in 1866, a mere fifty years before events in *A Farewell to Arms*, and regional disputes are evident all through Frederic Henry's conversations with Italian officers in the environs of Gorizia.

For example, Henry's friend, the priest, encourages him to visit his home region in the Abruzzi, and an Italian officer immediately argues against such a visit: "Listen to him talk about the Abruzzi. There's more snow there than here. He [Frederic] doesn't want to see peasants. Let him go to the centres of culture and civilization" (8). This town/country split sets the stage for Henry's transgression of the rural priest's hospitality. The priest extends a heartfelt hand of friendship in this scene only to have it ignored for reasons that even Henry cannot fully explain. Many travelers can plausibly recall this sort of encounter with authentic, rooted hospitality and their own failures to repay it adequately. Henry depicts his awkward exchange with the priest in stark terms:

> He had written to his father that I was coming and they had made preparations. I myself felt as badly as he did and could not understand why I had not gone. It was what I had wanted to do and I tried to explain how one thing had led to another and finally he saw it and understood that I had really wanted to go and it was almost all right. (13)

Hemingway's use of the word "almost" is crucial to this passage's final sentence. It reminds us that this disagreement between the cosmopolitan Frederic Henry and the provincial priest is fundamentally irresolvable. Underneath his misleading justifications, Henry has sided wholeheartedly with the dismissive Italian officers who regard the priest as an unsophisticated rube from the mountains, but he wants desperately to be better than this. Nicole Camastra's analysis of the scene explains these conflicted feelings in terms of sexual purity and defilement: "The juxtaposition of the 'whorehouse' with the 'cold, clear' Abruzzese country foreshadows the tension Frederic will soon negotiate between this 'passion and lust' in the nights, about which he tells the priest, and his longing for Catherine, described by Rinaldi as Frederic's 'lovely cool goddess'" (88). The Abruzzi represents an innocent pastoral ideal for Henry, and he knows that he is too corrupt to live up to it. Instead of admitting this by joining in the ridicule of the priest, he slinks away from this confrontation silently, preferring irresolution to confronting this ugly truth about himself. Later in the novel, after Henry's injury, the priest says, "[T]here in my country it is understood that a man may love God. It is not a dirty joke" (71), and the country to which he refers is not Italy; it is the Abruzzi. The priest has not bought into the unified Italian national identity, perhaps because of his more local orientation to his Abruzzi, or perhaps because of his more internationalist allegiance to the Roman Catholic Church.

As if these crypto-nationalist divisions within Italy were not enough, the Italian Army is also riven by strong class conflicts that come to a dramatic head in Henry's final conversation before his injury at Plava, a conversation with the ambulance drivers Passini, Gavuzzi, Manera, and Gordini, who "were all mechanics and hated the war" (48). These mechanics paint a sad picture of an Italian state in which a powerful minority uses violent coercion to compel its own citizens to fight. They tell a story of a division of *granatieri* (grenadiers) that "wouldn't attack and they [the *carabinieri*] shot every tenth man" (48). These mechanics do not hesitate to blame the war on Italy's ruling class: "There is a class that controls a country that is stupid and does not realize anything and never can. That is why we have this war" (51). The Marxist orientation of Passini's argument is hard to miss here, though Hemingway does not belabor it. Passini has little doubt about the failure of a common national identity to protect Italian soldiers from the destructive whims of their ruling classes, and he thus mounts a strong attack on the nationalist framework of Italy's prowar movement. And, in parallel with the Abruzzi priest's connection to transnational Catholic Church, Passini presumably has embraced Marx's call for an allegiance to a transnational proletariat, to the workers of the world.

So, from a battlefield that begins with two sides and one battle line between them, Hemingway derives endless complications that tangle up multiple conflicting lines of demarcation, alternate divisions and subdivisions of ethnicity, region, and class that thwart any simplistic, nationalist reading of the map of the Isonzo. It is against this chaotic background that we can return to our original question of what the American Frederic Henry is doing in Italy in an Italian military uniform in 1915. He is not, after all, Italian himself. In fact, he is not even the citizen of a country that is allied with the Italians in 1915, when he becomes an ambulance driver in Italy. This, as Michael Reynolds mentions in *Hemingway's First War*, distinguishes Henry from Hemingway himself, who joined the ambulance service in 1918 after the United States had entered the war in support of Italy and the rest of the allied nations (3), and this discrepancy between author and protagonist actually intensifies the ambiguities of national allegiance in the novel. When asked by the head nurse at the British hospital in Gorizia how he, as an American, has ended up in the Italian Red Cross Ambulance Corps, he replies, "I was in Italy . . . and I spoke Italian" (22), as if that explained anything. As the novel progresses, Frederic Henry's lack of national allegiance within the war context becomes an increasingly dangerous form of ambiguity. It is tempting to see him as a tourist who thought he would try out the "war thing" only to find out that the game had become dangerous as he got in over his head. As Ben Stoltzfus claims in an essay examining "Frederic's dialogic selves" (133), Henry's status as "an American in an Italian uniform" is a form of "masquerading and playacting" (129). Stoltzfus's observation is persuasive, and we should not disregard how playacting can have very serious, less playful consequences. Henry's lack of national allegiance to Italy, for example, is a precondition to his decision to cut off the stars on his uniform during the retreat from Caporetto and announce, "I was through. I wished them all the luck" (232). The pronoun "them" in this proclamation reminds us that he has, all along, been thinking of himself as an outsider on the Italian side of the war effort. William E. Cain contextualizes this decision as preferring "the beautiful clarity of life with Catherine [contrasting] powerfully with war's disarray, chaos, suffering and death," which, as he points out, is not necessarily a "perspective . . . that Hemingway shares" (386–87). But we should also consider this turn away from combat in terms of Hemingway's dispute with nationalism in this novel. Not fighting for his own nation, Henry has the luxury of abandoning the cause when he no longer sees the point of it: "I was through. I wished them all the luck. There were the good ones, and the brave ones, and the calm ones and the sensible ones, and they deserved it. But it was not my show any more and I wished this bloody train would get to Mestre and I would eat and stop thinking" (232). Notably, Henry has put himself at risk by being so good at the masquerade. A group of zealous *carabinieri* have arrested him during the retreat and accused him and every Italian officer they have intercepted of deserting. They do not understand that he is an American. Henry says, "It was not my show any more," but an Italian might ask whether it was ever really his show. According to the nationalist logic of the war, the Battles of the Isonzo could really only be his show if he were Italian. According to an alternative cosmopolitan logic of the war, of course, any war is everyone's show. Cosmopolitan soldiers enlist to battle injustice regardless of the nations involved, and this is a possibility that Henry renounces at this moment in the story in the face of the *carabinieri*'s murderous campaign against deserters.

Hemingway and his protagonist Frederic Henry can make various claims about how their efforts as Americans in Italy support the cause of justice. Beyond the actual assistance that they provide to wounded soldiers, both men contribute more abstractly to the facilitation of cultural exchange between the United States and Italy. Kim Moreland's article "Bringing 'Italianicity' Home: Hemingway Returns to Oak Park" provides extensive evidence from Hemingway's letters to his family of how he thought his time in Italy enriched him with a deep understanding of Italian culture surpassing the more superficial understandings of the average tourist to Italy. Hemingway was also, in Moreland's terms, able to play a crucial symbolic role as a carrier of Americanicity in Italy at a key moment in the development of the war: "In effect, Hemingway's fortuitous wounding, from the Italian government's perspective—he was the first American to be wounded and survive—expressed a message about America's military commitment, a message that the American government also wanted to send to the demoralized Italian troops" (55). Hemingway's presence there, in other words, represented a promise in the flesh by the American government that "the American Expeditionary Force" was on the way (55). Jeffrey Schwarz considers Hemingway's work as a cultural emissary in a different, much more political, light. He argues that depictions of Italians in the novel counteract American xenophobia, especially with regard to Italian immigrants to the United States, noting that many Italians in *A Farewell to Arms* do not recognize Frederic Henry as an American when they meet him. Once they find out that he is foreign, Schwarz writes, "he is nevertheless accepted and even embraced by the majority of the Italians he encounters" (110). Commenting on virulently xenophobic rhetoric applied to Italian immigrants, Schwarz provides an important and perceptive contextualization of *A Farewell to Arms* and its role in undoing harmful nationalist stereotypes in the United States. At the same time, the novel's account of the Caporetto retreat portrays a dysfunctional Italian state and could potentially reinforce anti-Italian stereotypes harbored by some of Hemingway's American readers.

If Hemingway was less xenophobic than most, he could attribute this to his cosmopolitan orientation. Cosmopolitanism is an appealing doctrine in this respect because it proposes that overcoming national divisions can bring about an end to war itself. There are significant virtues to being nonaligned in the context of war and of hewing to a principle that transcends the advancement of merely national interests. Of course, if that higher principle is economic self-interest, then the soldier becomes a mercenary, a soldier-for-hire who places his or her own needs above those of the larger community. Or, if that higher principle is enrichment of the soul, then the soldier becomes a tourist who seeks to acquire experience and knowledge by traveling overseas and interacting with the locals. There is, however, another category of participants in the theater of war with cosmopolitan attachments to a higher principle, and those are the advocates of impartial justice on the battlefield—travelers seeking to advance the cause of justice rather than economic or experiential benefits. *A Farewell to Arms* engages directly with this third category by situating its protagonist as an emissary of the International Committee of the Red Cross. In this sense, Frederic Henry owes his status on the World War I battlefield to an earlier battle that took place near Solferino fifty-six years earlier, in 1859. This was the site of a battle between the armies of Sardinia allied with French forces under Napoleon III and the armies of Austria-Hungary under the leadership of Emperor Franz Josef I, a battle that was crucial to the establishment of Italy as a modern nation-state. In the ensuing nine hours of heated combat, an estimated 300,000 soldiers split evenly between the two armies fought each other with bayonets and cannons in the environs of Magenta and Solferino. Six thousand died, and 30,000 wounded soldiers remained on the battlefield, many of whom were bayoneted by their enemies while lying helpless in the confusion that followed the battle's conclusion (Moorehead 2).

Swiss businessman Henry Dunant bore witness to this battle's aftermath and wrote about it in his book titled *A Memory of Solferino*, which came out in 1864. In this narrative, Dunant carefully positions himself as an outsider in this conflict: "I was a mere tourist with no part whatever in this great conflict; but it was my rare privilege, through an unusual train of circumstances, to witness the moving scenes that I have resolved to describe" (17). Dunant is in Italy to pay a visit to one of his customers—the French Emperor Napoleon III—and he provides a lengthy description of this battle and its aftermath. Dunant's narrative vividly recounts scenes from the battle and subsequent tragedies of the field littered with wounded and dead soldiers.

He pays particular attention to the logistical problems posed by so many in need of aid with so few resources to aid them. He describes wounded soldiers dying of thirst and drinking muddy, blood-filled water from puddles. The few field hospitals were completely overwhelmed, leaving many soldiers to die from preventable injuries. Though approximately 5,500 died in the actual battle, 40,000 more died as a result of poor conditions in the two months following the battle. Caroline Moorehead's book *Dunant's Dream: War, Switzerland, and the History of the Red Cross* (1998), offers an extensive history of the International Committee of the Red Cross and the fascinating story of the path from Dunant's visit to Solferino to the establishment of this organization in Geneva. She points out that, from the start, Dunant appealed to a notion of cosmopolitan justice through nonalignment, and that this was a notion that was also appealing to Europe's more pragmatic political leaders, who "wanted 'civilized' and 'humane' war, which could be invoked or set aside as a political instrument" (19). Upon returning home to Geneva, Dunant wrote a brief account of what he had witnessed at Solferino and published it himself as *A Memory of Solferino* in the hope that knowledge of this battle would lead to reforms in how European countries approached war. Dunant then distributed this document to influential people in Geneva, who responded to what they read by joining together to found the International Committee of the Red Cross and to write the first draft of the Geneva Convention. Both of these efforts laid the groundwork for organizations that were to become significant elements of modern warfare enlisting Ernest Hemingway, his protagonist Frederic Henry, and British members of the Voluntary Aid Detachment like Catherine Barkley. Consisting of medics, ambulance drivers, nurses, doctors, and food providers, this group was technically not aligned with one side or the other. Armies on both sides were supposed to see the Red Cross insignia and refrain from shooting at or shelling members of this third group that occupied a symbolic middle space somewhere outside of Italian or Austrian territory. This notion of a contingent of nonaligned, neutral caregivers, on the battlefield but outside of the conflict, was one of the key developments of the nineteenth century and continues to this day to define this external arbiter function regulating modern warfare. Frederic Henry's presence in the Battles of the Isonzo was predicated on a claim of humanitarian allegiances that transcended national differences and, in this context, functioned as a repudiation of the line dividing the Isonzo Valley.

The main problem with this reading is that Hemingway was known for eliding his neutral status in the war and for exaggerating his role as a combatant. In *The Young Hemingway*, Michael Reynolds tells of Hemingway's return to the United States and his evasions regarding his service in the Red Cross: "He told them about his wounding, showed them the scars. If they thought he had served with the Italian Army, Hemingway said nothing to dissuade them" (18). The older Hemingway who writes *A Farewell to Arms* is more straightforward about service in the Red Cross, and also more critical of its neutrality in war. For example, Frederic Henry notes that "we were required to wear an automatic pistol; even doctors and sanitary officers" (29). Arming health care workers is one way to muddle the Red Cross narrative of nonalignment, and Henry defines this policy as "the ridiculousness of carrying a pistol" and one that inspires "a vague sort of shame when I met English-speaking people" (29). Of course, this dismissive remark about the gun becomes less plausible when Henry actually uses this weapon during the Caporetto retreat and, in a break from his role as nonaligned caregiver, kills a deserting Italian sergeant. As Ellen Andrews Knodt argues, this scene is crucial because "it was important to Hemingway that Frederic Henry *not* be a hero, but a man caught up in events in love and war that he did not control, and yet also a man who was not merely a blameless victim of events" (154; emphasis in original). Hemingway's critique of Red Cross neutrality takes on added dimensions when he narrates Henry's encounter with an Italian soldier from Pittsburgh who complains of having a hernia and then confesses to aggravating this condition "so it would get bad and I wouldn't have to go to the line again" (35). The soldier from Pittsburgh successfully draws Henry into a small scheme to allow him to claim a fraudulent medical exemption from military service. Underlying this scheme is the truth that the health-care providers are key elements of the war effort. As the man from Pittsburgh says, "If I go back they'll make me get operated on and then they'll put me in the line all the time" (35). In other words, the doctors often patch up wounded soldiers in order to return them to the front, and this makes them active and energetic contributors to the war effort. By treating an ailment like the hernia of the man from Pittsburgh, the doctor provides genuine comfort. However, by returning this soldier to health, the doctor places him at greater risk of injury or death upon returning to the battle. Such potential contradictions are perhaps inherent in the Red Cross' mission from the start and are also perhaps indicative of how hard it is to remain neutral in war. In sum, just as it is impossible in *A Farewell to Arms* to draw a clear line between Italians and Austrians, it is impossible to draw such a line between the nonaligned Red Cross workers and the actively engaged combatants.

Whether Hemingway read *A Memory of Solferino* or not, there are plenty of parallels between *A Farewell to Arms* and Dunant's work. Both take place in the context of a battle between Italian and Austrian armies (though Italy did not quite exist in 1859). Both works focus more on the aftermath of war than on the elements of battle themselves. Much more of *A Farewell to Arms* focuses on Frederic Henry's time recovering in hospitals or fleeing from the battlefield than on any exploits on the battlefield itself. Henry Dunant and Frederic Henry follow similar trajectories from the horrors of the front line though remote field hospitals to the more established urban hospitals and eventually on to Switzerland. Dunant's arrival in Switzerland brings him home, where he can begin organizing a permanent relief mechanism for dealing with future wars, whereas Frederic Henry's arrival in Switzerland moves him in the opposite direction. In the place of Henry Dunant's self-sacrificing immersion in effective public-spirited reforms, we see Frederic Henry's self-interested withdrawal from all civic matters. Disenchanted with his own role in the Red Cross, the fruits of Dunant's activism, and the various contradictions attached to its battlefield work, Frederic Henry instead devotes himself to his individual development. Nonetheless, historical connections between Dunant's creation and Hemingway's novel help us understand a larger-scale development of a cosmopolitan sensibility on the heels of the emergence of European nation-states. War taught both figures important lessons about the dark side of nationalist power, and led both figures to a cosmopolitan counterargument against nationalism. In their different styles, both figures created lasting, persuasive arguments against the simplistic nationalist divisions that made the case for war.

Works Cited

Baker, Carlos. *Hemingway: The Writer as Artist*. Princeton, NJ: Princeton UP, 1963.

Cain, William E. "The Death of Love in *A Farewell to Arms*." *Sewanee Review* 121.3 (Summer 2013): 376–92.

Camastra, Nicole J. "'I Was Made to Eat': Food and Brillat-Savarin's Genesiac Sense in *A Farewell to Arms*." *Hemingway Review* 33.1 (Fall 2013): 86–92.

Dunant, Henry. *A Memory of Solferino*. Trans. Volunteers of the District of Columbia Chapter of the Red Cross. Washington, DC: American National Red Cross, 1939.

Frost, Robert. "Mending Wall." *A Boy's Will and North of Boston*. New York: Signet, 2001. 67–68.

Hemingway, Ernest. *A Farewell to Arms*. New York: Scribner, 1929.

———. "Soldier's Home." *In Our Time*. New York: Scribner, 1925.

Knodt, Ellen Andrews. "'Suddenly and Unreasonably': Shooting the Sergeant in *A Farewell to Arms*." *Hemingway's Italy: New Perspectives*. Ed. Rena Sanderson. Baton Rouge: Louisiana State UP, 2006. 149–57.

Mandel, Miriam. "Internal Structures: The Conservatism of *A Farewell to Arms*." *Hemingway's Italy: New Perspectives*. Ed. Rena Sanderson. Baton Rouge: Louisiana State UP, 2006. 174–84.

Moorehead, Caroline. *Dunant's Dream: War, Switzerland, and the History of the Red Cross*. New York: Carol & Graf, 1998.

Moreland, Kim. "Bringing 'Italianicity' Home: Hemingway Returns to Oak Park." *Hemingway's Italy: New Perspectives*. Ed. Rena Sanderson. Baton Rouge: Louisiana State UP, 2007. 51–61.

Reynolds, Michael. *Hemingway's First War: The Making of "A Farewell to Arms."* Princeton: Princeton UP, 1976.

———. *The Young Hemingway*. New York: Norton, 1986.

Schwarz, Jeffrey A. "Who's the Foreigner Now?: Rethinking American Prejudice in *A Farewell to Arms*." *Hemingway's Italy, New Perspectives*. Ed. Rena Sanderson. Baton Rouge: Louisiana State UP, 2007. 108–16.

Stoltzfus, Ben. "A Sliding Discourse: The Language of *A Farewell to Arms*." *New Essays on A Farewell to Arms*. Ed. Scott Donaldson. New York: Cambridge UP, 1990. 109–36.

Wood, Denis. *Rethinking the Power of Maps*. New York: Guildford, 2010.

IV

Across the River and into the Trees

11

Artifice and Reality

The Blending of Venice and America in *Across the River and into the Trees*

ADAM LONG

Critics of *Across the River and into the Trees* have almost universally recognized the importance of the novel's Venetian setting. Colonel Cantwell indeed loves Venice not only as a cultural and artistic crossroads but also as the deeply personal location of his first war experience and his coming to maturity. Despite Venice's importance, Cantwell frequently refers to America, often in comparison with Venice. However, there are moments in the text when Cantwell's love for Venice becomes entangled with his nostalgia for the United States. These entanglements prevent Cantwell's seeing Venice in a simple binary, where the New World fails in every respect in comparison with the Old. Instead, the references to America highlight the createdness of Cantwell's nostalgic vision of Venice. Just as the portrait of Renata is an idealized and unrealistic image of the woman, Cantwell's mental portrait of Venice and its charms is an idealized vision of a more complex reality. The references to America, then, are a part of the novel's larger attempt to distinguish artifice from reality.

Much criticism of *Across the River and into the Trees* has attempted to position it within Hemingway's career, asking how the novel "stacks up" to other Hemingway novels or asking how it addresses common Hemingway themes. By this standard, the novel is seldom seen favorably. The novel did not receive positive critical reception when it was first published, and many subsequent critics have found the character of Cantwell distasteful.

For instance, Kathleen Verduin generalizes, "Most difficult about Cantwell, however, is his arrogant bitterness, a bitterness that at times explodes into violence" (633). Such critics have read Cantwell as being a literary stand-in for Hemingway himself. A. Sidney Knowles finds *Across the River and into the Trees* to be a self-serving attempt for Hemingway to exorcise his own demons: "The last days of Richard Cantwell are Hemingway's bitter requiem for himself. [. . .] Equally, the novel serves as a settler of scores, old and new" (199). Though not all critics have stated this case as strongly as Knowles, finding biographical antecedents for characters in the novel has certainly been popular. Miriam Mandel has explored Giulio Brusadelli, Jeffrey Meyers has looked at Chink Dorman-Smith, and virtually everyone has speculated about Adriana Ivancich.

Other critics have focused more on the way in which *Across the River and into the Trees* develops literary themes begun elsewhere in Hemingway's work. Certainly, Hemingway returned to the soldier protagonist often in his career, changing this character in intriguing ways. Peter Lisca summarizes:

> Just as each Hemingway protagonist prior to Colonel Cantwell had embodied the experiences of earlier Hemingway protagonists, so in this old Colonel, Richard Cantwell, were subsumed the experiences of the youth Nick Adams, the Lieutenant Frederick [sic] Henry, the expatriate Jake Barnes, the Key Wester Harry Morgan, and the guerilla fighter Robert Jordan. In fact, the Colonel not only implicitly subsumes these characters, he refers directly to their experiences as being his own. (232–33)

Similarly, Knowles argues that the last days of Cantwell are a theme "presaged—but with greater objectivity on the one hand and a greater sense of fulfillment on the other—in the earlier deaths of Harry Morgan and Robert Jordan" (199). Central to these claims of continuity is the long-standing notion of Hemingway's "code hero." Cantwell, critics will argue, is an older code hero, one who is responding to the changes in society and in his life in ways consistent with the code followed by younger code heroes (Adams, Henry, Morgan, and Jordan). While this reading has led to some insightful criticism, Lisca also offers a note of caution: "Colonel Cantwell's obvious lineage has made it extremely difficult for critics to approach the novel with that freshness, that innocence, with which each new work of art must first be understood before it can justly be related to other works by the same artist or in the same tradition" (233). Bearing that caution in mind, this chapter will attempt a reading of *Across the River and into the Trees* as a cohesive and contained whole. After all, while Cantwell seems to reembody other Hemingway heroes, Hemingway's focus on Venice is found only in this novel, and thus it makes sense to understand this trope within the contained whole of this novel before considering how it connects to themes elsewhere in Hemingway's canon.

In exploring the presence of America in this Venetian novel, I will first turn to the moments in the text in which America is often used as a foil to build up an idealized Venice. Cantwell clearly identifies himself as more at home in the Old World. He says, "I have loved three [countries] and lost them thrice. Give a credit. We've re-took two" (160). The three countries he's referring to are France, Italy, and Spain. Cantwell's identification with Italy comes from his years serving there in World War I, years that were central in forming his adult character. He shares this coming-of-age experience with other Venetians, most notably the *Gran Maestro*. The narrator says, "Thus contact was made between two old inhabitants of the Veneto, both men, and brothers in their membership in the human race, the only club that either one paid dues to, and brothers, too, in their love of an old country, much fought over, and always triumphant in defeat, which they had both defended in their youth" (58). In addition to feeling a special connection with Venice and the Old World, Cantwell seems to feel an aversion to the New World, and specifically America. For instance, Cantwell compares the natural beauty of Renata with the artificial beauty of American women, which he sees as epitomized in their hair. Renata leaves her hair naturally wind-swept, but the American women curl their hair. Cantwell seems concerned about the artifice that this represents. He says, "In America, they make such things of wire and of sponge-rubber, such as you use in the seats of tanks. You never know there, whether there is any truth in the matter" (108). Importantly, this explanation of American artifice is used to highlight Renata's beauty, making her seem purer and more authentic.

One of the main distinctions that Cantwell makes between Venice and America is that Venice is a cradle for art and culture, whereas the United States is comparatively sparse in this area. Cantwell regularly shares his appreciation of Italian art, including the works of Tintoretto and Giotto. Similarly, he admires Venetian architecture, especially campaniles. Early in the novel, he discusses Italian art with his driver Jackson. Jackson mentions that he would love to bring a Titian back from the war with him, though he does not know what he would do with it. Though Cantwell mentions giving the painting to a local museum in the United States, Jackson notes the poor quality of his local museum. He says, "All they got in the local museum is arrow heads, war bonnets, scalping knives, different scalps, petrified fish, pipes of peace, photographs of Liver Eating Johnston, and the skin of some bad man that they hanged him and some doctor skinned him out. One of those women pictures would be out of place there" (24–25). Clearly, Cantwell's understanding of how fine art should be appreciated stands in contrast to Jackson's understanding of American museums. In this scene, Cantwell represents the cultured insider—the representative of Venice—and Jackson represents the typical American. This characterization supports Jackson's statement: Jackson and his museum are not ready to appreciate fine art.

Another of the main distinctions that Cantwell makes between Venice and America is propriety of behavior. American tourists are seen almost universally as distasteful. Cantwell complains of the American tourists, saying, "My countrymen sit down, or lie down, or fall down. Give them a few energy crackers to stall their whimpers" (183). He is particularly concerned about their artifice, stating that the version of "The Star-Spangled Banner" that can be heard on the radio is "a trick now. The radio can almost make the voice" (184). His distaste for American tourists is seen most clearly in his comments about the American writer, whom the *Gran Maestro* refers to as Cantwell's "pitted compatriot" (188). Cantwell describes this man's face as a "caricature" and suggests that "if he is a mediocre writer he will live forever" (130). Cantwell holds the "pitted compatriot" as one of the group of "[p]rofessional writers who had jobs that prevented them from fighting" (129). According to Cantwell, they "wrote of combat that they could not understand, as though they had been there," an act that Cantwell calls a "sin" (129). The "pitted compatriot," then, becomes a symbol for the artifice that Cantwell rejects in the Americans he meets.

In contrast to these Americans, Cantwell plays the role of the Old World aesthete well. He talks of art as an insider, instructing those he meets on its finer points. He is also an experienced gourmand. Michael Seefeldt notes the ways in which Cantwell serves as something of an aesthetic guide for Renata: "He selects the best wines (not best labels) and the best foods available in post-war Venice in the winter" (309). This is a reversal of the expected roles. Renata is, after all, a Venetian by birth and part of an established Venetian family. She should be the insider, but Cantwell sees himself in that role. In this way, Cantwell casts himself in the role of the chivalric hero. Despite the seeming impropriety of his sexual tryst with Renata, he sees himself as her protector. As Seefeldt asserts, "He has defended Renata's country, city, and personal honor" (308). Further, he inducts himself into a parody of a chivalric order. Despite the humor of the outward forms of this brotherhood, he seems to feel a genuine fraternal connection to its members, including the *Gran Maestro*. Unlike Jackson and the American tourists, then, Cantwell sees himself as a knightly figure, protecting Renata and Renata's city in a distinctively Old World way.

Having cast himself as one of the city's true protectors, Cantwell rejects the American soldier even more strongly than he rejects the American tourist. Cantwell calls the American troops "[s]ad, self-righteous, over-fed and under-trained" (61). Cantwell does not respect even the soldiers who did serve in the frontlines in combat. Of Jackson, he says, "[F]or all his combat infantryman badge, his Purple Heart and the other things he wore, [he] was in no sense a soldier but only a man placed, against his will, in uniform, who had elected to remain in the army for his own ends" (30). Specifically, Cantwell criticizes the motivation of American soldiers, claiming that they are more interested in making a good story than in making wise choices in battle. Cantwell says, "GI's somebody christened them. God how I hate that word and how it was used. Comic book readers. All from some certain place. Most of them there unwillingly. Not all. But they all read a paper called 'The Stars and Stripes' and you had to get your unit into it, or you were unsuccessful as a commander" (216). This indictment of the American military accuses not only the infantryman for being involved for the wrong motives but also the commanders for seeking publicity at the expense of loss of life.

Indeed, Cantwell's critique of American generals is severe, a fact that may be attributed to Cantwell's own demotion from the rank. Cantwell accuses American generals of having no practical military experience: "'In our army, you know,' he told the girl, 'practically no Generals have ever fought. It is quite strange and the top organization dislikes those who have fought'" (116). Cantwell prefers German generals such as Rommel to American generals such as Eisenhower and Patton. The results of this lack of experience are generals leading men into slaughters with little hope of success.

Cantwell's historical example is Custer's Last Stand. Of Custer, Cantwell says:

> That beautiful horse-cavalryman. I guess it is fun to be that way and have a loving wife and use sawdust for brains. But it must have seemed like the wrong career to him when they finished up on that hill above the Little Big Horn, with the ponies making the circle around them in all the dust, and the sage brush crushed by the hooves of the horses of the other people, and nothing left to him for the rest of his life but that old lovely black powder smell and his own people shooting each other, and themselves. (158)

Later in his confession about how he was busted from his general rank, Cantwell paints a similar picture of the generals giving the orders at both the Rapido and Hürtgenwald, particularly General Walter Bedell Smith, who commands from well behind the lines and thus makes poor decisions. This weakness in leadership is, for Cantwell, an intrinsic problem in the American system, not just a problem for Smith. Cantwell says, "He is not the villain. He only made the promises and explained how it would go. There are no villains, I presume, in a Democracy" (227–28). Generals such as Custer and Smith are different, in Cantwell's opinion, from himself, who failed because he was following these poor commanders' orders and then was scapegoated. In his characterization of American military, Cantwell portrays himself as something different from and other than the representatives of the New World.

The hatred of American generals is central to the novel; Cantwell's guilt over the battles seems to be the central event that Cantwell is trying to confess properly (and receive absolution for) as he prepares to die. This central obsession could help us understand Cantwell's negative attitude toward America and Americans. Knowles argues, "Throughout Cantwell's ruminations on the war, one is struck by the inability of the 'unjust bitter criticizer' to put aside matters that have run their course and now reside, unchangeably, in the past. How unlike, one must think, a professional officer in a victorious army" (205). Cantwell's focus on the past seems to stem from his desire to distance himself from the slaughter at these lost battles. Knowles continues, "One way to reestablish one's authority is to set oneself up as a critic, to demonstrate that he had a better grasp of the matter in which he feels he lost credit" (205).[1] Cantwell, then, is setting himself up as an authority outside of and other than the US military. As such, his distaste for America and identification with Venice is part of his desire to exorcise his own demons.

Running counter to this motif in the text are moments in which Cantwell undercuts his own idealization of Venice by nostalgically longing for America. He and especially Renata anxiously plan a trip to the United States. Renata and Cantwell imagine buying a house in the Venetian countryside, because Renata wants trees in the yard. Cantwell says that true trees can only be found in the United States. He says, "But you will never see trees, Daughter, until we go to America. Wait till you see a white pine or a ponderosa pine" (190). This leaves Renata wanting to "learn American" (191), both the language and the landscape. She asks Cantwell to teach her to say something in "true American" (192). The trip they imagine will be a road trip to the American West. Renata's desire for the trip seems to have been formed by the image of America she has internalized from American media. She tells Cantwell, "Unless you want to take the big Buick Roadmaster, with the Dynaflow drive. I've driven it all over Europe. It was in that last Vogue you sent me" (228). Renata wants to experience the "true" America through this trip.

But it is not only Renata who seems to long for America. Even Cantwell, who has experienced (as much as is possible) the "true" America and who has avowed his love for Venice, seems to long for America. Though he has returned to spend his last weekend in Venice before he dies, he does not spend his last day in Venice but in the marshes, emulating a duck hunt that is specifically more American than Venetian. He celebrates the fact that the ducks he will be hunting are not Venetian ducks but are migrating through, observing, "They shoot real ducks at this one. Good kids. Good shoot. Real ducks. Mallard, pin-tail, widgeon. Some geese. Just as good as at home when we were kids" (19). In addition, Cantwell does not die in Venice but on the battlefield in Northern Italy, where he repeats Stonewall Jackson's last words: "[L]et us cross over the river and rest under the shade of the trees" (282). Thus, despite his previous aversion to American generals, in his final moments he reenacts Stonewall Jackson's death, connecting him to the general.

At these times in the text, Cantwell casts himself as a New World intellectual. He is a modernist tragic hero, an almost stereotypical one. In response to the horrors he has experienced in modern warfare, he tries to create a world he can live in, often returning to classical art and myth to do so. Seefeldt summarizes Cantwell's existentialism:

> He reconstructs his own subjective, redemptive aesthetic life-order not by new discovery, but by referring reaffirmatively centuries back to old-world values: Renaissance Italy, especially with its North Italian painters; vulpine, time-wizened Venice, home to Old-Family Contessa Renata; and medieval European poets, like Dante and Villon, complete with their feuding, tortuous lives. (307)

Dante especially becomes a symbol for Cantwell's modernist approach. Verduin notes that Cantwell understands Dante as a modernist, not as a classicist, arguing that Hemingway "seems hardly to have known Dante at all: that is, he reveals no more than a superficial knowledge of Dante's actual writings" (635). Instead, Cantwell portrays Dante as a Byronic hero, an understanding of Dante that pervaded the Romantic period and continued into the twentieth century.[2] In this portrayal, Dante is a "proud and embittered exile, radiating scorn on all beneath him but capable of a profound and single-minded devotion" (635). The parallels with Cantwell are obvious, and it is unsurprising that he returns to this image to help explain his own behavior. This image is a Romantic creation favored by the modernists. In this case, Cantwell does not reveal himself to be a Venetian insider (Dante is a Florentine, after all). Instead, he shows himself as an insider in the American expatriate community.

So sometimes Cantwell seems to favor Venice at America's expense and other times he seems to favor America at Venice's expense. However, the binary is not so clear; many times in the text Venice and America don't seem that different at all. Cantwell compares the canals of Venice with the Mississippi River. He says, "Across the marshes, brown as those at the mouths of the Mississippi around Pilot Town are in winter, and with their reeds bent by the heavy north wind, he saw the squared tower of the church at Torcello" (33). Similarly, going to Mestre "was like going to New York the first time you were ever there in the old days when it was shining, white and beautiful" (39). Cantwell sees Venice itself as a tough town, one that compares to American towns such as Cheyenne and Memphis. In addition, Cantwell's Venice is filled with war profiteers who have replaced the ancient Venetian values with the capitalism of the New World, like the new money that Cantwell recalls seeing in Kansas City. In these passages, Venice does not stand out distinctly against the blight of the New World. Instead, Venice and America begin to blend together.

In many of these cases, the blending is more than an inevitability; it is, in fact, a positive. In his conversation with his water taxi driver, Cantwell offers to improve his boat by providing an American Jeep engine. Without the engine, the boat is "well built" and "pleasant," but not as "beautiful as a gondola" (48). The unimproved boat becomes for Cantwell a symbol of the old military spirit of Venice. He talks about its "gallantry" and compares it to "war horses," both American and Italian (55). He explains, "We have the gallantry of worn-through rods that refuse to break; the cylinder head that does not blow though it has every right to, and the rest of it" (55–56). Despite being a symbol of aging gallantry, Cantwell argues that the boatman should upgrade with the "smallest model Universal puts out. That's the best and lightest small marine engine" (47–48). Given that the Universal engine is too expensive, Cantwell promises to look into getting the man a "condemned" Jeep engine that he could "work... over" (48). For Cantwell, even an engine that is beyond use in America would be better than what the boatman has. Clearly, Cantwell tries to bring American expertise and technology to bear in improving the living conditions of Venetians.

Further, Cantwell sees the pioneer spirit that he associates with America as also being a trait of the founding Venetians. Cantwell says that it was "boys from Torcello" who "pioneered" Venice (35).[3] The choice of the word "pioneer" connects Venice in Cantwell's dialogue with his many references to the American West. Cantwell gives Torcello the full credit for establishing Venice, even saying, "It was a Torcello boy who was running arms into Alexandria, who located the body of St. Mark and smuggled it out under a load of fresh pork so the infidel customs guards wouldn't check him" (35). Cantwell's Torcello pioneer behaves much like the outlaws on the American frontier, the stories of whom Cantwell no doubt would have been inundated with in his youth. Later, Renata calls Cantwell a "Torcello boy" (151), completing the identification between Cantwell and these pioneers.

In addition to Venice blending with America, different versions of Venice begin to blend with each other, creating a complex symbolic structure for the novel. John Paul Russo notes that Hemingway draws from both the Classical and Romantic symbolic traditions associated with Venice. Classically, Venice was portrayed as a powerful empire, a center of art and finance. Russo gives the history of this symbolic tradition: "Renaissance humanists linked Venice to an ideal of republican *virtù* and liberty. This essentially classical myth, a 'civic cult of mystic patriotism,' goes back to the medieval period and the translation of Saint Mark's body from Alexandria to Venice" (154). Cantwell certainly admires the patriotism of Venetians, as when he praises the people of Torcello. In this symbolic system, Venice is the feminine object of desire (the "queen of the seas"), and the patriots of Venice her masculine heroes. As Russo notes, "Venice signifies the feminine, the unattainable, the sense of lack, the lure of death; Torcello with its square tower signifies completeness, phallocentrism, the masculine virtue of being closed up in oneself, autonomy" (161). When Cantwell aligns himself with Torcello, then, he inserts himself in Venice's classical symbolic system as the masculine admirer of the feminine city, and the embodiment of that city, Renata.

At other times, Hemingway draws on the Romantic symbolic system associated with Venice. For the modernists, Venice was no longer a symbol of power but instead a symbol of decay, a place of Eastern intrigue and loose morals. Nothing embodies this more than the Venetian Carnival. Russo points out that a major motif of the Romantic symbolic system is "play" and "fun" (161). On the most basic level, Cantwell has returned to Venice for one final weekend of fun before he dies. This fun is predicated on artifice, however, on pretending to be something other than what Cantwell is. He is masking impending death with a false image of fun escape through Renata. The character of Renata, after all, begins to blend with the character of Cantwell in certain ways. Lisca mentions that Renata is the same age as Cantwell was when he first visited Venice (and was injured in its defense). This would suggest that Renata should be read as a symbol for Cantwell's lost youth. Seefeldt writes that her name suggests rebirth (re-nata, in Italian), in this case a rebirth of Cantwell's youth (314). Thus, in spending his final weekend of fun with Renata, he is masquerading as the younger man he used to be.

The blending of Venice and America and of Renata and Cantwell are two examples of the complex symbolic blending that takes place elsewhere in the novel as well. Ben Stoltzfus explains that the way in which the art mentioned in the novel tends to merge with the representation of Renata. He says, "Venus, Venice, and Renata rising from the sea on a scallop shell are arresting images" for Renata (26). Stoltzfus traces similar symbolic blendings, such as that of the stones of St. Mark's Square with Renata's family gems (27). He further suggests that *Across the River and into the Trees* represents a "simultaneity of the past and the present" (23). The bridge image proposed by Lisca, however, captures the nuance slightly better. Lisca writes, "Standing over all the opposites that meet, for reconciliation or definition, is a symbol which is itself very much a part of the Venetian setting—the bridge" (247). We can see Cantwell trying to cross one of these bridges in some of his references to America. It is true that sometimes he tries to make himself a Venetian insider at the expense of all that is American. It also true that at other times he writes himself as a New World modernist, looking down on the decay of Venice. More often than either of these, however, America and Venice are part of a system of blended symbols. Cantwell is on the bridge between the Old World and the New.

So what do we make of these mentions of America in this Venetian novel? Does Cantwell idealize Venice, does he long for America, or is he able to blend the two together? We are not invited to form simple conclusions. The treatment of the theme is complex, even contradictory at times. I would argue that Cantwell's claim that the local is inescapable is important in coming to terms with these contradictions. Late in the novel, Cantwell apologizes to Renata for using highly localized language. He says, "Everybody sat on folding chairs as for a Chautauqua lecture. I'm sorry about these local terms; but we are a local people" (218). Apparently, Cantwell uses local terms, because local terms are what he knows. They are the only language he has to describe what he means. In Italy, too, he finds the substance of his narration in observation rather than in speculation. When visiting the fish market, he says, "A market is the closest thing to a good museum like the Prado or as the Accademia is now" (178). Though he is interested in art, he is drawn in his last weekend not to the Accademia but to the fish market and the duck blind.

The complex symbolic system of Venice is death in masquerade, a brightly costumed Venetian parading around at Carnival. But occasionally Cantwell recognizes the real behind the mask. He expounds upon the concrete things with which he is familiar, things he knows in the "local terms." Not surprisingly, these local things that he knows are often, though certainly not always, American, given that many of his experiences have taken place in America. In the final scene before Cantwell leaves the hunting lodge, he formally absolves himself of the complex symbolic system of Venice-Renata and leaves for the country, for the trees that remind him of America. This move can be seen as a choice of the local and concrete, since the last actions he takes in the countryside similarly are a shedding of the complex symbolic system. In his conversation with Barone Alvarito, he acknowledges and accepts a budding romance between Renata and Alvarito. This conversation is held indirectly (perhaps passive-aggressively), with Venice standing in for Renata. The two discuss their mutual love of Venice, with Alvarito acknowledging that Cantwell loved it "best of all" (277). It is clear from the context that what they are really talking about is Renata. Charles Oliver suggests, "There is understanding here between the two men; each is aware of the other's love for Renata, and there is respect" (150). For Oliver, this conversation is part of Cantwell's taking "some control over the circumstances of his own death" (150–51). Cantwell is preparing for death by shedding some of the artifice he has created. On the practical level, Renata's relationship with Alvarito will assure that she is "taken care of" after his death. Cantwell may believe this is necessary, though it is difficult to imagine that Renata really needs such chivalry. Further, in acknowledging Renata and Alvarito's relationship, Cantwell is acknowledging the appropriateness of their match. Alvarito is the Italian baron, and she the Italian countess. They are logical partners, the two Italian insiders. Cantwell is the one who has been pretending (or at least trying to), and this final acknowledgment of their relationship purges him of this artifice. He then returns to the landscape he knows, the forest so foreign to Venice, to a place he can speak of in "local terms," and there dies as the American general had before him.

Colonel Cantwell wants very much to be comforted by false idealizations, but he cannot be, because he knows these images are false. He idealizes his love for Renata, comparing the portrait of her to an image of the Virgin Mary or to *Venus Rising from the Sea*. Yet he recognizes that his love for Renata must soon end, and could not have been permanent anyway. He idealizes certain war heroes, but he undercuts this heroism with repeated portrayals of needless slaughter. He sees himself as a victim of poor leadership, but he also sometimes takes responsibility for failing. And, of course, he idealizes Venice as a center of art and culture, but undercuts his love of the city, realizing that it, too, has been built upon artifice. Venice is Byron's home, writ large: the furnishings are "not sacred, nor relics. They are just extra beds that were not used afterwards for various reasons" (52). Cantwell's final struggle, then, is to face death with no comfort from illusion. He must "cut out everything phony about the illusion" (213). And he must do this no matter how strong the siren song of Venice is.

Notes

1. Knowles is making a larger biographical argument here. He is suggesting that in addition to Cantwell purging himself of his wartime memories, Hemingway is also trying to purge himself of the shame incurred by the fallout of his experiences at Rambouillet.

2. On this point, see Ellis.

3. Lisca reminds us that the real story of Torcello is much more complex than the myth that Cantwell is telling. I would add that often the myth of the American pioneers similarly oversimplifies historic complexities.

Works Cited

Ellis, Steve. *Dante and English Poetry: Shelley to T. S. Eliot*. New York: Cambridge UP, 1983.

Hemingway, Ernest. *Across the River and into the Trees*. New York: Scribner, 1998.

Knowles, A. Sidney, Jr. "Hemingway's *Across the River and into the Trees*: Adversity and Art." *Essays in Literature* 5 (1978): 195–208.

Lisca, Peter. "The Structure of Hemingway's *Across the River and into the Trees*." *Modern Fiction Studies* 12.2 (1966): 232–50.

Mandel, Miriam. "*Across the River and into the Trees*: Reading the Brusadelli Stories." *Journal of Modern Literature* 19.2 (1995): 334–45.

Meyers, Jeffrey. "Chink Dorman-Smith and *Across the River and into the Trees*." *Journal of Modern Literature* 11.2 (1984): 314–22.

Oliver, Charles M. "Hemingway's Study of Impending Death: *Across the River and into the Trees*." *Hemingway in Italy and Other Essays*. Ed. Robert W. Lewis. New York: Praeger, 1990. 143–52.

Russo, John Paul. "To Die Is Not Enough: Hemingway's Venetian Novel." *Hemingway in Italy and Other Essays*. Ed. Robert W. Lewis. New York: Praeger, 1990. 153–80.

Seefeldt, Michael. "Hemingway's Paradoxical Protagonist: Colonel Cantwell, New-World Knight and Old-World Connoisseur." *North Dakota Quarterly* 68 (2001): 303–16.

Stoltzfus, Ben. "The Stones of Venice, Time, and Remembrance: Calculus and Proust in *Across the River and into the Trees*." *Hemingway Review* 22.2 (2003): 19–29.

Verduin, Kathleen. "Hemingway's Dante: A Note on *Across the River and into the Trees*." *American Literature* 57.4 (1985): 633–40.

12

Across the River and into the Trees

A Trigonometric Mirror

MARINA GRADOLI

There comes a time when a man stops along the stream of life to reflect and decides not to follow that stream anymore. The flow of the stream has constantly distorted his reflections, but toward the end of life, if he reaches a place where the water comes to an almost standstill, that water becomes a mirror into which he can reflect and get a clear image of himself... then he decides to go "across that river."

Venice is where the water—still moving—comes to an almost complete standstill, and it helps such reflections. In Venice, with its thousand rivulets, where the palaces themselves seem to come to life in their gently moving reflections, a man can look back upon his life, reflect, and finally accept death not as a tragic event but as an acceptance of life.

Across the River and into the Trees is the result of such a reflection: a special encounter between a writer and a town on water. Hemingway was hurt by the negative reactions of the critics to his book. They had not understood what he was trying to do: from "arithmetic" he had moved into "calculus" (Bruccoli, *Conversations* 62). *Across the River and into the Trees* is not a trivial love affair between a sick old man and an improbable Lolita. Rather it is an attempt to enact a myth.

Renata—as her very name may remind the reader—is the rebirth of youth, the remembrance of past love. Renata is the mirror, as Venice is, and thus she helps Cantwell to reflect and to remember so as to live in the eternal present. Renata is Venus, the goddess of beauty and love born by the sea, with her long unkempt hair. Renata is Beatrice, Dante's guide to the kingdom of God. Renata is obviously also Adriana Ivancich, the beautiful and unattainable Venetian lover.

Renata is a living myth, as Joseph Campbell has taught us to understand myth, not as a fantastic account of reality but rather as a true representation of real events. In order to reach a mythical dimension in an account we must be able to see it multidimensionally, from different points of view, from various temporal perspectives. For instance: if I think back to a particular event when I was a child or when I was an adolescent or an adult, I can give a realistic account of those events and share that experience with another person; but if I can see all those experiences simultaneously and see my life from beginning to the almost end (when death is so close I can almost experience it), in that simultaneity I reach a new dimension of time: I am out of "time's winged chariot," I coincide with time infinite. My time comes to a full circle where my end and my beginning meet and I am immersed in a mythological time. I myself become a myth contemplating the different stages of my life. I don't discard, I don't forget any of those stages; each event is as valuable as the others because they all contribute to make the man I am, a unique irreplaceable human being: I am mythical, according to Joseph Campbell's idea of myth. In this sense, not only Renata but Colonel Cantwell himself is a mythical character (or should I say "persona"?)

Hemingway has partially failed in transforming a true myth into a true woman or a true man, yet the truth of the living myth comes through: fellow writers (such as Vittorini and Montale in Italy) acknowledged the existential experience Hemingway was trying to convey.

In this novel Hemingway has tried to compress the whole world in a nutshell. The everyday life and globalism; politics and military strategy; a town marketplace and zoology; Bruegel and Eleonora Duse or Ida Lupino. From anthrax to botulism, there is no realm that Colonel Cantwell (and obviously Hemingway) does not discuss as an expert. Renata herself protests, "You know many, many things. . . . About pictures and about books and about life" (*ARIT* 194). In *Across the River and into the Trees* the narrative material seems so pointlessly banal and chaotic that the critics could not understand and did not approve. In spite of a few excellent analyses (such as those by Baker and Lisca in the past, then by Williams and Tintner, and, more recently, by Meredith and Stoltzfus), this novel is mainly neglected by both readers and critics. Maybe *Across the River and into the Trees* was too ambitious a project and consequently was destined to failure. Yet, in spite of its flaws, it is a sound and strong piece of art. Metaphorically it could be compared to the monumental Cathedral of Siena. The gigantism of its conception (the church as we see it today was intended as a mere wing of the transept) dispels the spiritual and aesthetic delight it should bestow.

If you go inside you'll find treasures to be discovered and analyzed, but the overall atmosphere of emotional enjoyment of the art is missing. If you want to feel that enjoyment, go and sit in front of the facade of the cathedral of Orvieto and stay there in all seasons and in any hour of the day.

In all arts there must be an equilibrium between craftsmanship and emotion. In reading *Across the River and into the Trees*, apart from the opening scene in the lagoon, one does not feel emotion. There is a myriad of practical information. The book is a Baedeker of how to eat, what to see, even what to read. A quotation from Whitman strikes one as particularly inappropriate: the young Renata is not culturally equipped to make such a quote (195). There is a donnée here that escapes the reader and prompts him to go back and read Whitman. What he finds may shock him as an epiphany:

> These are really the thoughts of all men in all ages and lands, they are
>   not original with me,
> If they are not yours as much as mine they are nothing, or next to
>   nothing,
> If they are not the riddle and the untying of the riddle they are nothing,
> If they are not just as close as they are distant they are nothing.
>   ("Song of Myself" lines 355–58)

These are really the thoughts of all men . . . if they are not yours as much as mine they are nothing. Suddenly we realize the truth of these lines and how "Song of Myself" and that solitary song which is *Across the River and into the Trees* are akin. We go on reading. "This is the grass that grows wherever the land is and the water is" ("Song of Myself" l. 359). This is the same grass that grows in Proust's land. Proust, who took the trouble to insert a quotation from Victor Hugo at the end of his *Recherche*: "Il faut que l'herbe pousse et que les enfants meurent" (It is necessary that the grass sprouts and children die; 1038).

Proust comments:

> I say that the cruel law of the art is that people die and we ourselves will die consuming all sufferings so that the grass may grow, not the grass of oblivion, but the grass of the eternal life, the thick grass of creative works of art, over which generations will merrily come without any concern of those who sleep underneath and make their "déjeuner sur l'herbe." (1038)

How quickly this image brings us back to the beautiful passage in which Colonel Cantwell muses about all the fine places he would like to be buried in:

> I could be a part of the ground where the children play in the evenings, and in the mornings, maybe, they would still be training jumping horses and their hoofs would make the thudding on the turf, and trout would rise in the pool when there was a hatch of fly. They were up on the causeway from Mestre to Venice now with the ugly Breda works that might have been Hammond, Indiana. (*ARIT* 40)

These cadences and rhythms and thoughts are Hemingway's, but his art is connecting us with so much else, awakening distant places and voices . . ."If they are not yours as much as mine they are nothing, or next to nothing" ("Song of Myself" l. 356). We may be willing to follow Hemingway's references and the thin threads he is offering, but the canvas is much too complex to decipher.

Hemingway was confident that readers would detect his allusions, at least at a subliminal level. I myself have experienced something of the sort in reading the marginal episode of the cyclist and the unsuccessful attempt of Colonel Cantwell to see the title of the newspaper the man is reading.

This episode made me think of another traveler in another story, "The Revolutionist" who, meaningfully, is carrying paintings' reproductions wrapped in a copy of the *Avanti*. This personal transfer I imputed to the fact that soon after, Colonel Cantwell mentions Mantegna, and Mantegna is the painter that the titular revolutionist stubbornly objects to. The reading of *Across the River and into the Trees* becomes very complex, and I compare its structure to a diagram I have seen on the Italian TV illustrating the relation between various institutions in an Italian region. The result of their complex interdependency makes the final calculus of partnership almost impossible.

This diagram prompts me to draw a similar structure to account for the complex world of the novel.

Hemingway himself synthesized the contents of the novel in an authoritative cable to *Time* on September 11, 1950:

> The present novel is about love, death, happiness and sorrow. It is also about the city of Venice and the Veneto, which Hemingway has known and loved since he was a young boy....
>
> It is the best novel that Hemingway can write, and he has tried to make a distillation in it of what he knows about the above subjects plus one other subject, which is war. (qtd. in Bruccoli, *Conversations* 57–58)

But the book is much more. It is an experiment in writing. The famous "iceberg theory," Hemingway's major contribution to the art of writing, is still operating here, but he has gone further in his experimentation: from arithmetic he has moved into calculus. One eighth of *Across the River and into the Trees* shows above the water level, but it is what dwells under the surface that gives dignity of movement to that tip. Underneath it is very crowded.

I will offer just a few examples; each reader may sketch his own iceberg according to what he himself is willing to bring to the reading of the novel.

I will start with Whitman, since he triggered my adventures in reading.

In "Song of Myself" we read: "A morning-glory at my window satisfies me more than the metaphysics of books. / To behold the day-break!" (ll. 549–50). This is the same feeling experienced by Cantwell, who wants his windows always open to observe nature and the natural world of man.

Elsewhere, Whitman describes:

> The work of fishermen, the work of the eel-fisher and clam fisher;
> I come with my clam-rake and spade . . .
> I have a small axe to cut holes in the ice . . .

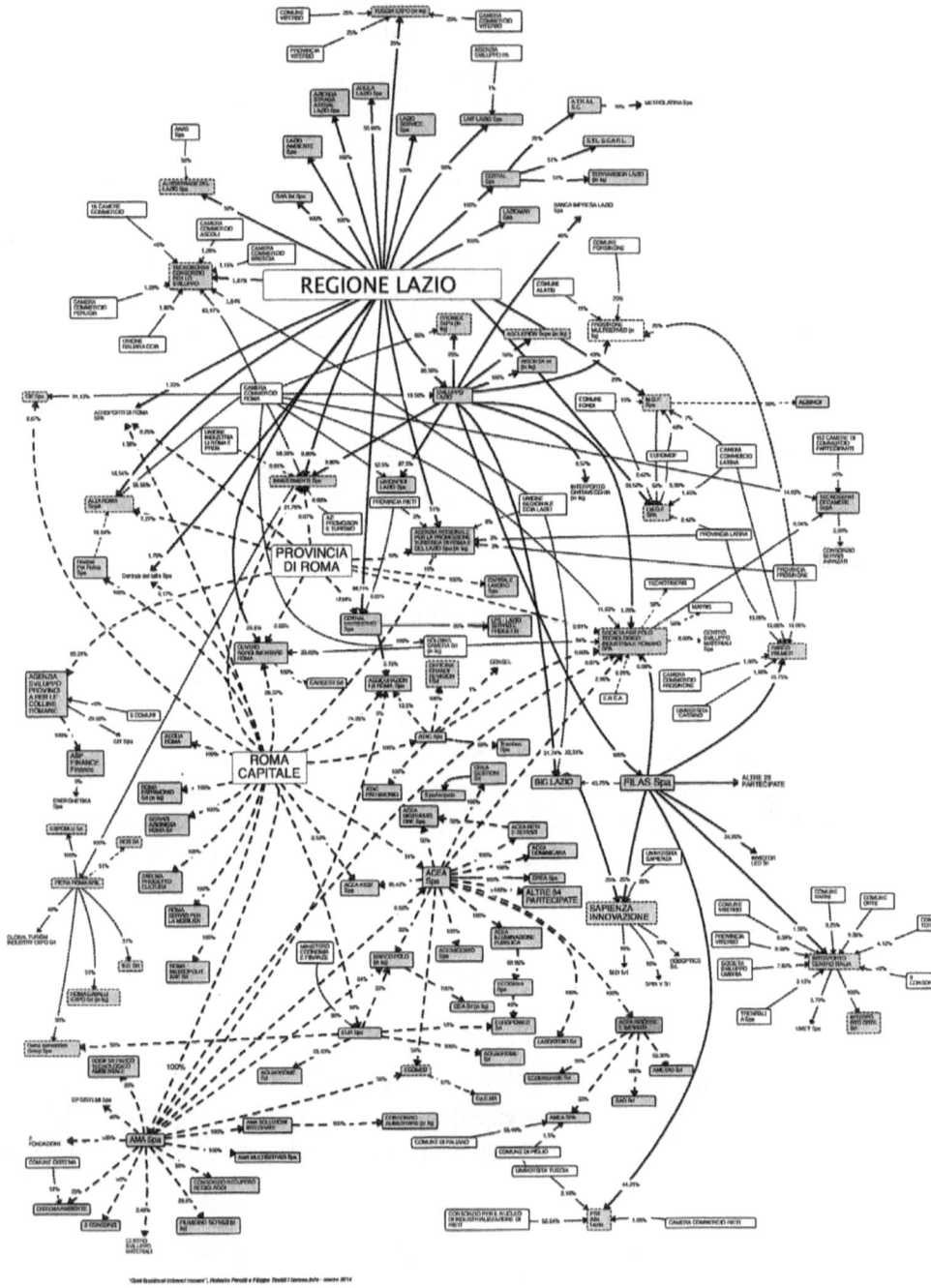

Figure 12.1. Diagram of partnerships between among of Regione Lazio. Courtesy of Marina Gradoli.

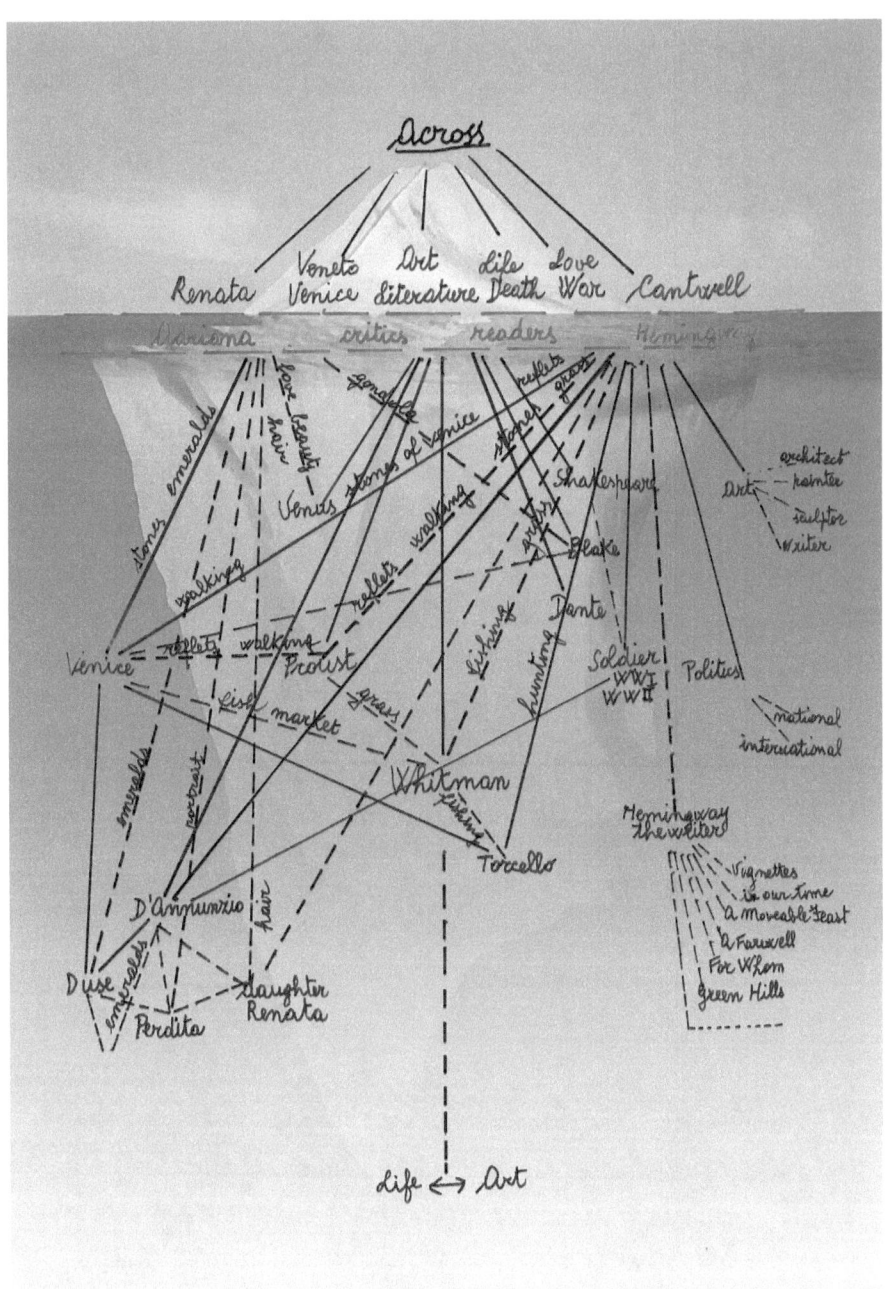

Figure 12.2. The iceberg theory in *Across the River and into the Trees*. Courtesy of Marina Gradoli.

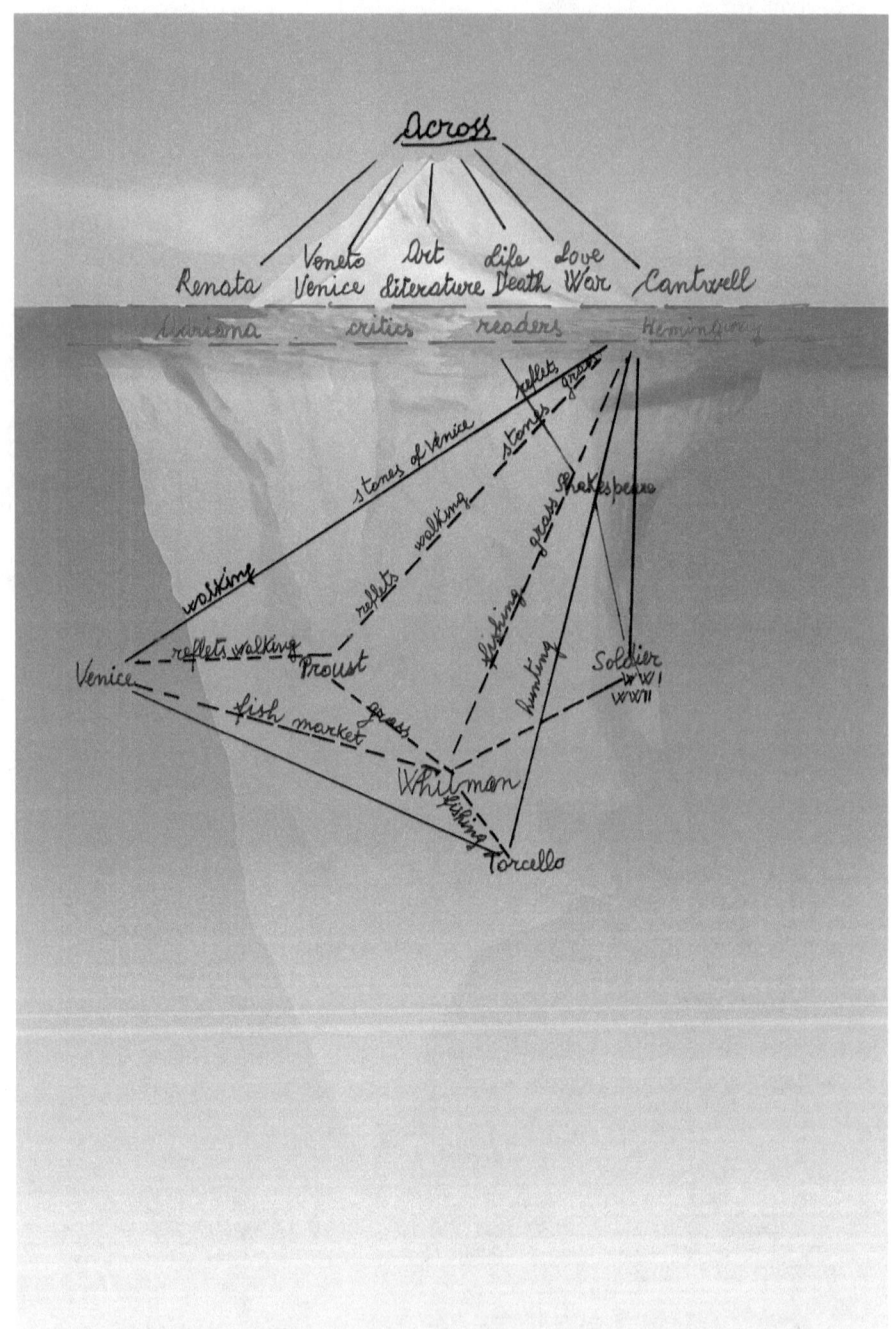

Figure 12.3. Whitman's connections under the surface. Courtesy of Marina Gradoli.

> the dark green lobsters are desperate with their claws as I take them
> out, I insert
> wooden pegs in the joints of their pincers . . .
> There in a huge kettle of boiling water the lobsters shall be boil'd till
> their color
> becomes scarlet. . . .
> mackerel-taking,
> Voracious, mad for the hook, near the surface, they seem to fill the
> water for
> miles ("A Song of Joys" ll. 35–36, 39, 45, 47–49)

This is Whitman who brings us close to Cantwell who "breaks the ice" in the lagoon and goes to the fish market to observe

> the heavy, gray-green lobsters with their magenta overtones that pre-
> saged their death in boiling water. They have all been captured by
> treachery, the Colonel thought, and their claws are pegged.
> . . . There were a few albacore and bonito. . . . looked like boat-tailed
> bullets
> . . . not made to be caught except for their voraciousness. . . . these rov-
> ing bullets, in their great bands, live in blue water and travel through
> all oceans and all seas.
> A nickel for your thoughts now, he thought. Let's see what else they
> have. (*ARIT* 178–79)

The reader is willing to give more than a nickel to know Cantwell's thinking while he observes the medium-sized shrimps "gray and opalescent, waiting their turn too, for the boiling water and their immortality"—although only the artist can give "immortality" to a boiled shrimp.

Reading Whitman and Hemingway side by side is a new literary expe-rience, albeit one must keep in mind that "no classic resembles another" (Bruccoli, *Conversations* 61).

> the tale of the murder in cold blood of four hundred and twelve young
> men
> . . . Their colonel was wounded and their ammunition gone . . . ("Song
> of Myself" ll. 875, 878)

This is Whitman but could as well be Hemingway: choose your own quote. War memories are similarly compelling and traumatic in the two authors, and, while those memories cannot be removed, they might become appreciable, as Whitman indicates: "O to resume the joys of the soldier! / To feel the presence of a brave commanding officer—to feel his sympathy! ("A Song of Joys" ll. 65–66). This sentiment anticipates the sympathy and comradeship the young lieutenant Cantwell offered his soldiers who were untimely in applauding Gabriele D'Annunzio's harangue (*ARIT* 54).

D'Annunzio is another interesting presence under the surface. Going up the Grand Canal, Cantwell sees "the little villa . . . ugly. . . . There *he* lived" (*ARIT* 49; emphasis in original). "He" stands for D'Annunzio. Here we have an unaccountable inaccuracy of Colonel Cantwell / Hemingway. D'Annunzio never lived in that villa with Eleonora Duse, but was assisted there by his own "daughter" Renata after he was wounded in the eye in the aircraft accident.[1] Actually D'Annunzio's Renata is a much more pregnant source for the name of Cantwell's "daughter" Renata.

D'Annunzio is not just a name thrown in by the author to show off his erudition. Hemingway's portrayal of the Vate, the things Cantwell likes or dislikes of the man, helps us to decipher the persona of Cantwell as well as of Hemingway himself. According to Reynolds (115), in 1920 Hemingway owned *The Flame of Life* (*Il Fuoco*), a copy of which he presented to Dorothy Connable (Baker 580). In 1938 he owned a copy of the biography written by D'Annunzio's friend/secretary Tom Antongini; he even sent a copy of the book to his sister-in-law Virginia Pfeiffer (Reynolds 93). Hemingway's persistent interest in D'Annunzio through the years is testified moreover by the presence in the Finca Vigía library of Frances Winwar's biography published in 1956 (Tintner 13).

In Antongini's biography, Adeline Tintner found the anecdote of the three precious emeralds Eleonora Duse gave to her lover, an episode that points to the family emeralds Renata gives to Colonel Cantwell. Through a close analysis of D'Annunzio's *Notturno* (the work that Colonel Cantwell highly praises in *Across the River and into the Trees*), Tintner convincingly argues that D'Annunzio's work is a major inspirational source for Hemingway's novel. By 1924 Hemingway had read *Notturno*, probably a 1923 French version of the book or, we may guess, the original version in Italian, a lan-

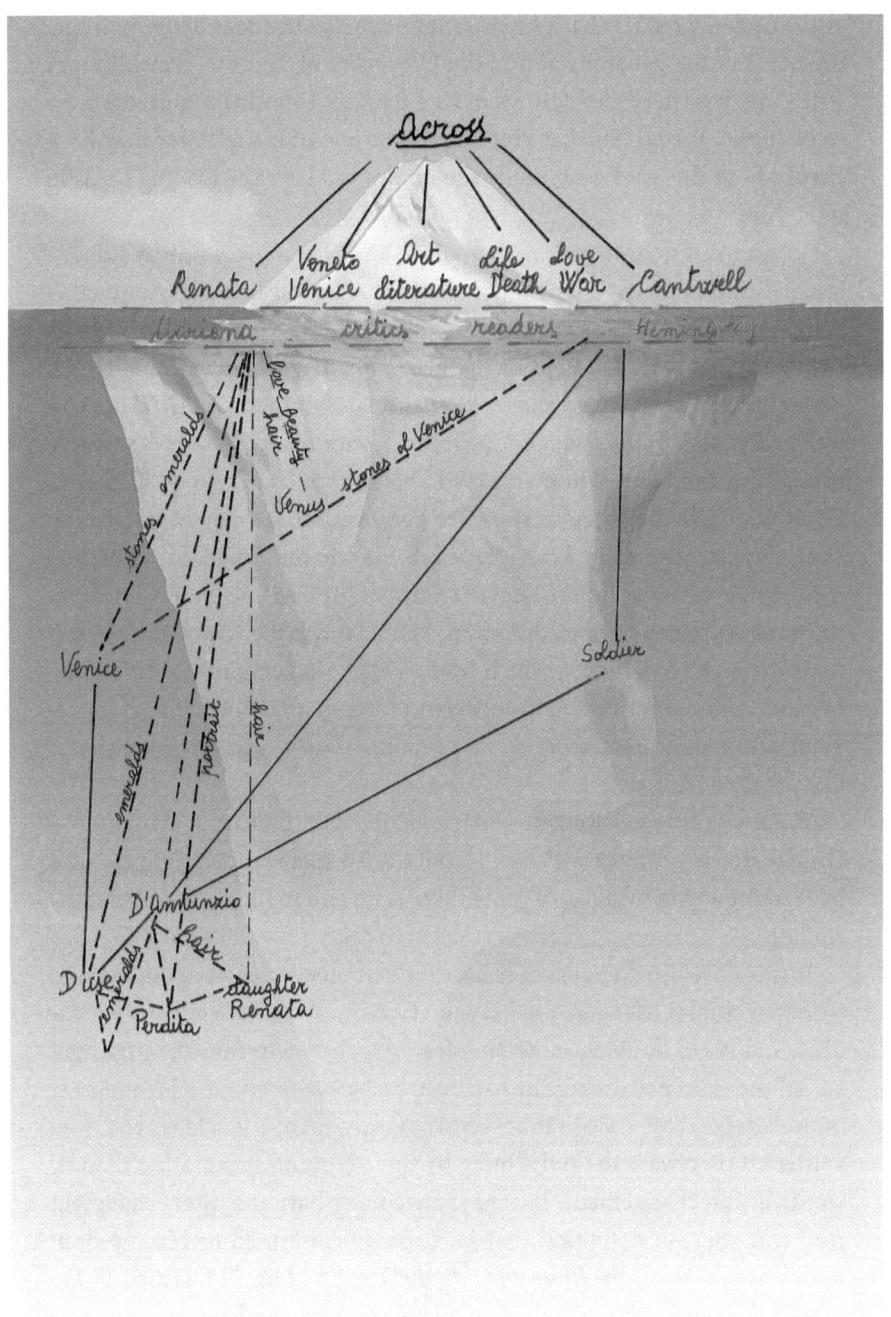

Figure 12.4. D'Annunzio's connections under the surface. Courtesy of Marina Gradoli.

guage he could read. What a surprise to find on the last page of the facsimile the name of the generous donor, the University of Toronto, which in 1923 (the same year the Hemingways moved back to Toronto) acquired a copy of *Notturno*. It suggests that Hemingway or one of his relatives may have checked out the book (hopefully the library has kept the loaning cards in its archives).

As with Whitman, reading D'Annunzio and Hemingway side by side is a fascinating literary experience. The alive texture of the hair of D'Annunzio's daughter is comparable to the often-praised hair of Renata by Cantwell. Its rich blackness is reminiscent of the blackness of a Venetian gondola, the perfect profile of which recalls Blake's celestial "symmetry" (*ARIT* 140), as well as Renata's profile, which "could break your heart" (78) as "the curve of her [Eleonora Duse] fore-arm could break your heart" (50)—Eleonora Duse, who gave the precious stones to her lover, stones that eventually become "square stones" in *Across the River and into the Trees* (103), which in their turn evoke the uneven square stones of the Baptistery of Saint Mark that rocketed Proust from Combray to Venice and to the scintillating reflections through his window, which lead us to the reflections on the ceiling of Cantwell's room through his open window: an unending circular movement of the mind collecting literary reminiscences in "the perfect circle" like Giotto (*ARIT* 57).

Blake—gondola—Renata—black hair—D'Annunzio's daughter—Duse—stones—Proust—Venice . . . once the reader accepts being engaged by Hemingway in his literary game there is no end to the enjoyment of the reading.

In this novel we do not simply have hidden silenced parts of the iceberg; we have complex triangulation between facts. In *Across the River and into the Trees*, Cantwell, "looking across the river[,] . . . had determined, by triangulation" the exact place where he had been badly wounded (26). Hemingway himself defined his style in these terms as early as 1929, in a letter to Owen Wister: "I try always to do the thing by three cushion shots rather than by words or direct statement. But maybe we must have the direct statement too" (*SL* 301)—a definition that he strongly confirmed to Harvey Breit in defense of *Across the River and into the Trees*, adding, "In writing I have moved through arithmetic, through plane geometry and algebra, and now

I am in calculus. If they don't understand that, to hell with them" (qtd. in Bruccoli, *Conversations* 62). Hemingway's "calculus" is not a mere calculus (as James Meredith has aptly illustrated) between discrete fragments brought back into an integral unity; rather it is a trigonometric calculus.[2] In a trigonometric calculus, if we have three cognitae, we may find the other three incognitae according to our ability,[3] but "if they are not yours as much as mine they are nothing, or next to nothing" (Whitman, "Song of Myself" l. 356).

This trigonometric calculus can be worked out for D'Annunzio as well as for a myriad other instances in the novel, and the reading of *Across the River and into the Trees* becomes much more meaningful and gratifying.

We are well aware of Hemingway's interest in Native Americans, but maybe we should better investigate his interest in Indian literary heritage. Hemingway's poems such as "Bird of Night" and "Translations from the Esquimaux: There Are Seasons" might testify to such an interest, but, even more, the rhythms and repetitions of his prose seem to echo Indian poems such as "Where the Fight Was." This could account for the alleged Indian blood, one-eighth, Hemingway boasted of, which was never confirmed by family or biographers. While it is of some interest that Hemingway repeated this fib to Lillian Ross during the famous interview in 1950 it is far more telling to note that the ratio, one-eighth, is the same of the famous iceberg theory. In the deep waters under the iceberg of *Across the River and into the Trees* Hemingway engaged again in a titanic struggle between life and art to see whether he will be destroyed or defeated.

Appendix 1—Elevator

What we have outlined for Whitman and D'Annunzio may apply to other writers mentioned in the novel such as Dante, Proust, Shakespeare, etc., or painters such as Giotto, but it may as well apply to Hemingway's previously published works. Sometimes they are openly referred to with captions such as *A Farewell*, *In Our Time*, *Out of Season*, or less obviously: "But that was in another country and besides the wench is dead" (*ARIT* 196); *"fraîche comme au jour de la bataille"* (250); the length of the lover's hair; "I want to be like you" (134); "I wish to serve you" (135), all sentences echoing various works by Hemingway which reverberate in the novel enriching its imagery. Without denying the interesting correlations that Ben Stoltzfus makes between Cantwell's failing heart and the working of the elevator, the following passage from *Across the River and into the Trees* gains in meaning and feeling when juxtaposed with a passage from *A Farewell to Arms*:

> "... should I come up to your room?"
> "Which do you wish?"
> "To *come to your room*, of course, and see how you live and how things are there."
> "What about the hotel?"
> "Everything is known in Venice anyway."
> ...
> "Good," the Colonel said. "By stairs or elevator?"
> "*By elevator*," she said, and he heard the change in her voice. "You can call a boy or we can run it ourselves."
> "We run it ourselves," the Colonel said. "*I checked out on elevators long ago.*"
> It was a good ride with a slight bump, and a rectification at the end, and the Colonel thought: Checked out, eh? You better be checked out again.
> The corridor was now not simply beautiful, but exciting, and *putting the key into the lock was not a simple process, but a rite.*
> ...
> "Say once more, first, that you love me and *make the buttons very tight.*"
> "I love you," the Colonel said quite formally.
> Then he whispered into her ear as gently as he knew how to whisper, as his whisper was when they are fifteen feet away and *you are a young lieutenant on a patrol*, "I love you only, my best and last and only and one true love." (*ARIT* 104–6; emphasis added)

* * *

> Well, I knew I would not be killed. Not in this war. It did not have anything to do with me.... After supper I would go and see Catherine Barkley. I wish she were here now. I wished I were in Milan with her.

I would like to eat at the Cova . . . and go to the hotel with Catherine Barkley. Maybe she would. Maybe she would pretend that I was her boy that was killed and we would go in the front door and the porter would take off his cap and I would stop at the concierge's desk and ask for the key and she would stand by the elevator and then *we would get in the elevator and it would go up very slowly clicking at all the floors and then our floor and the boy would open the door and stand there and she would step out and I would step out and we would walk down the hall and I would put the key in the door and open it and go in* and then take down the telephone and ask them to send a bottle of capri bianca in a silver bucket full of ice and you would hear the ice against the pail coming down the corridor and the boy would knock and I would say leave it outside the door please. Because we would not wear any clothes because it was so hot and the window open and the swallows flying over the roofs of the houses and when it was dark afterward and you went to the window very small bats hunting over the houses and close down over the trees and we would drink the capri and the door locked and it hot and only a sheet and the whole night *and we would both love each other all night* in the hot night in Milan. That was how it ought to be. I would eat quickly and go and see Catherine Barkley. (*FTA* 37–38; emphasis added)

The above is just one example of a myriad possible interrelations between the novel and previous Hemingway works mentioned or implied in the novel. This novel is a multiple layered work and a single interpretation might hamper its full meaning. The title itself has been too easily dismissed as a clear reference to the last words of General Stonewall Jackson while it may also pay tribute to an Indian song/poem titled "Where the Fight Was," printed in *Poetry: A Magazine of Verse* (the same magazine that published Hemingway's early poems and a vignette in January 1923).

Appendix 2—"Where the Fight Was"

It is suggestive to think that the title of the novel may not only be indebted to General Jackson's last words but may also pay tribute to an Indian poem, "Where the Fight Was," printed in *Poetry: A Magazine of Verse* (the magazine that published Hemingway's early poems and a vignette in January 1923).[4] In the place where the fight was

> Across the river,
> In the place where the fight was
> Across the river:
> A heavy load for a woman
> To lift in her blanket,
> A heavy load for a woman
> To carry on her shoulder.
> In the place where the fight was
> Across the river:
> The women go wailing
> To gather the wounded
> The women go wailing
> To pick up the dead.

We are well aware of Hemingway's interest in Native Americans, but maybe we should better investigate his interest in Indian literary heritage. Poems such as "Bird of Night" (*Poems* 36) and "Translations from the Esquimaux: There Are Seasons" (*Poems* 59) might testify to such an interest, but, even more, the rhythms and repetitions of his prose seem to echo Indian poems such as "Where the Fight Was." This could account for the alleged Indian blood (one-eighth, the same ratio of the iceberg) Hemingway boasted of, which was never confirmed by family or biographers. It is of some interest that Hemingway repeated this fib to Lillian Ross during the famous interview in 1950.

Notes

1. For this useful information I am indebted to Adeline Tintner.
2. Trigonometry is the branch of mathematics that deals with the relations between the sides and angles of planes or spherical triangles and the calculations based on them; methods of deducing from given parts other required parts.
3. I am referring to that branch of mathematics that calculates all the elements of a given triangle (that is, the values of all three sides and all three angles) given only three of these values (one of which must be one side of the triangle.). To de-

termine the three unknown elements it suffices to have three independent analytical relations linking the known elements to the unknown ones. Applying this trigonometric calculus to the known or implied relations in the novel, we may deduct a connecting side between two distinct elements, for instance, Colonel Cantwell and D'Annunzio or Eleonora Duse and Renata.

4. This song and five others ("Listening," "Buffalo Dance," "The Wind," "Courtship," and "Parting") by Alice Corbin, inspired by the literal translations of Chippewa songs by Frances Densmore, were published in *Poetry: A Magazine of Verse*. They have been republished in *American Indian Poetry: An Anthology of Authentic Songs and Chants*, ed. Gorge W. Cronyn, (New York: Ballantine Books, 1972), 239, by arrangement with Liveright Publishing Corporation (copyright 1934; renewal copyright by Gorge W. Cronyn in 1962). This anthology was originally published under the title *The Path on the Rainbow: An Anthology of Songs and Chants from the Indians of North America* (New York: Boni and Liveright, 1918) and was a great hit that couldn't have escaped Hemingway's attention.

Works Cited

Baker, Carlos. *Ernest Hemingway: A Life Story*. New York: Scribner, 1969.
———. *Hemingway: The Writer as Artist*. Princeton: Princeton UP, 1963.
Bruccoli, Matthew J., ed. *Conversations with Ernest Hemingway*. Jackson: U of Mississippi P, 1986.
———, ed. *Ernest Hemingway and the Mechanism of Fame*. Columbia: U of South Carolina P, 2006.
Hemingway, Ernest. *Across the River and into the Trees*. 1950. New York: Scribner, 1996.
———. *A Farewell to Arms*. 1929. New York: Scribner, 1995.
———. *Complete Poems*. Ed. Nicholas Gerogiannis. Lincoln: U of Nebraska P, 1992.
———. *Selected Letters, 1917–1961*. Ed. Carlos Baker. New York: Scribner, 1981.
Lisca, Peter. "The Structure of Hemingway's *Across the River and into the Trees*." *Modern Fiction Studies* 12 (Summer 1966): 232–50.
Proust, Marcel. *Time Regained*. Vol. 7 of *In Search of Lost Time*. Trans. C. K. Scott Moncrieff and Terence Kilmartin. Rev. D. J. Enright. New York: Modern Library, 1999.
Reynolds, Michael. *Hemingway's Reading, 1910–1940: An Inventory*. Princeton: Princeton UP, 1981.
Stoltzfus, Ben. "The Stones of Venice, Time, and Remembrance: Calculus and Proust in *Across the River and into the Trees*." *Hemingway Review* 22.2 (Spring 2003): 19–29.

Tintner, Adeline R. "The Significance of D'Annunzio in *Across the River and into the Trees.*" *Hemingway Review* 5:1 (Fall 1985): 9–13.
Whitman, Walt. *Leaves of Grass and Other Writings.* Ed. Michael Moon. New York: Norton, 2002.
Williams, Wirt. *The Tragic Art of Ernest Hemingway.* Baton Rouge: Louisiana State UP, 1981.

13

The Italian Translation of *Across the River*

Will It Ever Reach the Juncture?

PIERO AMBROGIO POZZI

TRANSLATED AND REVISED BY ALLYSON MCKAY

In February 1965, over three years after Ernest Hemingway's death, the Italian version of *Across the River and into the Trees* was published in Mondadori's Medusa collection, under the Italian title *Di là dal fiume e tra gli alberi*. In May of the same year, Gallimard launched *Au-delà du fleuve et sous les arbres* in France. Hemingway had prevented the publication of foreign-language editions (*Dear Papa* 308)—or film versions—of the book to try to preserve the reputation of Adriana Ivancich, his primary source of inspiration and the physical model for his female protagonist, Renata. Encouraged by derisive newspaper articles, the public likened Renata's behavior to that of Adriana, who was persecuted by the irresponsible gossip that persisted until her suicide in 1983, and even to this day.

The Italian version of the book was entrusted to Fernanda Pivano, who had previously translated other works by Hemingway, notably *A Farewell to Arms* (1949) and *The Old Man and the Sea* (1952).

A Farewell to Arms gave Pivano an air of courage and competence. It was said that following a raid on the offices of the publishers Einaudi in Torino, the Gestapo had arrested Pivano because they found the contract for the translation of the novel that had offended the Italian Army, which had been defeated by the Austrians and Germans at Caporetto during World War I. What really happened, as narrated in Pivano's *Leggende americane*, was that Pivano rushed to the Gestapo headquarters in the Albergo Nazionale to get her brother off the hook after a misunderstanding had gotten him arrested (39). All she had to do was deny her involvement; besides, it is unlikely that the Germans would have been offended, since they won at Caporetto. In any case, Einaudi did not publish *A Farewell to Arms* but instead ceded the rights to Mondadori, which printed Pivano's version a few years later.

Pivano translated *The Old Man and the Sea*, the 1952 novella that earned Hemingway his Pulitzer Prize and furthered his Nobel cause, adding glory to Pivano's reputation as an Americanist and launching her definitively with Italy's cultural establishment. The Italian translation of *The Old Man and the Sea*, which was either poorly or never revised by Mondadori, contained—and still contains—a number of unfortunate translation choices that, to the best of my knowledge, were never queried until I pointed them out (see a brief selection of these choices, retranslated into English, in the appendix to this article). The Italian version of *A Farewell to Arms* was better, which I attribute to the careful editing that books underwent in those days, and to the fact that there were two existing translations of the book, one by Bruno Fonzi, which was illegally printed by Jandi Sapi in Rome in 1945, and one by Dante Isella, Giansiro Ferrata, and Puccio Russo, which was published by Mondadori in 1946.

The first edition, a 5,934-copy run of *Addio alle armi* was published in June 1946 as part of the elegant Il Ponte collection (cover price 500 lire), which was presented to Hemingway as "a new collection [. . .] which collects the best names in the international literary field." The book was translated "with reverence" by Isella, Ferrata, and Russo in Fribourg during their exile in Switzerland. The illustrations were by Renato Guttuso.[1]

We know that Pivano was familiar with Fonzi's translation since she is quoted as saying it was "nice" (Pivano 40). Isella, Ferrata, and Russo's translation was also published by Mondadori, but I cannot find any mention of it by Pivano. She mentions a third translation, published in Switzerland, which "took heavily from the French version, I mean with the same phraseology as the French version" (40). This clearly refers to the Swiss version of the Isella-Ferrata-Russo translation, which was also published in 1946, by Ghilda del Libro in Lugano. There were therefore two Italian versions and one French version available for consultation—no meager resource.

Mondadori commissioned Pivano's version even though it already had the Isella-Ferrata-Russo version listed in its catalogue because Hemingway had not been able to come to an agreement with Alberto Mondadori himself concerning the specifications for publications of his works until *after* the 1946 Swiss Italian publication of *A Farewell to Arms*. This agreement also covered the choice of translator. The same goes for *Across the River and into the Trees*, as demonstrated by the letter dated March 23, 1950, that Hemingway wrote from the Île-de-France shortly after saying goodbye to Adriana at Le Havre, where he also reserved the right to choose the illustrator of the dust cover.[2]

* * *

Pivano's much-anticipated translation of *Across the River*, which was published without serious revision, was terrible. It was not until forty-five years later that Mondadori "reprinted" the translation in an Oscar edition in which the most obvious errors had been secretly corrected by an unnamed editor who probably used some of the corrections I sent to Mondadori,[3] or at least my *Diario di traduzione* (Translation diary), which was published in installments in 2005 on Giuseppe Iacobaci's renowned blog *Intramel*. *Diario* was followed by several other articles and tables.[4] As far as I know, no one else had previously attempted to have the damage remedied or to question the legitimacy of Fernanda Pivano's legendary reputation. I do not expect that Mondadori ever considered a radical retranslation of *The Old Man and the Sea* or *Across the River and into the Trees* in the interests of protecting the myth—and their rather sizeable catalogue of publications by "Nanda." Any other motivation—even that of respecting a contract in which the well-intentioned but unwitting Hemingway made Pivano the translator—does injustice to one of the leading lights of twentieth-century literature.

Many errors were simply patched over, while others remained untouched. One of the funniest was on the back cover (see figure 13.1), in a quotation from chapter 38: "C'è sempre un tale silenzio quando muore un pesciolino rosso" (*Di là* 207). This sad, empty sentence is supposed to give an idea of the book's content. In reality, it is just a bad translation of the supreme secret of the imaginary Ordine Militar, Nobile y Espirituoso de los Caballeros de Brusadelli, as revealed by its founder, Colonel Cantwell, during Renata's induction: "Love is love and fun is fun. But it is always so quiet when the gold fish die" (198). Rather than the single goldfish of the Italian, they are talking about plural goldfish in a colorful yet subtle allusion. Their motto has a double meaning, and while you could use poetic license to translate "gold fish" as *pesce rosso* in the singular so that it rhymes,

Figure 13.1. Cover of the Mondadori translation of *Across the River and into the Trees*. Photo by P. A. Pozzi. ã 2014 Mondadori.

it does require a definite article. For example: "L'amore è amore e lo spasso è spasso. Ma c'è sempre tanta pace quando il pesce rosso giace." The double entendre is incredibly subtle, even to native speakers of English. However, Hemingway confirms it in Renata's comment after her investiture: "I am very proud and happy to be a member of the Order," the girl said. "But it is, in a way, a rather *rough* order" (198; emphasis added).

The new cover is remarkable also for the photograph, a sad black-and-white image of a pensioner feeding pigeons on the pier at San Marco, with the island of San Giorgio Maggiore in the background. This ridiculous image, which was supposed to introduce a novel about love, honor, and death, was signed off by no fewer than three professionals!

The bound Meridiani edition of *Across the River* still features Fernanda Pivano's original translation. This incredibly careless version has prevented an audience potentially more open to understanding Hemingway's narrative—the Italian public—from enjoying it to the full. The characters and settings resulting from the fallacious Italian interpretation of the precise, intricate work were unrecognizable, even to people who lived there and could therefore have appreciated the controversial novel. Others—like myself, who retranslated the novel out of personal curiosity—were more fortunate but would nevertheless have benefited from a decent translation, which would have allowed us to glimpse into the author's personal story between the lines.

Hemingway wrote *Across the River* with the risk, or possibly with the hope, of being understood at a secondary level, thanks to his cryptic, but sincere self-portrait in the form of Colonel Cantwell. If readers are prepared to believe in his sincerity, it is there to be deciphered and they can enjoy it with him. Thus, we magically start to find clues, similarities, and the keys to understanding the literary expression of a private life that was full of suffering, imbued with a love that remained largely silent, in the correspondence and writings of those who were close to Hemingway at the time; above all Adriana Ivancich, but also Marlene Dietrich and Aaron Hotchner.

* * *

Chapter 13 opens with a host of cryptic references. The love scene with the army blanket in the gondola fits with Hemingway's encounter with Marlene Dietrich in 1934 on a much bigger boat, the black transatlantic liner *Paris*, with the same Perrier-Jouët champagne in the ice bucket (*SL* 580–81; Hendrickson 25–26). Coincidentally, the outing in the black gondola starts with Cantwell inviting Renata to imagine that they are taking a carriage ride around the Bois de Boulogne—in Paris! The reference is outlandish given that they are in the city that he loves most of all, Venice, which is already so charming on its own that it would never occur to you to think of another— normally. I therefore think that the scene is a wink at Marlene, which is supported by Marlene's dedication to him on a photograph: "Papa—I write this on a picture so that you can't lose it so easily. I love you unconditionally. That excludes being angry, offended etc. etc. It includes Plein Pourvoir for you concerning me. How do you like it now, Gentlemen" (*SL* 716).[5] It is also corroborated by a letter to Marlene from September 1949 that Hemingway wrote shortly before he finished *Across the River*:

> Daughter, please try to keep contact from now on as I am finishing a book and should be through in around three weeks. I think that you will like it very much. Will give you carbon of manuscript if you like. You are in it and nobody else is in it because it is all made up. But it is made up as well as I can make it. (*SL* 677)

Evidently Ernest was not being entirely sincere with Marlene, but I do think Marlene is really there, and it can only be her. Marlene is most prominently present in chapters 13 and 14. These episodes stand out from the rest of the novel and is introduced with an unlikely pretext: the romantic dinner in chapters 11 and 12 sees the couple drinking a bottle of white Capri wine, a bottle of Valpolicella, and two bottles of Roederer champagne without either of them appearing to get even remotely drunk. The wine at dinner is preceded by three Montgomeries each at Harry's Bar. Montgomeries are almost pure gin! The pretext serves to finish off the restaurant's stock of chilled Roederer in the Gritti Hotel during the off-peak season, before they get to the bottle of Perrier-Jouët that they take with them in the gondola. Here there is an alcohol-fueled change of scene, with *another* Renata. The change of scene also provides an opportunity for a literary embellishment. Chapter 13 starts with a quotation from "The Tyger," taken from William Blake's *Songs of Experience*. It begins:

> They went out the side door of the hotel to the *imbarcadero* and the wind hit them. The light from the hotel shone on the blackness of the gondola and made the water green. She looks as lovely as a good horse or as a racing shell, the Colonel thought. Why have I never seen a gondola before? *What hand or eye framed that dark-ed symmetry?* (110; emphasis added)

And here is the first stanza of Blake's poem:

> Tyger! Tyger! burning bright
> In the forests of the night,
> *What immortal hand or eye*
> *Could frame thy fearful symmetry?* (ll. 1–4; emphasis added)

The black gondola is first likened to a good horse or a race boat, and we would be perfectly justified in thinking that Ernest is again referring to Adriana, whom he used to call the Great Black Horse, but Hemingway then goes straight into Blake's quote, evoking the bright tiger who burns in the forests of the night. I am convinced that it was his intention to switch to the very blond Marlene, who burned feline bright in the dark movie theatres and forests of male dreams, who was a sex symbol by definition. For two chapters she would palpitate under Colonel Cantwell's damaged hand, in a scene filled with a palpable erotic tension incompatible with the as yet secret femininity of an eighteen-year-old noblewoman with a rigid Catholic education who devotes her time to charitable works and who has not yet fallen in love, despite being as beautiful and exuberant as she—Adriana—might be.

The Blake quotation does not appear to have been picked up on by critics or biographers, and they have certainly not read it as a clue, a message in a bottle, so to speak. Despite writing poetry herself, not even Adriana mentioned it. Marlene, who was warned ("You are in it . . ."), would certainly have seen it. Adriana, on the other hand, would have noticed the Elizabethan "dark-ed" with the hyphen in "dark-ed symmetry," with its two syllables instead of one, like "fearful," because it was she who told Ernest that in the seventeenth century the plague had sent the gondolas into mourning, where previously they had been variously colored and richly decorated (Ivancich Biaggini 46).

And then, in the penultimate stanza of "The Tyger" goes:

When the stars threw down their spears,
And water'd heaven with their tears,
Did he smile his work to see?
Did he who made the Lamb make thee? (ll. 17–20, emphasis added)

Who knows if, in quoting "The Tyger" for Marlene, Hemingway did not also think of Adriana in the penultimate stanza, and in Blake's sister poem, "The Lamb," from the preceding *Songs of Innocence* in the same book. Why? Because Adriana and Marlene could be *Shewing the Two Contrary States of the Human Soul*, along with the subtitle of Blake's *Songs of Innocence and of Experience*: Adriana the Lamb and Innocence, Marlene the Tyger and Experience:

Little Lamb, who made thee?
Dost thou know who made thee? (ll. 1–2)

* * *

In chapter 6, as they chug past Gabriele D'Annunzio's Casetta Rossa (Little Red House) on the Canal Grande, Colonel Cantwell encourages his chauffeur, Jackson, to read *Notturno*, the work that influenced and informed Hemingway's novel. In *Notturno*, we meet Sirenetta, or Cicciuzza (D'Annunzio's daughter with Maria Anguissola Gravina, Countess of

Figure 13.2. D'Annunzio's Casetta Rossa on the Canal Grande (seen from the Guggenheim Museum). Photo by P. A. Pozzi.

Ramacca) who prepared the *cartigli*, the strips of paper upon each of which Il Vate (The Poet) wrote a single line of text in the dark with his eyes bandaged due to a war wound (D'Annunzio 3). Sirenetta transcribed the words from the strips, thereby liberating her father's writing, with an effect similar to that which Adriana had on Ernest's writing. Sirenetta's birth name was Eva Renata Adriana. There is no doubt that Hemingway was aware of the coincidence, which became a source of inspiration: the female archetype becomes the Renata of his novel, who is also his Adriana, his forbidden fruit. The Colonel and Ernest, respectively, call Renata and Adriana "Daughter." The reference to *Notturno* is testimony of Hemingway's debt to Gabriele D'Annunzio, of his gratitude for—among other things—Adriana. In quoting *Notturno*, Hemingway allows the reader to discover the key to the mystery behind the name Renata.

The structure of *Notturno* is very similar to that of *Across the River*. As Elena Ledda wrote in the preface to the Garzanti edition of D'Annunzio's book:

The work seems to be founded on a sort of fantastical, hallucinatory overlapping of three alternating temporal planes: the present of the moment of writing and illness, the recent past of the war episodes, the distant past of the childhood memories [. . .]. Then there were the few, but essential elements around which the fragmented story unfolded: death, war, blindness, women. (lii)

Simply replace "blindness" with "a weak heart" and the canvas is identical. Beyond the structure, the setting is also parallel: the wounded D'Annunzio lets his memories of war, life, and death flow as he lies on the bed in the Casetta Rossa, while the dying Colonel Cantwell gives free rein to similar thoughts as he lies on a bed in the nearby Hotel Gritti, in the San Marco *sestiere* (quarter) in Venice.[6] And they often talk about the same battlefields in the Carso and Pasubio ranges, or in the Basso Piave area. They also both talk about "Sister Death," whom Cantwell refers to as Thanatos, the brother of Sleep.

As if that were not enough, it is also noteworthy that as a young man D'Annunzio was attracted to the "hereditary gems" that Roman noblewomen wore. He later received a gift of emeralds to be worn as a talisman from his mistress Eleonora Duse, the "great, sad, and never properly loved actress" (*ARIT* 37). The Colonel also receives a gift of hereditary emeralds from Renata to be kept on his person at all times, like a talisman. This gift is too unusual not to have been inspired by D'Annunzio.

Mark Cirino notes a 1985 study of which I was unaware by the late Adeline Tintner touched on many of the similarities with D'Annunzio that I have noticed. I hope that my observations also will serve to disprove any parallels with *Across the River and into the Trees* and Thomas Mann's *Der Tod in Venedig* that were particularly promoted by Carlos Baker (267), in favor of a more plausible Italian reference.

* * *

Across the River and into the Trees points to Hemingway's great Italian love: Cantwell and Renata's story starts and finishes on the spot where Ernest and Adriana first met, at the Quattro Strade crossroads in Latisana (Ivancich Biaggini 7),[7] 500 yards as the crow flies from the Ivancich's villa in San Michele al Tagliamento. The Colonel's big Buick arrives from the east, from

Trieste, and materializes in Latisana, where the Ernest's big Buick arrived from Codroipo, in the north. The action unfolds after that, in chapter 3:

> They made a curve and crossed the Tagliamento on a temporary bridge. It was green along the banks and men were fishing along the far shore where it ran deep. The blown bridge was being repaired with a snarl of riveting hammers, and eight hundred yards away the smashed buildings and outbuildings of what was now a ruined country house once built by Longhena showed where the mediums had dropped their loads. (9)

Hemingway's source of inspiration could not be clearer. The story starts in the place where Ernest met Adriana. From the tip of Friuli, the Colonel enters Veneto via the Tagliamento, sees Renata's bombed house, then steps into her life for three days, as if in an impossible dream, which he abandons when he leaves Veneto at the end of the third day. He reenters Friuli, and turns left at the Quattro Strade, heading north toward Codroipo on the road that took Ernest to Adriana. In chapter 45, we read: "'Turn left,' the Colonel said. 'That's not the road for Trieste, sir,' Jackson said" (223). They head toward Codroipo. For no apparent reason, the Colonel cites General Stonewall Jackson: "No, no, let us cross over the river and rest under the shade of the trees" (224).

The river is real, and across the Tagliamento and into the trees is Renata's house, the forbidden place of rest. The Colonel dies on the back seat of the big Buick, with Renata's portrait beside him.

Jackson turns back, "facing south toward the road juncture that would put him on the highway that led to Trieste" (225).

The Quattro Strade, "the road juncture." Not "junction" or "intersection" or "crossing," but *"juncture,"* "a particular point in events or time" (according to *The New Oxford American Dictionary*). A particular point—the key to the entire novel, and the author's life. The crossroads, where the story began, is where the big Buick returns to from Codroipo, as if a new, dreamed-of story could begin. And it well might have, in September 1950, when the first edition of *Across the River* was published. Adriana was about to board the ship that would have taken her to him, in Cuba, on October 27. The scandal that erupted in Italy following the publication of *Across the River* prompted her departure on February 7, 1951. Ernest and Adriana did not see

Figure 13.3. "Across the river and into the trees": the Ivancich villa at San Michele al Tagliamento, seen from Latisana. Photo by P. A. Pozzi.

each other again until 1954, when they met in Venice, Percoto, and Nervi. However, Adriana held a place in Ernest's heart until death, and beyond.

Appendix: A Few of the Inaccuracies Found in Fernanda Pivano's Translations

The Old Man and the Sea

Original Text	Pivano's Translation	Pivano's Translation Back-translated
... and had butchered their marlin out...	... *e avevano già squartato i loro marlin*...	... and had quartered their marlin...
... had taken them to the shark factory...	... *li avevano portati allo stabilimento*...	... had taken them to the factory...
... when they were brought alongside...	... *quando venivano rimorchiati*...	... when they were towed ...
... there was a picture in color of the Sacred Heart of Jesus and another of the Virgin of Cobre...	... *vi era una fotografia a colori del Sacro Cuore di Gesù e un'altra della Vergine di Cobra*...	... there was a photograph in color of the Sacred Heart of Jesus and another of the Virgin of Cobra...

(continued)

Original Text	Pivano's Translation	Pivano's Translation Back-translated
...How would you like to see me bring one in that dressed out over a thousand pounds?...	...*Ti piacerebbe vedermene portare a casa uno da mezza tonnellata?*...	...How would you like to see me bring one in that weighs a thousand pounds...
...But then I think of Dick Sisler and those great drives in the old park...	...*Ma poi ripenso a Dick Sisler*...	...But then I think of Dick Sisler...
...Each line, as thick around as a big pencil, was looped onto a green-sapped stick...	...*Ogni lenza, spessa come una grossa matita, era fissata a un bastoncino instabile*...	...Each line, as thick as a big pencil, was fixed to an unstable stick...
...each line had two forty-fathom coils...	...*per ogni lenza c'erano due duglie di quaranta tese*...	...each line had two forty-toise fakes...
...Now the man watched the dip of the three sticks over the side of the skiff...	...*Ora il vecchio vide cadere tre bastoncini fuori dalla barca*...	...Now the man saw three sticks dropping outside the skiff...
...It had a wire leader and a medium-sized hook...	...*Aveva un bozzello di ferro e un amo di misura media*...	...It had a steel pulley block and a medium-sized hook...
...made it fast to a ring bolt in the stern...	...*diede volta alla lenza su una bitta a poppa*...	...tied it up on a bitt in the stern...
...of the sort that poison ivy or poison oak can give...	...*come quelle prodotte dal veleno dell'edera e della quercia*...	...of the sort that ivy or oak poison can give...
...compact and bullet shaped...	...*compatto e a forma di palla*...	...compact and ball shaped...
...The old man hit him on the head for kindness and kicked him, his body still shuddering, under the shade of the stern...	...*Il vecchio per bontà lo colpì sulla testa e lo prese a calci, mentre il corpo ancora tremava all'ombra della poppa*...	...The old man hit him on the head for kindness and kicked him, his body still shuddering under the shade of the stern...

Original Text	Pivano's Translation	Pivano's Translation Back-translated
...the hand-forged hook...	...*l'amo curvato a mano*...	...the hand-bent hook...
...cut the line against the wood of the gunwale...	...*tagliò la lenza contro la barchetta*...	...cut the line against the skiff...
...The wire must have slipped on the great hill of his back...	...*Forse il filo gli è scivolato sulla schiena*...	...The wire must have slipped on his back...
..."Fish," he said softly, aloud, "I'll stay with you until I am dead."...	..."*Pesce*" *disse con sommessa voce "resterò con te fino alla morte.*"...	..."Fish" he said in a whisper "I'll stay with you until I am dead."...
...It would not be bad to eat with a little lime or with lemon or with salt...	...*Non sarebbe cattivo, a mangiarlo con un po' di arancio o limone o sale*...	...It would not be bad with a little orange or with lemon or with salt...
...His sword was as long as a baseball bat and tapered like a rapier...	...*La spada era lunga come una mazza da baseball e appuntita come un'alabarda*...	...His sword was as long as a baseball bat and pointed like a halberd...
...He will start circling soon...	...*Presto incomincerà a rotolare*...	...He will start rolling soon...
...Then he stepped the mast and, with the stick that was his gaff and with his boom rigged, the patched sail drew...	...*Poi armò l'albero e la vela rattoppata si rizzò*...	...Then he stepped the mast and the patched sail rose...
...the shark plowed over the water as a speedboat does...	...*il pescecane sbattè l'acqua come un motoscafo*...	...the shark beat the water as a speedboat does...
...the lights of the beach colonies along the shore...	...*le luci dei villaggi rivieraschi lungo la spiaggia*...	...the lights of the coastal villages along the shore...
..."Tiburon," the waiter said. "Eshark."...	..."*Tiburón*" *disse il cameriere.* "*Pescecane.*"...	..."Tiburon," the waiter said. "Shark."...

Across the River and into the Trees

Original Text	Pivano's Translation	Pivano's Translation Back-translated
...low as he was, no foothills showed, and the mountains rose abruptly from the plain...	...in basso com'era, non vedeva i piedi delle colline, e le montagne si alzavano di colpo dalla pianura...	...low as he was, he didn't see the feet of the hills, and the mountains rose abruptly from the plain...
...that's beech, isn't it?...	...quella è betulla, vero?...	...that's birch, isn't it?...
...beech is, to an open fire, as anthracite coal is to a stove...	...la betulla vicino al fuoco è come carbone di antracite in una stufa...	...birch near fire is as anthracite coal in a stove...
...I should be a better man with less wild boar blood...	...dovrei essere migliore, con meno sangue di orso selvatico...	...I should be a better man with less wild bear blood...
...he was alive and a dark green and completely unfriendly...	...era viva e giovanissima e molto ribelle...	...he was alive and very young and very rebellious...
...just hold me very tight and hold the high ground, too...	...tienimi soltanto stretta e tienimi tutta...	...just hold me tight and hold me all over...
...the other arm held the high ground now...	...con l'altro braccio la tenne tutta...	...with the other arm he held her all over...
...twenty-eighth division...	...diciottesima divisione...	...eighteenth division...
...General Fat Ass Franco on his shooting stick...	...il generale Franco Culo Grosso col suo fucile...	...General Big Ass Franco with his rifle...
...combat boots...	...scarponi da montagna...	...mountaineering boots...
...that could be used as a Brooklyn icepick...	...che avrebbe potuto servire come piccozza per il ghiaccio di Brooklyn...	...that could be used as a piolet for Brooklyn's ice...
...I took nothing but an Admiral's compass because I had a small boat at that time on Chesapeake Bay...	...Io ho preso soltanto la bussola di un ammiraglio, perché in quel periodo nella baia di Chesapeake avevo una nave troppo piccola...	...I took nothing but an Admiral's compass because I had a too small ship at that time in Chesapeake Bay...
...But we had all the Wehrmacht stamped Martell...	...Ma trovammo tutto il falso Martell stampigliato dalla Wehrmacht...	...But we found out all the imitation Martell stamped by Wehrmacht...

Original Text	Pivano's Translation	Pivano's Translation Back-translated
... Then, there were draft dodgers, (...), insiders, cowards, liars, thieves and telephone racers ...	... Poi c'erano gli imboscati, (...), intriganti, codardi, bugiardi, ladri e ficcanaso ...	... Then, there were draft dodgers, (...), schemers, cowards, liars, thieves and nosy parkers ...
... I don't know, she said, I think we should just leave here. I love to have people see us, but I don't want to see anybody ...	... Non so, disse la ragazza, credo che dovremmo vivere qui. Mi piace che la gente ci veda, ma non voglio vedere nessuno ...	... I don't know, she said, I think we should live here. I love to have people see us, but I don't want to see anybody ...
... walking with the girl ...	... andava a spasso con una ragazza ...	... walking with a girl ...
... I wish to hell she was here though, if this were a double blind, and have her looking to the west just in case one string did come in ...	... Accidenti se vorrei che fosse qui, però, se questo fosse un appostamento doppio, e farle guardare a ovest nel caso che arrivasse una punta ...	... I wish to hell she was here though, if this were a double blind, and have her looking to the west just in case one sting did come in ...
... on the bow of the boat ...	... sulla poppa della barca ...	... on the stern of the boat ...
... and put him in the burlap bag that was under the bow ...	... e lo mise nel sacco che c'era sotto la poppa ...	... and put him in the bag that was under the stern ...
... The head game-keeper was standing on the bank in his high boots, his short jacket and his pushed back old felt hat, and he looked critically at the number of ducks on the bow of the boat as they came alongshore ...	... Il custode era in piedi sulla riva con gli stivaloni alti, la giacchetta corta e il vecchio cappello di feltro spinto all'indietro, e guardò con aria critica il numero di anatre a poppa della barca mentre si accostavano a terra ...	... The keeper was standing on the bank in his high boots, his short jacket and his pushed back old felt hat, and he looked critically at the number of ducks on the stern of the boat as they came alongshore ...
... But don't you ever run into anything, or let any [making sure that this is run-in with the above box "let any sparks ... all the same box] sparks strike you, when you're really souped up on nitroglycerin. They ought to make you drag a chain like a high-octane truck ...	... Ma non bisogna correre e non bisogna avvicinarsi al fuoco se si è miscelati a nitroglicerina. Dovrebbero metterti un riduttore come agli auto carri a nafta ...	... But don't you ever run and don't approach fire when you're mixed up with nitroglycerin. They ought to put a gearbox on you like a diesel truck ...

(continued)

Original Text	Pivano's Translation	Pivano's Translation Back-translated
...manual of minor tactics for the heavy pressure platoon...	...manuale di esercitazioni leggere per il battaglione di quelli che hanno la pressione alta...	...manual of light exercises for the hypertensives battalion...
...If they did not lift the shelling...	...Se non avessero cessato il bombardamento...	...If they did not cease the shelling...
...they always lifted it and moved it back ahead...	...lo cessavano sempre e lo spostavano...	...they always ceased it and moved it...
...My attention has been faulty again...	...La mia attenzione è di nuovo fuori posto...	...My attention is out of place again...
...He looked at himself in the mirror, set in the half closed door. It showed him at a slight angle. It's a deflection shot, he said to himself, and they didn't lead me enough...	...Si guardò nello specchio, applicato alla porta socchiusa. Lo rifletteva leggermente d'angolo. È una fotografia presa di scorcio, disse fra sé, e non mi hanno fatto posare abbastanza a lungo...	...He looked at himself in the mirror, set in the half closed door. It reflected him at a slight angle. It's a foreshortened snap, he said to himself, and they didn't have me posing long enough...
...he never used command cars...	...non comandava mai automezzi...	...he never was in command of cars...
...or must a vehicle have wheels or be tracked?...	...oppure è necessario che un veicolo abbia le ruote o sia sui binari?...	...or must a vehicle have wheels or be on rails?...
...looked like boat-tailed bullets...	...parevano sgombri...	...looked like mackerels...
...but these other roving bullets...	...ma questi altri sgombri erranti...	...but these other roving mackerels...
...never discuss casualties...	...non devi mai discutere i danni di guerra...	...never discuss war damages...
...esses...	...sergenti...	...sergeants...
...S-2...	...sergente maggiore...	...staff sergeant...
...Tree burst wounds hit men where they would never be wounded in open country...	...Tre ferite laceranti colpirono gli uomini dove non sarebbero mai stati feriti se fossero stati in zona aperta...	...Three tearing wounds hit men where they would never be wounded in open country...

Original Text	Pivano's Translation	Pivano's Translation Back-translated
...And the place we were going to fight in, (...) was going to be Passchendaele with tree bursts...	...E il luogo dove dovevamo combattere, (.. .) sarebbe stato Passchendaele, con tre attacchi ...	...And the place we were going to fight in, (...) was going to be Passchendaele, with three attacks ...
...It was Passchendaele with tree bursts, he told nobody except the wonder light on the ceiling...	...È stato Passchendaele con tre attacchi, disse alla luce meravigliosa sul soffitto ...	...It was Passchendaele with three attacks, he told to the wonder light on the ceiling...
...general (Brevetted) George Armstrong Custer...	...generale (effettivo) George Armstrong Custer ...	...general (Regular) George Armstrong Custer ...
...They killed several men from the Academy at Gettysburg...	...Hanno ucciso parecchi che uscivano dall'Accademia di Gettysburg...	...They killed several men leaving the Gettysburg Academy ...
...the two stakes chained together...	...i due pontili galleggianti tenuti insieme con le catene...	...the two floating wharves held together with chains...
...until the great lantern that was on the right of the entrance to the Grand Canal...	...fino al grande faro sulla destra dell'imboccatura del Canal Grande...	...until the great lighthouse on the right of the mouth of the Grand Canal...
...a gondola working up the Canal against the wind...	...una gondola che risaliva faticosamente il Canale contro corrente...	...a gondola going wearily up the Canal against the tide...
...by lounging in the lee of the Gritti...	...a ridosso del caseggiato del Gritti...	...close to the block of the Gritti...
...she [the gondola] looks as lovely as a good horse or as a racing shell...	...la ragazza era bella come un buon cavallo o un proiettile lanciato...	...the girl was as lovely as a good horse or as a flying shell...

Notes

1. "'Crazy for You': Hemingway e Mondadori" / "'Publishing All Your Works': I contratti," online journal of the Fondazione Arnoldo e Alberto Mondadori, *Quanto Basta* 14 (March 2011), http://www.fondazionemondadori.it/qb/article.php?issue_id=53&article_id=250.

2. Hemingway, letter to Alberto Mondadori, March 23, 1950, http://www.fondazionemondadori.it/qb/download.php?attachment_id=1236.

3. Email of September 8, 2004, with in attachment "Across the River and Into the Trees—Sunto appunti su trad. Pivano.doc." Subsequent contact with the head of Meridiani occurred in September 2005. There are numerous other documented examples.

4. See www.retididedalus.it, www.biblit.it, and www.enciclopediadelledonne.it.

5. Notice that Hemingway used the phrase "How do you like it now, Gentlemen?" out of the blue, without explaining its significance or origin. It comes from the 1671 parody of the Second Duke of Buckingham, George Villiers, titled *The Rehearsal*.

6. The Gritti is 160 yards from Casetta Rossa, on the same bank of the Canal Grande. The Casetta Rossa is opposite Ca' Venier dei Leoni; the Gritti is opposite Ca' Dario. Ca' Venier dei Leoni and Ca' Dario are on the other bank of the Canal Grande.

7. As far as I can tell, the Quattro Strade "juncture" is today's Piazzale Osoppo, at the intersection of Via Vittorio Veneto, Via Egregis Gaspari, Via Guglielmo Marconi, and Via Vendramin.

Works Cited

Baker, Carlos. *Hemingway: The Writer as Artist*. Princeton: Princeton UP, 1972.
Blake, William. *Canti dell'Innocenza e dell'Esperienza, a cura di Roberto Rossi Testa. Testo originale a fronte*. Milano: Classici UE Feltrinelli, 2009.
D'Annunzio, Gabriele. *Notturno*. Milano: Garzanti Editore, 1995.
Hemingway, Ernest. *Across the River and into the Trees*. London: Arrow Books, 1994.
———. *Dear Papa, Dear Hotch: The Correspondence of Ernest Hemingway and A. E. Hotchner*. Ed. Albert J. DeFazio III. Columbia: U of Missouri P, 2005.
Di là dal fiume e tra gli alberi. Trans. Fernanda Pivano. Milano: Mondadori, 2012.
———. *Selected Letters, 1917–1961*. Ed. Carlos Baker. London: Panther Books, 1985.
Hendrickson, Paul. *Hemingway's Boat: Everything He Loved in Life, and Lost, 1934–1961*. London: The Bodley Head, 2012.
Ivancich Biaggini, Adriana. *La Torre Bianca*. Milano: Mondadori, 1980.
Pivano, Fernanda. *Leggende americane*. Milano: Bompiani, 2011.
Tintner, Adeline R. "The Significance of D'Annunzio in *Across the River and into the Trees*." *Hemingway Review* 5.1 (Fall 1985): 73–87.

14

Across the Associate Editorship of the Harvard *Lampoon* and onto the Wall above the Urinal

The Reach and Legacy of E. B. White's "Across the Street and into the Grill"

KIRK CURNUTT

Only one month after the publication of *Across the River and into the Trees*, the October 14, 1950, issue of the *New Yorker* featured E. B. White's "Across the Street and into the Grill." This one-page parody became an immediate cause célèbre, at once epitomizing and crystallizing the critical disgruntlement with the first Hemingway novel since the blockbuster success of *For Whom the Bell Tolls*, already a decade in passing. According to A. E. Hotchner, the attention that White's parody received from newspaper and magazine columnists so irritated Hemingway that he denounced the art of parody itself: "The parody is the last refuge of the frustrated writer," he supposedly told Hotchner. "Parodies are what you write when you are the associate editor of the Harvard *Lampoon*. The greater the work of literature, the easier the parody. The step up from writing parodies is writing on the wall above the urinal" (70).[1] Hemingway seems not to have remembered that on numerous occasions when he felt competitive or insecure he had dabbled in this apprentice form of water-closet graffiti, firing off often injudicious takeoffs of Gertrude Stein, Louis Bromfield, and, most notoriously, Sherwood Anderson.[2] For White's part, maintaining his affable public persona necessitated adding a subtitle to republications of the parody to assure audiences that his spoof was not intended to disparage: "With respects to Ernest Hemingway," the piece would insist to future readers.[3]

In the six decades since its initial publication, "Across the Street and into the Grill" has become the single most famous Hemingway parody. This is no mean feat, no matter White's reputation as among the greatest of American wits and essayists. As Louis Menand has noted (also in the *New Yorker*), Hemingway parodies are as plentiful as "zucchini in August: you cannot give them away" (108). Since White himself first collected the piece in *The Second Tree from the Corner* in 1954, "Across the Street and into the Grill" has been reprinted close to two dozen times, usually in humor or genre anthologies such as Dwight Macdonald's *Parodies: An Anthology from Chaucer to Beerbohm—and After* (1960) or the *New Yorker* compilation *Fierce Pajamas: An Anthology of Humor Writing from The New Yorker* (named after another White parody). Although Carlos Baker is oddly silent on White, no subsequent biography can fail to mention the parody's effect on Hemingway's reputation before the comeback of *The Old Man and the Sea* resuscitated it in 1952, paving the way to his winning the Nobel Prize.[4] Perhaps the best evidence of the perceived centrality of White's burlesque to perceptions of Hemingway's career development is the way it pops up in ephemeral media mentions. The *New York Times*' 1961 Hemingway obituary, for example, digresses from a fairly unsurprising account of the author's life and works to mention that *Across the River and into the Trees* "touched off" "Across the Street and into the Grill," "probably the supreme parody of Hemingway" (6). And in a 1983 *Times* article called "Hemingway's Status Revives among Scholars and Readers" that quotes several founding members of the Hemingway Society, Edwin McDowell devotes an entire section to White, writing that "Hemingway's spare, laconic style had always invited parody, but [*Across the River*] served as the target for the most devastating parody of all... 'Across the Street and into the Grill.'"[5]

Equally if not more important than Hemingway criticism, studies of the art of parody also discuss White's piece as a representative example of the mode's aims and ends. In *Parody: The Art that Plays with Art* (2010), Robert Chambers analyzes White's attack as an example of how "a principal chore of parody is to satirize stylized or tired conventions, to kill them off" and asserts that White "parodically eviscerated" mannerisms of Hemingway's that had grown stale (23). By virtue of such references, it seems safe to say that not only is "Across the Street" the most famous Hemingway spoof ever, but one of the most famous parodies period. Specialists can certainly name famous literary ribbings from the tradition of Western literature: Henry

Fielding's *Shamela* (1741), Max Beerbohm's *A Christmas Garland* (which, among others, parodies Henry James; 1912), Donald Ogden Stewart's *A Parody Outline of History* (whose targets include Sinclair Lewis, F. Scott Fitzgerald, and Ring Lardner; 1921), and perhaps even timelier ones such as Fanny Merkin and Andrew Shaffer's *Fifty Shades of Earl Grey*, a parody of E. L. James's best-selling kinky-sex phenomenon *Fifty Shades of Grey* (both 2012). With the exception of *Shamela*, though, time has diminished most of these works, however; it seems doubtful that general readers have ever heard Beerbohm or Stewart, and just a few short years after its appearance, Merkin and Shaffer's goof on James's "mommy porn" is out of print. White's parody has avoided that fate.

The obvious but unexplored question is why: what makes White's exercise in mocking imitation, whether affectionate or not, any better than Cornelia Otis Skinner's "For Whom the Gong Sounds" or Alan Coren's "The Pooh Also Rises" (which is, thankfully, an A. A. Milne mash-up and not a hymn to scatology)? The most obvious explanation would be that White's is simply the best of the bunch—the cleverest, the most pointed, the funniest. Yet most critics would hesitate to ground an argument in such a strictly qualitative criterion as "the best." Such a judgment is merely an opinion, after all, wholly unprovable because it is subjective and therefore useless as a reliable measure. If we do try to search for quantitative justifications for the reputation enjoyed by White's piece, two reasons quickly stymie us: (1) in critical discussions of parody, there is far more emphasis on defining what parody is and what it does than what might make it "good"; and (2), perhaps related, we lack to date any in-depth analysis of the parodic devices and techniques employed in "Across the Street and into the Grill" that would help us identify exactly what constituent parts make it so damned good. The closest we come are a smattering of paragraphs in Edward C. Sampson chapter on *The Second Tree from the Corner* in his 1974 Twayne author series study of White and a 1989 *American Literature* article on Hemingway parodies in general. In the former, Sampson seems to echo the critical commonplace when he writes that "in a style like Hemingway's there is a thin dividing line between effectiveness and affectation—like the thin line between sentiment and sentimentality in much of Charles Dickens" and that "one of the functions of the parodist is to discover these fine lines and, by crossing them, to show the dangers and vulnerability of the style" (124). In the latter, James C. McKelly catalogues the range of stylistic tics that Hemingway parodists zero in on to generate their comedy. "Across the Street and into the Grill," McKelly notes, seems "most disturbed by Hemingway's proclivity for inappropriate, muddled, and incorrect grammatical constructions" (548). White's focus is not surprising given the assiduous devotion to syntactical clarity he would express in his 1959 revision of William J. Strunk's *The Elements of Style* (originally published in 1920). One easily sees in "Across the Street" the parodist poking fun at the nonsense possible with fussily symmetrical sentence structures in lines such as "He took another swallow of [alcohol], and it was a good and careful swallow" (28). Why Hemingway's sometimes arthritic rhythms are targeted more than his propensity for simple words or the faux British dialect lesser-known parodists fixate on is not a question McKelly explores, however. Thus, the question of why "Across the Street" is more famous than the other parodies he surveys—many of which, curiously enough, are drawn from the pages of *The Hemingway Review* in the initial years after its 1981 founding—goes unexamined.

As a second explanation for the notoriety of "Across the Street," we might argue that both White's and the *New Yorker*'s authority as cultural arbitrators of taste are responsible for the parody's enduring fame. In terms that Dwight Macdonald might appreciate, the magazine's "highbrow" wit and craft mock Hemingway's "midcult" aesthetics, assuring the magazine's urbane, elite, non-Dubuque-dwelling readership that the author's popularity is proof of the mass audience's inability to distinguish good and bad literature. (Founding editor Harold Ross famously quipped that the *New Yorker* was "not for the little old lady in Dubuque").[6] If mocking Hemingway as "middlebrow" literature is White's point, the explanation would carry the added irony that the writer himself only published in the *New Yorker* once in 1927, and his piece, "My Own Life," happened to be a parody of Gertrude Stein (among lesser-known literary figures).[7] We will explore this possibility in more depth shortly, but for now we note that even if a Macdonaldian critique of "midcult" literary status is the point, that still doesn't explain the preeminence of "Across the Street." White was far from the only regular *New Yorker* contributor to send up Hemingway, after all. As Menand notes, White's close friend and collaborator, James Thurber, who also knew a thing or two about humor, published "A Visit from Saint Nicholas (in the Ernest Hemingway Manner)" in 1927. Menand calls this piece a "pitch-perfect imitation of Hemingway stichomythia" (what a Dubuque resident might call "dialogue") and suggests Thurber's piece deserves at least as much attention as "Across the Street" since it appeared long before Hemingway parodies were as plentiful as summer vegetables (108). We should also note that "Across the Street and into the Grill" is not the only humor piece about Hemingway that White himself composed for the *New Yorker*. In April 1934 he published "The Law of the Jungle," a bit of light verse inspired by the *New York Herald-Tribune*'s breathless account of Hemingway's return from his African safari. Although not a parody of a specific text since it is written in the form of doggerel, the piece does mock Hemingway's macho public image. I suspect most readers would deem "Across the Street and into the Grill" a cleverer exercise than "The Law of the Jungle," but that does not mean it is necessarily funnier. White's earlier takeoff is actually more accessible, its humor more immediate:

> When hot for sport and ripe to kill,
> The average novelist shoots at will.
> But that, my friends, I'm glad to say
> Is not the case with Hemingway,
> Whose sporting life is so subtle
> Where leopards roam and lions scuttle,
> Whose fowling piece doth never bungle
> The oldest law of Afric's jungle,
> Who stands his ground in time of danger
> But only shoots a total stranger. (1–10)

Compare this to the opening line of "Across the Street and into the Grill": "This is my last and best and true and only meal, thought Mr. Pirnie as he descended at noon and swung east on the beat-up sidewalk of Forty-fifth Street" (28). Readers unfamiliar with *Across the River and into the Trees* likely have no clue what White is even saying here; the humor relies on a much more specific point of contrast than the Great White Hunter persona satirized in "The Law of the Jungle." Why this earlier piece remains all-but-forgotten except to a few discerning scholars while "Across the Street and into the Grill" is considered a classic certainly has nothing to do with the accessibility of the comedy. Despite this difference, both White pieces as well as Thurber's "A Visit from Saint Nicholas" target fairly predictable excesses, albeit in different ways: Hemingway's heroic code, his propensity for bluster, his cartoonish masculinity. While the *New Yorker*'s position on the middlebrow aesthetics that accounts for Hemingway's popularity is apparent enough, reading the three in succession offers no clear reason why "Across the Street" would attain such distinction while the other two would remain so little known.

A final conjectural reason White's parody enjoys the notoriety it does may be less complimentary to its author. Whether in a biography or in a discussion of literary parody in general, commentators inevitably note that by the time of *Across the River and into the Trees* Hemingway's style was so mannered and his themes so predictable that he'd lapsed into self-parody. For Menand, this is another reason Thurber's Hemingwayesque retelling of *The Night Before Christmas* deserves more attention: it appeared in 1927, only a year after *The Sun Also Rises*, when Hemingway's stylistic traits seemed singular and groundbreaking instead of hindering (108). To put it another way, Hemingway was wrong when he told Hotchner that "[t]he greater the work of literature, the easier the parody" (70). The laughs that parodies aim to spark seem to come easier when making fun of a *lesser* work, or at least one more disparaged, as *Across the River and into the Trees* was, than a critically praised work such as, say, "Big Two-Hearted River" or "Indian Camp." While there is some truth to such an assertion, it also does not stand as a universal rule. Unfortunately, *Across the River* is far from the only inferior work in the Hemingway canon. *To Have and Have Not* is in many ways a far worse book, and yet when it was published in 1937 the lone parody it inspired did not make one-tenth of the splash that White's did. In fact, until Robert W. Trogdon recently rediscovered Kenneth Campbell's "An Appreciation of Hemingway" in the July 1938 issue of the *American Mercury*, it was so little known that Audre Hanneman failed to list it in the 1967 comprehensive bibliography upon which most Hemingway scholars still rely. Shooting fish in the barrel of an inferior work by no means guarantees a parody's visibility.

If we cannot identify a qualitative reason that White's parody has survived while dozens of others are forgotten then perhaps the answer lies in function rather than execution. We tend to think of parody as simple imitation with exaggeration without necessarily appreciating how different parodic strategies and techniques serve varying ends. One thing to note immediately about "Across the Street and into the Grill" is that its humor does not depend upon what we might call third-party intertextuality. That is, White does not employ an ancillary text as a foil for the main target, avoiding what we today might call the "mash-up" approach. One reason Thurber's "A Visit from Saint Nicholas (in the Ernest Hemingway Manner)" never achieved the same notoriety as White's parody is because it ribs Clement Clarke Moore's schmaltzy 1823 verse as much as Hemingway's style: "The children were in their beds. Their beds were in the room next to ours. Mamma and I were in our beds. Mamma wore a kerchief. I had my cap on. I could hear the children moving. We didn't move. We wanted the children to think we were asleep" (17). While we giggle at the abbreviated sentences and repetition, we also chortle at how the application of Hemingway to Moore transforms the sentimentality of the original by rephrasing its treacly holiday story within bursts of hard-boiled back and forth:

> "I saw him," I said.
> "Sure."
> "I did see him."
> "Sure you saw him." She turned farther toward the wall.
> "Father," said the children.
> "There you go," mamma said. "You and your flying reindeer." (Thurber 17)

Are we laughing more at Hemingway or at Moore here? On a basic level, readers may say they can process the humor without feeling their attention divided between the twin targets of mockery. Nevertheless, the ancillary text in parody creates an interpretive distraction by simple virtue of its presence; we must cognitively bounce back and forth between the two texts, evaluating, for example, the absurdity of flying reindeer at the same time we evaluate the exaggerated repetition and laconic terseness of the dialogue.

One sees this same competition for attention in numerous other Hemingway parodies, some of which set their sights on literary targets just as towering in influence as Hemingway. George Plimpton's "The Snows of Studiofiftyfour" (1979), for example, is described by one reviewer as "a skillful mutation of Hemingway's writing style and a Truman Capote–esque sensibility" (Collins 10). Published at the peak of the 1970s disco craze, the parody describes "snow" that is decidedly *not* of the natural, frozen-water flake variety depicted in "The Snows of Kilimanjaro." The humor of Plimpton's piece relies on a contrast between the faddishness of the infamous New York discotheque where cocaine was as readily served as cocktails and the high seriousness of Hemingway's theme of death and compromised principles. Here, for example, is the opening note of "Studiofiftyfour," a takeoff on Hemingway's prefatory definition of Mount Kilimanjaro and the frozen leopard carcass near its peak: "Studiofiftyfour, a converted movie theater fifty-seven feet above sea level, was said to have been the liveliest discotheque in New York City. Close to the top seats in the balcony was discovered a matchbook cover bearing the White House seal. No one knows what the White House aide was seeking at that altitude" (70). Once again, however, who is the butt of the joke here? Most readers may snort (no pun intended) at the skillful appropriation of sparse imagery and italicized stream of consciousness passages from Hemingway's classic 1936 story, but it is Capote's latter-day reputation as a social gadfly that is targeted. In this case, Hemingway serves the role Moore does in Thurber's piece: he is the device more than the target.

Yet just because White's "Across the Street and into the Grill" avoids this sort of intertextual dependency on a second source does not mean its comedy arises solely out of Hemingway materials. As Linda Hutcheon notes, all parodies rely on some foreign element, some new presence not in the primary text, to alter readers' perceptions of the originals (32). In this regard, it is interesting to note what aspects of *Across the River and into the Trees* are *not* in the parody. As Edward Sampson notes, White focuses on two particular chapters of the novel, 11 and 12, or Colonel Cantwell's romantic dinner with Renata at the Gritti Palace. "His technique is to select certain words and phrases Hemingway used," Sampson writes, "[and by] placing them in a slightly different context, he pinpoints the foolishness of the original" (141). "Slightly different context" is a bit of an understatement, however, for there is very little *beyond* the burlesque of Hemingway's style to indicate that the parody mocks *Across the River and into the Trees*. White transposes the Colonel's story from Italy to New York, makes the Hemingway hero an assistant treasurer at the Guaranty Trust Company instead of a demoted general, and even depicts his Mr. Pirnie as an effete drone, arguably a version of Hemingway's own Hubert Elliot from "Mr. and Mrs. Elliot" from *In Our Time* (1925). White may indeed echo certain phrases and cadences of *Across the River and into the Trees*, but those are merely the catalyst of the comedy. What makes the parody funny is not the foolishness of the original but the absurdity of the assertion of the Hemingway ethic in the banal existence of their doltish hero, Mr. Pirnie. Sampson analyzes a key example of White's revision of Hemingway's original:

There is something contrived and untrue when the Colonel and the *"Gran Maestro"* reminisce about the past and each asks the other if he remembers certain events: "And we would throw the empty fiascos at the station guards from the troop trains." And: "We would throw all the left-over grenades away and bounce them down the hillside coming back from the Grappa." This passage cries for the parody that White provides: "Boticelli, do you remember when we took all the mailing envelopes from the stock room, spit on the flaps, and then drank rubber cement till the foot-soldiers arrived?" (142)

In the most extended example of White's technique, the parody has Mr. Pirnie describe the dangers faced in the modern office place. The assistant treasurer's knuckles are "scarred and stained by so many old mimeographings." As the hero tells the girl he seeks to impress:

"The stockroom men were very brave . . . but it is a position where it is extremely difficult to stay alive. Just outside that room there is a little bare-faced highboy and it is in the way of the stuff that is being brought up. . . . First you clean out the baskets and half-wits, and all the time they have the fire escapes taped. They also shell you with old production orders, many of them approved by the general manager in charge of sales."

It may be, as Sampson writes, that White "singles out for ridicule" tonal elements of "the posed and phony heroism" and "the pseudo-realistic, irrelevant details" that constitute Hemingway's style. What makes them funny, however, is their application to the drudgery of labor in the mailing room. In other words, we can argue that White's central comedic method is to show how utterly inapplicable the Hemingway hero's "grace under pressure" code is to the workaday world of the average wage earner. Lest we miss the point, White emphasizes it as Mr. Pirnie walks down Forty-fifth street, waiting for his day to end: "I commute good, thought Pirnie, looking at his watch. And he felt the old pain of going back to Scarsdale again."

More than any exaggeration of Hemingway's style, the reference to Scarsdale may be the key clue to understanding White's humor. It is almost as significant as Henry James's choice of Schenectady as the hometown of the eponymous heroine of *Daisy Miller* (1878), a central indicator of the utter gaucheness that the Miller family represents. The point can be demonstrated through a more apropos comparison to yet another contemporaneous takeoff of *Across the River and into the Trees*. In May 1951, parodist Ira Wallach opened his collection *Hopalong Freud and Other Literary Characters* with a spoof called "Out of the Frying Pan and into the Soup." Four years later, comic book publisher William Gaines reprinted the piece in the first issue of his newly reconstituted *MAD Magazine*. Gaines had recently redesigned *MAD* from a comic book into a magazine format as his company, EC Comics, was hounded out of business in the aftermath of the Estes Kefauver–led Senate hearings on juvenile delinquency, which had been prompted by Dr. Fredric Wertham's notoriously hysterical critique of comic books' supposedly baleful effect on American children in *Seduction of the Innocent*.[8] The inclusion of a previously published parody in *MAD* makes for interesting speculation; considering the magazine's "charter" was "to squirt soda in the face of mainstream America" through a "mish-mash of topical parody *made for young eyes*" (Hajdu 324; emphasis added), it is tempting to suggest Gaines reprinted the piece to make a generational statement. By the time the new *MAD* hit newsstands in July 1955, the Nobel Prize had institutionalized Hemingway, making him ripe for burlesquing for teenage and collegiate readers as the favorite writer of old fogeys. Whatever the reason for reprinting Wallach, Gaines added a mock editorial note to the piece, crediting the novel to "Ernest Heminghaw," famous for his "gut-gripping Heminghaw action": "Only one trouble," the note ends in suitably staccato style: "Following novel is written by ELI WALLACH."[9]

"Out of the Frying Pan" itself targets all the requisite failures of *Across the River*. There are passages of pointless repetition, such as the conversation between Wallach's Colonel Cantwell figure (a corporal demoted to a private, or "Pfc," instead of a general busted down to colonel) and his friend Pierre regarding Mignonette, the parody's Renata:

> "She's [at the restaurant La Chienne Morte]," he said, "but not alone, Mon Pfc."
> "Not alone?"
> "No, Mon Pfc," Pierre said.
> "There are people with her?"
> "Yes, there are people with her," said Pierre.
> "She is not alone," said the Pfc.
> "No. She is not alone. There are people with her." (4)

Wallach also takes potshots at the sentimentality Hemingway voices through his endless strings of bland, abstract adjectives ("'I love you true,' he said. 'I love you straight. I love you honest. I love you sincere'"; 6). And as with White's parody, much of Wallach's humor arises from absurdity: his lovers take romantic waterway rides in a submersible phone booth instead of a gondola. Unlike "Across the Street and into the Grill," the spoof also integrates Hemingway himself in the humor, as in *MAD*'s aforementioned reference to "Ernest Heminghaw." Interestingly, that prefatory note replaced the original one that Wallach included in *Hopalong Freud*, which took a direct poke at Hemingway's reputation for sports, machismo, and gunplay: "This was written in Ebbets Field while a relief pitcher—guy by the name of Hemingway—was coming in from the bull pen. Hemingway pitched one strike and two cojones. Then he shot the batter" (1).

For our purposes, the defining difference between "Out of the Frying Pan" and White's "Across the Street" is the setting. Wallach does not retain *Across the River*'s Venetian vistas either, but neither does he wrench it entirely out of a familiar Hemingway context. Instead of New York, he relocates the plot to Paris, with a closing reference to another key Papa site, Pamplona. The result is a sealing off of the referential borders of the comedy, grounding us in Hemingway's world and precluding the need, as much as possible, for an intertextual contrast.[10] This is not to say that *Across the River and into the Trees* is the only source of Wallach's humor. He crafts jokes from *The Sun Also Rises*' constant references to Parisian restaurants that Hemingway made famous, such as the Closerie des Lilas or Madame Lecomte's ("La Chienne Morte," i.e., "The Dead Dog"). More obviously, Wallach borrows the oft-derided "expletive deleted" device Hemingway employs in *For Whom the Bell Tolls*: "Fornicate the river!" the Pfc barks (7). As a result of this referential constriction into Hemingway's textual world, the mockery of such trademark characteristics as heroism, perfection of craft, and connoisseurship (the Pfc guzzles Citronella '16) is hermetically sealed. To be funny, the humor relies first and foremost upon readers' familiarity with its primary subject and not with the parodist's own identity or with the values the medium of publication embodies. To appreciate this point, consider how idiosyncratic "Out of the Frying Pan" seems alongside such other contents in *MAD* issue 24 as its takeoffs on "Dale Carnegie-style self-improvement guides" and its "fake advertisements that simultaneously mocked pillars of American commercial culture, such as Band-Aids and

Jell-O, and Madison Avenue's cynical exploitation of the public's willing gullibility" (Hajdu 324). Even the accompanying illustration by Bernard Krigstein seems out of place next to visuals by *MAD* mainstays Will Eider and Jack Davis.[11] Instead of a cartoon, the image is a straightforward representation of a soldier with a gun. While the figure bears no resemblance whatsoever to Hemingway (the Pfc does not even look sixty, as the parody states his age to be), the lack of caricature has the effect of further distinguishing the piece, distancing its comedy from *MAD*'s anarchic style and reminding us in the process that it is a reprint of a selection from a previously published book.

Such is not the case with "Across the Street and into the Grill," whose humor is entirely of a piece with the *New Yorker*'s brand of urban/urbane comedy. As a commuter, White's Mr. Pirnie is the type of stock character the magazine (and many New York–based writers) loved to mock: the suburbanite, as opposed to the denizen of the metropolis, the cosmopolitan attuned to the invigorating excitement of big cities. Scarsdale marks Mr. Pirnie as bourgeois, as the type of visitor to New York who likes to eat at Schrafft's, the one-time candy company that by the 1950s had expanded into a restaurant chain, operating upwards of fifty eateries in the city. With its relatively cheap menu and high-volume service, Schrafft's was hardly fine dining, offering in the Eisenhower era one-dollar deviled-tongue-and-cheese sandwiches and turkey on toast.[12] To ridicule Hemingway's gastronomic reputation, White has the chain serve "mayonnaise in fiascos" and "green pokeweed salad." The use of Schrafft's as the anti–Gritti Palace allows White to deflate Hemingway's reputation as a globe-trotting connoisseur, associating his values instead with hopelessly middle-class tastes. By extension, White depicts Hemingway's literary values as squarely midcult: sentimental and grandiose, self-absorbed, and lacking in cultivation.

Cultivation does not simply mean aesthetic taste (although it is impossible to imagine the *New Yorker* printing Wallach's joke about "pitch[ing] one strike and two cojones"). For White's generation, cultivation meant the emotional detachment that *New Yorker* writers of the time valued as a signature of literary and critical professionalism.[13] As Daniel Tracy has argued, one appeal of "smart magazines" such as the *New Yorker* and *Vanity Fair* was that they assured upper-middle-class audiences that they possessed the requisite judgment to distinguish high culture from populist diversions that might absorb and assimilate traits of Art with a capital A. Even in their humor (one might say *especially* in their humor), these publications grounded their authority to discern the cultural strata of highbrow vs. middle- and lowbrow in their sense of professionalism. In writing parodies, *New Yorker* mainstays such as White, Thurber, Dorothy Parker, Corey Ford, and S. J. Perelman demonstrated their ability to mock a variety of writing modes, whether avant-garde or popular, through the mastery of imitation and a wit that was dry rather than agenda-driven. That is, their parodies were not sparked by feuds, jealousies, or other subjective motives, as Hemingway's inevitably were. Instead, the humorists presented themselves as policing the excesses of literary prominence and reputation, whether that notoriety was obtained because of the writer's posturing ego or merely the glaring individuality of his or her style. As Tracy insists, "These editors and writers secured professionalism through a primary appeal not to a particular aesthetic program but through their commitment to critical reason that anyone might exercise; the irony and iconoclasm came not from modernism but from a commonsense rationality that could see coolly through pretension. The smart magazine appeal to critical reason secured professional authority and readers' trust—for all wit's potential to draw lines of distinction, it also would make a chatty friend" (57).

In this context, it is not hard to read "Across the Street and into the Grill" as ridiculing the "pretensions" of the Hemingway hero—the preoccupation with death, the struggle to assert individual valor, the terseness of a style designed to convey the stoic resolve of survival—by redefining them for the ideal "smart" reader as a bourgeois preoccupation, as concerns of unhappy people in ticky-tacky houses like those of Scarsdale who lack the discernment to appreciate that "real" art is about craft, not sentimental anxieties. This inscribed intention is ultimately the reason that White's parody enjoys the reputation it does while equally witty exercises such as Thurber's and Wallach's have been consigned to relative obscurity: the underlying questions of "Across the Street" are "What is literature and who is it written for?" Is literature about the life and death matters that so preoccupied Hemingway, or is it about exercising that "commonsense rationality" that would allow sophisticated readers to deem Hemingway's concerns melodramatic and overblown? By transplanting the Hemingway hero to Scarsdale, White firmly sided with the latter opinion, associating Hemingway with that midcult audience that, in Macdonald's view, strained for "Universal Significance" at the expense of judgment, portentous profundity at the expense of taste (*Masscult and Midcult* 38). In a sense, one can argue that Thurber's intertextually dependent parody takes the focus off of teaching the reader the judgment necessary for literary critique thanks to the distracting presence of Clement Clarke Moore; equating Hemingway's hard-boiled dialogue with Moore's stentorian rhythms and rudimentary rhyme scheme effectively negates both. However, Wallach's more hermetic parody is so interiorized in Hemingway's world that it offers no synoptic vantage point from which to draw those "lines of discernment." To put it another way, Wallach fails to inscribe into his parody an image of the ideal Hemingway reader who falls for Papa's pomposity. With Mr. Pirnie, however, White created just such a figure. Had the parodist explicitly depicted his faux protagonist as a Hemingway fan, perhaps by quoting Hemingway or showing Mr. Pirnie reading a Hemingway book, he would have made his point a little too obvious. But by making him a middle-class commuter imagining his life more glorious and heroic than his surroundings would suggest, White gives us a portrait of the type of reader for whom Hemingway would provide a fantasy existence, the sort whom literature would encourage to imagine himself a grand hero, a tastemaker, and the consummate lover.

The point that, for White, Hemingway's writing was less about craft and discernment than self-aggrandizing fantasy is best demonstrated by a 1962 letter the essayist wrote to John Updike. In it White defines his idea of literature and, by contrast, what good writing is not: "I keep trying to discover what it is (what mysterious thing) that elevates writing to the level where combustion takes place, and I guess it is simply that in writing there has to be an escape of gases or vapors from the center—Core Gas, that is" (*Letters* 446). The metaphor of "combustion" reminds one of T. S. Eliot's description of literature as a chemical reaction in "Tradition and the Individual Talent" (1919). For Eliot, authorial personality or sensibility is a mere catalyst that sparks the process by which two gases combine; the catalyst is unchanged by the process and, more importantly, it leaves no trace of itself in the newly formed substance (7). The separation of the authorial self from the work is the essence of Eliot's theory of the impersonality of art. White reverses the metaphor, depicting the essence of literature as the elemental gas that escapes the combustive process of creativity, purified of those distracting traces of the writer's personality. Both critics would likely agree that Hemingway's main fault was the inseparability of his persona from his art. White takes his chemical imagery in a far bawdier direction, however. "And even this explanation is unreliable," White says of his Core Gas metaphor, "because God knows there was always a lot of gas escaping from Hemingway but a lot of the time it reminded me of the farting of an old horse" (*Letters* 446).

At the risk of beating a gassy horse to death, we might say that transplanting *Across the River and into Trees* to New York and making Mr. Pirnie a suburbanite is White's way of dismissing Hemingway heroism as pure flatulence.

Notes

1. Hemingway improvised his own parody of *Across the River* for Hotchner called "In Harry's Bar in Venice." For many years it was only available on an LP (and subsequent formats) titled *Ernest Hemingway Reading* (1965), released by Caedmon Records. More recently, Mark Cirino includes the text of the piece in his reader's guide to the novel (210–11).

2. As is well known, Hemingway parodies Anderson mercilessly in his 1926 *Torrents of Spring*. Less well known is his unpublished takeoff on Stein, "The Autobiography of Alice B. Hemingway," his reaction to the insults Stein leveled at him in *The Autobiography of Alice B. Toklas* in 1933. For a discussion of various parodic attacks Hemingway mounted on various friends and foes, see my essay "Literary Friendships, Rivalries, and Feuds."

3. See White's *Second Tree from the Corner*, 140. Occasionally in anthologies the note reads "With *my* respects to Ernest Hemingway" (emphasis added).

4. See, for example, Lynn 556; and Reynolds 228.

5. It is tempting to suggest here that "Across the Street" remains a touchstone of the critical response to Hemingway because it is often discussed in the same breath as the *New Yorker*'s other 1950 reassessment of the author, Lillian Ross's notorious profile "How Do You Like It Now, Gentlemen?" Ross's piece appeared in the May 13 issue, roughly four months before White's parody, and catalyzed the downturn in Hemingway's reputation even before *Across the River and into the Trees* was published. That downturn owes much to Hemingway's own self-presentation: speaking in pidgin English, boasting of knocking Tolstoy and Dostoevsky out of the literary boxing ring, he comes off in Ross's profile at worst as an insufferable braggart and at best as a drunk.

6. Of course, the implicit question here is whether the *New Yorker*'s audience was itself "midcult" in the sense that it looked to acquire highbrow tastes by reading "smart magazines." For an investigation of this possibility and the magazine's rhetorical construction of sophistication, see Tracy.

7. "My Own Life" has never been reprinted in its entirety; I do include the Stein section, "The True Story of My Break with Gertrude Stein," in *The Critical Response to Gertrude Stein* (254–55).

8. The first issue of *MAD Magazine*, as opposed to *MAD* the comic book, was nevertheless numbered issue 24, not issue 1, mainly "so Gaines could piggyback on the old *Mad*'s postal license" (Hajdu, *Ten-Cent Plague*, 324).

9. At the pedantic risk of ruining this joke, Eli Wallach (1915–2014) was a consummate character actor, best remembered today for *The Magnificent Seven* (1960), *The Misfits* (also 1960), and *The Good, the Bad, and the Ugly* (1966). In the midfifties Wallach had yet to break into film; he was instead a fixture on Broadway, where he had recently starred in Tennessee Williams's *The Rose Tattoo* (1951) and John Patrick's *The Teahouse of the August Moon* (1953). Coincidentally, Wallach appears in *Hemingway's Adventures of a Young Man*, A. E. Hotchner's 1962 effort at stringing together several of Hemingway's Nick Adams stories into a single screenplay.

10. This claim may seem to contradict my earlier assertion that no parody can exclude a "foreign element" or intertextual connection. In Wallach's case, I would suggest the decision to make Hemingway's protagonist a private instead of a colonel associates the Cantwell figure with the diverse representations of enlisted men during World War II, from Bill Maudlin's Willie and Joe cartoons in *Stars and Stripes* to Private Snafu propaganda cartoons. The reclassification functions the opposite way of White's parody: if Mr. Pirnie turns the Hemingway hero into a bourgeois commuter, Wallach's private ironically emphasizes Hemingway's own association with the officer class, quietly signaling his distance from the average soldier.

11. Bernard Krigstein (1919–1990) has garnered a cult reputation as an illustrator whose work did not quite fit into the comic book format. As Art Spiegelman writes, he "had the privilege and the misfortune of being an Artist with a capital 'A' working in an Art Form that considered itself only a Business." As Spiegelman adds, "What reputation [Krigstein] has rests on a handful of short stories he illustrated in 1954 and 1955 for EC comics (the folks [Gaines] who brought you *Tales from the Crypt* and *Mad*), but one of those stories, 'Master Race,' was an accomplishment of the highest order—a masterpiece" ("Bernard Krigstein's Life," 72). For our purposes, it is useful to contrast Krigstein's staid illustration for "Out of the Frying Pan" with his panels for *Mad*'s parody of James Jones's *From Here to Eternity*, "From Eternity Back to Here!," especially considering how much Hemingway resented Jones's novel for its massive success (Lynn, *Hemingway*, 558–59; Reynolds, *Hemingway*, 244). Krigstein's illustrations for this spoof are far more in the caricature tradition than the illustration for the Wallach parody.

12. The New York Public Library has a variety of Schrafft's menus from throughout the years posted online. See http://menus.nypl.org/menu_pages/56754. For a history of the chain, see Slomanson, *When Everybody Ate at Schrafft's*.

13. This does not mean the *New Yorker* did not appreciate the value of potential Hemingway contributions. As Francis J. Bosha has shown, founding editor Harold Ross courted the writer between 1942 and 1948, hoping to secure a story (though not a fishing essay) from him.

Works Cited

Beerbohm, Max. *A Christmas Garland*. London: Heinemann, 1912.
Bosha, Francis J. "Ernest Hemingway and *The New Yorker*: The Harold Ross Files." *Hemingway Review* 21.1 (2001): 93–99.
Campbell, Kenneth. "An Appreciation of Hemingway." *American Mercury* 14.7 (July 1938): 288–91.
Cirino, Mark. *Reading Hemingway's* Across the River and into the Trees. Kent, OH: Kent State UP, 2016.
Collins, Geneva. "For Whom Parodists Toil." *Victoria Advocate*, July 30, 1989, 10.
Coren, Alan. "The Pooh Also Rises." *Chocolate and Cuckoo Clocks: The Essential Alan Coren*. Ed. Giles and Victoria Coren. San Francisco: Canongate, 2008. 113–14.
Curnutt, Kirk. *The Critical Response to Gertrude Stein*. Westport, CT: Greenwood Press, 2000.
———. "Literary Friendships, Rivalries, and Feuds." *Ernest Hemingway in Context*. Ed. Debra A. Moddelmog and Suzanne del Gizzo. New York: Cambridge UP, 2012. 163–72.
Eliot, T. S. "Tradition and the Individual Talent." *Selected Essays, 1917–1932*. New York: Harcourt, Brace, 1950. 3–11.
Fielding, Henry. *An Apology for the Life of Mrs. Shamela Andrews*. Ed. Sheridan W. Baker, Jr. Berkeley: U of California P, 1953.
Hadju, David. *The Ten-Cent Plague: The Great Comic Book Scare and How It Changed America*. New York: Farrar, Straus, and Giroux, 2008.
Hanneman, Audre. *Ernest Hemingway: A Comprehensive Bibliography*. Princeton: Princeton UP, 1967.
Hemingway, Ernest. *Across the River and into the Trees*. New York: Scribner's, 1950.
———. "The Autobiography of Alice B. Hemingway." Unpublished item 256. Hemingway Collection, John F. Kennedy Library, Boston, MA.
———. "In Harry's Bar in Venice." *Ernest Hemingway Reading*. 1965. Caedmon Records. TC 1185. LP. Rptd. in Mark Cirino. *Reading Hemingway's* Across the River and into the Trees. Kent: Kent State UP, 2016.

———. "My Own Life: After Reading the Second Volume of Frank Harris." *New Yorker*, February 12, 1927, 23.

———. *The Torrents of Spring*. New York: Scribner's, 1926.

"Hemingway's Prize-Winning Works Reflected Preoccupation with Life and Death." *New York Times*, July 3, 1961, 6.

Hotchner, A. E. *Papa Hemingway: A Personal Memoir*. 1966. New York: Random House, 2005.

Hutcheon, Linda. *A Theory of Parody: The Teachings of Twentieth-Century Art Forms*. London: Methuen, 1985.

James, E. L. *Fifty Shades of Grey*. New York: Random House, 2012.

Krigstein, Bernard. "From Eternity Back to Here!" *Mad* 12 (June 1954): 1–5.

Lynn, Kenneth S. *Hemingway*. New York: Simon & Schuster, 1987.

Macdonald, Dwight. *Masscult and Midcult: Essays Against the American Grain*. 1963. New York: New York Review of Books, 2011.

———. *Parodies: An Anthology from Chaucer to Beerbohm—and After*. Ed. Dwight Macdonald. New York: Random House, 1960.

McDowell, Edwin. "Hemingway's Status Revives among Scholars and Readers." *New York Times*, July 26, 1983, A1.

McKelly, James C. "From Whom the Bull Flows: Hemingway in Parody." *American Literature* 61.4 (December 1989): 547–62.

Menand, Louis. "Parodies Lost: The Art of Making Fun." *New Yorker*, September 20, 2010, 107–9.

Merkin, Fanny, and Andrew Shaffer. *Fifty Shades of Earl Grey: A Parody*. New York: DaCapo Press, 2012.

Plimpton, George. "The Snows of Studiofiftyfour." *Harpers Monthly* (November 1979): 70–75.

Remnick, David, and Henry Finder, eds. *Fierce Pajamas: An Anthology of Humor Writing from the New Yorker*. New York: Random House, 2002.

Reynolds, Michael S. *Hemingway: The Final Years*. New York: Norton, 2000.

Ross, Lillian. "How Do You Like It Now, Gentlemen?" *New Yorker*, May 13, 1950, 36, 38–40, 42–56.

Sampson, Edward C. *E. B. White*. Boston: Twayne, 1974.

Skinner, Cornelia Otis. "For Whom the Gong Sounds." *American Literature in Parody*. Ed. R. P. Falk. New York: Twayne, 1955. 241–44.

Slomanson, Joan Kanel. *When Everybody Ate at Schrafft's: Memories, Pictures, and Recipes from a Very Special Restaurant Empire*. Fort Lee, NJ: Barricade Books, 2007.

Spiegelman, Art. "Ballbuster: Bernard Krigstein's Life between Panels." *New Yorker*, July 22, 2002, 72.

Stewart, Donald Ogden. *A Parody Outline of History*. New York: Doran, 1921.

Thurber, James. "A Visit from Saint Nicholas (in the Ernest Hemingway Manner)." *New Yorker*, December 24, 1927, 17–18.

Tracy, Daniel. "Investing in 'Modernism': Smart Magazines, Parody, and Middlebrow Professional Judgment." *Journal of Modern Periodical Studies* 1.1 (2010): 38–63.

Wallach, Ira. "Out of the Frying Pan and into the Soup." *Hopalong Freud and Other Modern Literary Characters*. New York: Abelard-Schuman, 1951. 1–9. Rptd. in *MAD Magazine* 24 (July 1955): 17–19.

White, E. B. "Across the Street and into the Grill." *New Yorker*, October 14, 1950, 28.

———. "The Law of the Jungle." *New Yorker*, April 14, 1934, 31.

———. *Letters of E. B. White: Revised Edition*. Ed. Dorothy Lobrano Guth and Martha White. New York: Harper, 2007.

———. *The Second Tree from the Corner*. New York: 1954.

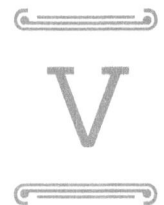

The Fables

15

Dear Children (Good and Bad), You Are Cordially Invited to a Roasting of Instructional Literature

CAM COBB

Pause for a moment and make a mental list of some of the times and places Hemingway experienced in his life. If you are familiar with his writing, your list is probably a long one. After all, he wrote about the Midwest of the early 1900s, Italy in World War I, Paris and Spain of the twenties, Kenya of the early thirties and fifties, the Spanish Civil War, and Cuba both during and after the Great Depression. You may also have noted that he was based in Key West for nearly a decade, and settled in Ketchum, Idaho, in his final years. Traveling and sojourning were significant aspects of Hemingway's storytelling and they are central to his image, both as a literary innovator and as a cultural icon.

A growing body of research is devoted to the different places that formed a part of Hemingway's life, including Kansas City, Toronto, Paris, Key West, Kenya, Cuba, and even China. While Hemingway the writer and Hemingway the traveler seem to be inseparable, his destinations have not all received equal attention. Moreover, not every period of his writing career has received equal attention. Some aspects of his career and work have been downright neglected over the years. One overlooked aspect of Hemingway's life is the time he spent in Northern Italy in the late forties and early fifties (Cirino 130). Perhaps this neglect stems from the fact that his time there was sporadic, totaling less than twelve months over a five-and-a-half-year period (Reynolds 364–66). Perhaps it is because *Across the River and into the Trees*—the novel he produced during this period, and set in

Venice—was so poorly received upon its publication (Stoltzfus 19). Amid this swirling neglect, Hemingway's compact fable "The Good Lion" has lurked on the edge of the critical radar since it was first published.

"The Good Lion"—A Fable of Hypocrisy, Parody, and Racial Identity

After a decade-long short story drought, Hemingway burst out with two fables in the March 1951 issue of *Holiday*. While *Holiday* may not have had the same literary clout as the *New Yorker*, as a travel magazine it was an appropriate venue for a well-known globe-trotter. Titled "The Good Lion" and "The Faithful Bull," the fables were illustrated by Adriana Ivancich—Hemingway's Italian muse—and were written for her young nephew, Gherardo Scapinelli (Roth 137–38). Both stories have been republished over the years, in collections such as *The Complete Short Stories of Ernest Hemingway: The Finca Vigía Edition*. While "The Good Lion" has thus far garnered scant critical attention, the variety of responses to the story is striking.

Questioning the quality of the fable as well as Hemingway's motives in writing it, Susan F. Beegel disparages, "The aging Hemingway, with lucrative magazine offers readily available and ever-increasing financial obligations, occasionally lowered his standards [. . .] to publish embarrassments like 'The Good Lion' in *Holiday*" (7–8). While Beegel's response represents one end of the critical spectrum, others view the story far more favorably. Surveying the lack of writing on the fable, Miriam Mandel remarks, "I am only sorry that . . . no one has yet bothered to say anything about his very funny fable, "The Good Lion," which features a pasta-eating African lion" (Mandel 28). According to Marc Dudley, the story "is a little-discussed and oft-forgotten fablesque short story that deserves attention" (138).

In George Monteiro's view, "The Good Lion" is, at its core, a narrative about hypocrisy. At its outset, the story establishes a sharp contrast between the winged lion, who is "so good" and "noble," and his ravenous companions, who are "all bad" and "wicked." Unimpressed with his fellow lions, the "good" lion refuses to follow their customs and adheres to his own eating habits. Rather than eating Hindu traders, he "will eat only pasta and scampi" (433). In this dichotomy, the "good lion" morally judges his fellow lions, commenting, "What savages these lions are" (Hemingway 483). As Monteiro observes: the "good" lion soon "emigrates to Italy. There he heads right for Harry's Bar. He promptly orders a dry, very dry martini—a

Gordon's gin martini" (433). Yet the story does not end with Gordon's gin. As Monteiro notes, the "good" lion orders his martini "only after he asked (Africa has changed him) for a 'Hindu sandwich'" (433). It would seem that the "good" lion does eat Hindu traders after all—and his unfavorable moral verdict of his companions in Africa is thus insincere. "So much for the impregnability of high principle" (433), Monteiro concludes.

While "The Good Lion" punctuates the duplicity of hypocrisy, the story could also be seen as an exercise in stylistic self-parody. Taking stock of the fable, Jayne Widmayer notes, "The elements which make Hemingway's writing so distinctive are present in the fables—the simple sentences, the simple words, the repetitions—but are pushed just to the point of being overdone" (436). Like a number of Hemingway's characters, the "good" lion is a world traveler who finds himself in caught up an escalating dispute and eventually winds up in a popular European bar. In fact, he could be compared to Colonel Cantwell, the protagonist of *Across the River and into the Trees* (436–38). According to Widmayer, "He and Colonel Cantwell return to Venice after experiences that have shaped their values and formed their characters. Both are at home at Harry's Bar and both drink Gordon's gin martinis, very dry" (437). Moreover, both protagonists surround themselves with gourmets and both are linguists (437). Summing up the closing scene in the story, Widmayer notes that the "good" lion is "happy because in Venice, unlike in the jungles of Africa, he can indulge himself in his affectations and can impress people by them. He is, of course, even worse than the bad lions in the jungle since they, at least, are not hypocrites" (434). Regarding the writer's possible frame of mind in constructing this story, Widmayer speculates: "Hemingway was surely indulging himself in showing how easily his style could become the appropriate language of a child's bedtime story and yet how different his own use was" (436). From this perspective, the story can be interpreted as "a parody of the way the Hemingway hero acts" (438).

By examining how the "good" lion's hypocrisy troubleshoots racial constructs, Marc Dudley pushes analysis of the story into new territory. While the fable creates a world of racial and cultural contrasts—as exhibited in the clear divide between the "good" lion and his "wicked" companions, as well as the landscapes of Africa and Venice—the story also challenges these supposed (and socially constructed) divides. Dudley observes, "[A] narrative intention to simply build on the dark-light, good-evil, civil-savage polarities strongly underscores underlying assumptions and simultaneously (and most importantly) interrogates the paradigm's inherent veracity" (143). Presenting a multilinguist, and morally judgmental (yet ultimately disingenuous) traveler, Hemingway "exposes the malleability of (racial) identity... [which] ultimately brings us back to the question [...] Is race essential?" (144). Although the twist ending renders the "good" lion as a fraud, it has additional connotations. When the "good" lion's predilection for Hindu sandwiches becomes clear, the narrator states, "Africa had changed him" (CSS 484). On one level, this comment seems to indicate "that the 'primitive' African continent, in all its ignobility, has infected our protagonist" (Dudley 144). Yet, as Dudley asks, was the lion really changed by Africa, "[o]r did it just expose him for what he truly was?" (144). It appears that the "good" lion straddles overlapping worlds and racial constructs—worlds and constructs that are not distinct.

While "The Good Lion" has not received a heap of critical attention since its debut, those who have discussed it have portrayed it as a tale of hypocrisy and self-parody, and a statement on binary thinking, as it links to and radicalized identity and stereotypes. While the story is all of these things, it also roasts instructional children's literature.

Instructional Children's Literature

In today's literary landscape, a number of children's stories are thoughtful, some are tragic, and a few are controversial. Some are all three. Characters and situations in these stories are complicated and the lines between right and wrong, and hero and villain, are often blurred. Protagonists wrestle with tough decisions and sometimes struggle to find meaning in their lives. Whether it is Parvana striving to feed her family in war-torn Kabul, Caitlin coping with Asperger's and the loss of her brother in a school shooting, or Joey Pigza reconnecting with a father who abandoned him long ago, contemporary children's literature can be weighty indeed. Yet these were not the sorts of stories Hemingway grew up with as a child.

Born on the eve of the twentieth century, Hemingway was raised on fiction that is much different from that read by the young audience of today. Sure, he had social commentaries like *Adventures of Huckleberry Finn* on his bookshelf, but he also had *A Child's Garden of Verses* (Brasch and Sigman). And this means that as a young reader, Hemingway had the edifying constrictiveness of "A Good Boy," the racial elitism of "Foreign Children," and the binary thinking of "Good and Bad Children." "A Good Lion" could be read as a roasting of three pillars of instructive children's literature. After all, the fable parodies the naïveté of didactic storytelling, the arrogance of racial elitism, and the extremism of binary thinking.

You Are Cordially Invited to a Roasting

Reading "The Good Lion" as a parody of instructional children's literature enriches the way we experience the story. It adds a level of humor to the story. With verve and deceptive simplicity, the compact fable lampoons didactic storytelling, racial elitism, and binary thinking. To discuss these three aspects of instructional children's literature (as well as their presence in "The Good Lion"), this essay will draw from Robert Louis Stevenson's collection, *A Child's Garden of Verses*. According to Julia Briggs and Dennis Butts, the well-known book is "the most important collection of serious poems for children of the century" (162).

Didactic Storytelling

Much of the instructional children's literature of the 1800s and early 1900s was didactic in nature (see Briggs and Butts 130–66 ; Briggs 167–91; Ostry 27–56). Such stories—whether expressed in prose, song lyrics, or poetry— were designed to provide moral tales for families to vicariously experience and learn from. More pointedly, these lessons were constructed to instill particular values and encourage normative behaviors in parents and children (Ostry 28). Some of the values and behaviors championed in these stories include obedience, modesty, and courtesy (28–29). As teaching tools, these stories often tell the audience how to respond to characters, situations, and actions.

Stevenson exemplifies this didactic approach in *A Child's Garden of Verses*. The ten-line poem "A Good Boy," for instance, chronicles a day in the life of a young boy, cataloguing his words and actions. According to the "good boy" (who narrates the poem): "I woke before the morning, I was happy all day / I never said an ugly word, but smiled and stuck to play" (1–2). As these two lines indicate, the poem acts as a vehicle of teaching manners, encouraging young boys to awake early, remain content, and refrain from using "ugly" language. In "Good and Bad Children" Stevenson extends this didactic approach, using the poem as a way of directly addressing children:

> Children, you are very little,
> And your bones are very brittle;
> If you would grow great and stately,
> You must try to walk sedately.
>
> You must still be bright and quiet,
> And content with simple diet;
> And remain, through all bewild'ring,
> Innocent and honest children. (1–8)

In these two stanzas, Stevenson utilizes the word "must"—a modal of requirement—twice when instructing children how to act. The underlying message is that good children must be sedate, bright, quiet, innocent, and honest. Here, Stevenson directly tells his audience what sorts of behaviors they should value and exhibit in their day-to-day lives. Consequently, these didactic poems leave little to their audience's imagination.

Hemingway mimics the didactic approach to storytelling in "The Good Lion." Throughout the fable, readers are informed who is good and who is bad, as well as which words, actions, and behaviors are acceptable and which are not. Early in the story, Hemingway tells readers, "The other lions were all bad lions and every day they ate zebras and wildebeests and every kind of antelope" (CSS 482). Extending this depiction of "bad" lions, Hemingway elaborates, "Sometimes the bad lions ate people too. They ate Swahilis, Umbulus, and Wandorobos and they especially liked to eat Hindu traders" (482). Having sketched out the "bad" characters of the story, Hemingway turns the reader's attention to the protagonist.

When describing the hero of "The Good Lion," Hemingway is just as direct as he is when portraying the villains. More specifically, when introducing the protagonist, he directs readers: "But this lion, that we love because he was so good, had wings on his back" (482). Like didactic children's stories, Hemingway tells his audience which character they should sympathize with and indeed "love." Continuing with this approach, he later tells readers that the lions who tease the protagonist for eating pasta are "very bad and wicked lions indeed" (482). One lioness, who threatens to kill the "good" lion—and eat him "wings and all"—"was the wickedest of them all" (483, 482). Hemingway's message is explicit: there is one "good" lion we love, and there are many "bad" lions we do not love.

Throughout the "The Good Lion," Hemingway's use of vocabulary—adjectives in particular—directs readers how to respond to the characters and situations that unfold in the story. He uses the word "good" twelve times, "noble" once, "and "dutiful" once to portray the positive nature of the protagonist. When describing the African counterparts of the "good" lion, Hemingway uses the word "bad" five times, "wicked" five times, and "wickedest" once. Because "The Good Lion" tells its audience how to respond to characters and events, it does not invite readers to interpret the story. Yet while the story's moral dimension seems to be explicit, it is not. The eventual hypocrisy of the "good" lion—as revealed when he orders a Hindu trader sandwich at the closing of the story—shatters the preceding didactic statements that litter the story (Widmayer 433–34). It appears that Hemingway is at once demonstrating and lampooning didactic storytelling.

Racial Elitism

While a fair amount of instructional children's literature set out to teach manners didactically, some stories also carried with them an underpinning message of racial elitism (Bradford 197; Briggs 184). A worldview of racial hierarchy permeated Western Europe during the late eighteenth and early nineteenth centuries (Bradford 196–98). It was rooted in what is known today as scientific racism. While race-based elitism was certainly not a new concept in the 1800s, the publication of Charles Darwin's works on evolution led to the phenomenon of social Darwinism. As Darwin's ideas of natural selection and survival of the fittest gained acceptance (and indeed prominence), they were eventually applied to sociology, politics, and literature (Lerer 172–89). Some viewed Darwin's biological theories as a way of explaining why the imperial powers, such as Britain, came to exert force and hold power over others cultures in the world (Mackenzie 154). Within this rubric, which drew from age-old notions of a civilization-barbarism dichotomy, ethnoracial and ethnocultural identities around the world were appraised and ultimately ranked. This elitist worldview led some to explain—and indeed excuse—the practices of enslavement and conquest (Bradford

199–202). It is important to note that the lens of scientific racism was not only widespread but was also persistent. It crossed generations.

Scientific racism, as an idea and worldview, was lasting, in part, because it was taught to children when they were young. This indoctrination can be seen in some of the European children's literature of the 1800s and early 1900s (Richards 1–10). Stevenson's poem "Foreign Children," for instance, exemplifies racial elitism. In the opening stanza, Stevenson sets up a sharp contrast between domestic (British) children and foreign children (the original peoples of North America, the Japanese, and the Turks). He imagines that the foreign children all have an innate desire to be British:

> Little Indian, Sioux or Crow,
> Little frosty Eskimo
> Little Turk or Japanee
> O! don't you wish that you were me? (1–4)

After setting up a hierarchical foreign-domestic dichotomy, Stevenson goes on to explain his thinking behind the hierarchy itself. Through the poem's speaker, Stevenson addresses the foreign children of the world, stating:

> You have seen the scarlet trees
> And the lions over seas;
> You have eaten ostrich eggs,
> And turned the turtles off their legs.
>
> Such a life is very fine,
> But it's not so nice as mine:
> You must often, as you trod
> Have wearied not to be abroad.
>
> You have curious things to eat,
> I am fed on proper meat;
> You must dwell beyond the foam
> But I am safe and live at home (5–16)

The supremacy of British children is explicit throughout the short poem. British children eat "proper meat" instead of "curious things." Moreover, they are "safe" and live in a "home." While the foreign children described in the poem may see and experience certain things that British children cannot (such as "scarlet trees"), they ultimately "wish" they were British. While Stevenson does not morally judge the foreign children to whom he is speaking, he sees them as something lesser than their British counterparts. He pities them. And Hemingway parodies this racial elitism through the colonialism and hypocrisy in "The Good Lion" (Monteiro 433; Widmayer 433–34; Dudley 143–44).

Racial elitism lurks both on and beneath the surface of "The Good Lion." For the most part, the elitism that pervades the story stems from its didactic moral message as well as its either-or, binary worldview. The protagonist and his father, who live in Venice, are "noble" and "dutiful." The protagonist's father, a majestic winged lion, lives in a city of palaces where bronze horses "have one foot in the air because they fear him" (483). The father's subjects include "a thousand pigeons" that "make a noise like a rushing river" when flying (482, 483). Venice is a city of manners, where a son kisses "his father on both cheeks" and the conscientious father sends a message to Cipriani—who runs Harry's Bar—that he "will be in someday soon to see about [his] bill" (483). The "dutiful" son and his majestic father are both "good," and in contrast with this most noble pair are the lions of Africa.

The lions of Africa lack the refinement of the "good" lion and his father. Instead of luxuriating at Harry's Bar, they "drink his blood, going lap, lap, lap with their tongues" (482). The wicked lioness has bad breath and is never able to get Hindu blood off of her whiskers. Because the bad lions of Africa mock the protagonist for eating pasta and scampi and having wings, they are discriminatory. Because they refuse to believe what they are told about the wonders of Venice, they are untrusting and close-minded. Even their language appears to be lacking. While the "good" lion answers his father politely "like a dutiful son," and speaks in "beautiful Spanish" and "exemplary French," the angry African lions "roared and growled in African lion dialect" (483). In short, the "good" lion is a "lion of culture" while the African lions are, in the words of the protagonist, "very savage" (483).

Yet while Hemingway sets up a clear dynamic of racial hierarchy, he undercuts it at the story's end (Dudley 143–44). The "good" lion drinks gin and orders a Hindu trader sandwich—not pasta or scampi—at Harry's bar. Even the grace of Venice is implicated in the "good" lion's hypocrisy. After all, what can be said about Venice's supposed high culture when the proprietor of Harry's Bar himself assures the protagonist that he "can get some" Hindu sandwiches for him (CSS 484). "The Good Lion" at once presents and deconstructs the questionable nature of racialized dichotomy and racial elitism, which pervaded a fair amount of the instructional children's stories of Hemingway's youth.

Binary Thinking

In addition to didactic storytelling and racial elitism, children's literature in English has roots in binary thinking (Nodelman 9). Instructional stories, used to teach children manners, presented a world of extremes, where actions, people, and ideas—such as good and bad—were firmly locked into oppositional relationships. Reflecting on this sort of thinking, curriculum theorist John Dewey noted as far back as 1938: "Mankind likes to think in terms of extreme opposites. It is given to formulating its beliefs in terms of Either-Or, between which it recognizes no intermediate possibilities" (17). An example of this sort of binary thinking pervades a number of poems in Stevenson's *A Child's Garden of Verses*.

In "Good and Bad Children," for instance, the traits of two very different groupings of children are presented separately, as though they are distinct from one another. Within this dichotomy, good children are stately, sedate, quite, innocent, honest, and happy. They are "content with [a] simple diet" (6). Conversely, bad children are unkind, unruly, they cry, and are ultimately "[h]ated" (19). They also "eat unduly" (20). Here, there is a line that sharply divides two very different sorts of children. In this schema of extremes there is also a distinct line between civilized domestic children and uncivilized foreign children. In Stevenson's poem "Foreign Children," the children of the original people of North America, Turkey, and Japan are compared to the children of Britain. Here, the habits of foreign children, their food, and their geography is portrayed as unpleasant and "curious" (13), while the British child's world is described as "safe" (16). While the foreign world of "lions," "scarlet trees," and "ostrich eggs" might be exotic (5–7), it is not "proper" (14). Moreover, these two settings are separate from one another. As Dewey noted, there are two extremes in this worldview—and no "intermediate possibilities" in between (17).

Like the either-or view of many instructional children's stories, "The Good Lion" is a fable rooted in a world of extremes. It is a world governed by binary oppositions. Good lions are the polar opposite of bad lions, and Venice is sharply contrasted with Africa. More specifically, good lions, as exemplified by the story's protagonist, are noble and dutiful. They eat pasta and scampi, and speak various European languages, such as Spanish and French. Bad lions, on the other hand, are wicked. They eat animals as well as humans—especially Hindu traders. Bad lions threaten to kill good lions, as the "most wicked" lioness does. They also taunt the "good" lion throughout the story, calling him a "pasta-eating lion" and "a worthless liar and the son of a griffon" (482, 483). Yet the unpleasantness of the bad lions goes beyond their words and actions. The wicked lioness has bad breath, "because she never brushed her teeth ever" (483). Even her appearance is objectionable, as "she could never get the blood of Hindu traders off her whiskers even when she rubbed her face in the grass" (482).

The dualism of the "The Good Lion" is not only depicted by the good-bad lion dichotomy but is also visible in the story's two landscapes. In terms of geography, Hemingway contrasts the initial African setting with the world of Venice. Africa is populated by zebras, wildebeests, and antelope, while Venice is populated by a griffon, as well as the pigeons of Saint Mark's Square. While Africa is inhabited by Swahilis, Umbulus, and Hindu traders, Venice is inhabited by men who travel "on foot or in boats" and frequent Harry's Bar (483). It is also inhabited by Cipriani himself, who runs Harry's Bar. Africa does not seem to have any monuments and, in the words of the "good" lion, is a land of "savages" (483). Conversely, according to the "good" lion: "There are more palaces in my father's city than in all of Africa" (483). Venice has bronze statues (the horses of Saint Mark's), piazzas, a basilica, and Harry's Bar. While these two worlds seem to exist on separate planes, they begin to collide when the "good" lion flies from one space to another.

This collision deepens when the "good" lion orders a Hindu trader sandwich while relaxing in the comfort of Harry's Bar. It would seem that after establishing a system of binary opposition, Hemingway punctures the very system he established. After all, the "good" lion, who eats pasta and scampi in Africa, is also a "bad" lion who eats Hindu traders in Venice. And the elevated nature of Venice itself is questioned when Cipriani offers to procure a Hindu trader sandwich for his celebrated (and well-traveled) guest. Rather than existing as separate realities, it seems that Venice and Africa are, in actuality, worlds that overlap (Dudley 143–44).

Conclusion

Hemingway's time in Northern Italy in the late forties and early fifties has been overlooked over the years, and yet there is much to be learned from this period of his life, as well as from the work it produced. While "The Good Lion" has lurked on the edge of the critical radar since it first appeared in 1950, the story has much to offer. Critical responses to the story have thus far pointed out its elements of hypocrisy, self-parody, and racial stereotyping and deconstruction (Monteiro 433; Widmayer 433–34; and Dudley 143–44). Yet, in addition to these things, the fable is also a roasting of instructional children's literature.

In fact, "The Good Lion" lampoons three key aspects of instructional literature. It simultaneously mimics and questions the direct messaging of didactic storytelling, presents and then deconstructs the hierarchy of racial elitism, and sets up a world of binary opposition and then summarily punctures it in one fell swoop. Hemingway's writing superimposes Africa with Venice and the world of grown-ups with the world of children. Recognizing "The Good Lion" as a lampoon of instructional children's stories highlights its comedic dimension. And reading the story in this way enriches one's experience, and appreciation, of its humor. Hemingway is not only exemplifying (and indeed hyperbolizing) instructional children's literature, but he is also having fun with it. After all, where else can you find a globe-trotting, pasta-eating hypocritical lion who drinks dry martinis and cavorts with Cipriani at Harry's Bar?

Works Cited

Beegel, Susan F. *Hemingway's Neglected Short Fiction: New Perspectives*. Tuscaloosa: U of Alabama P, 1982.

Bradford, Clare. "The End of Empire? Colonial and Postcolonial Journeys in Children's Books." *Children's Literature* 29 (2001): 196–218.

Brasch, James Daniel, and Joseph Sigman. *Hemingway's Library: A Composite Record*. New York: Garland Publishing, 1981.

Briggs, Julia. "Transitions (1890–1914)." *Children's Literature: An Illustrated History*. Ed. Peter Hunt. New York: Oxford UP, 1995. 167–91.

Briggs, Julia, and Dennis Butts. "The Emergence of Form (1850–1890)." *Children's Literature: An Illustrated History*. Ed. Peter Hunt. New York: Oxford UP, 1995. 130–66.

Cirino, Mark. "Hemingway's Veneto (review)." *Hemingway Review* 31.2 (2012): 130–33.

Dewey, John. *Experience and Education.* 1938. New York: Simon and Schuster, 1997.

Dudley, Marc. *Hemingway Race and Art: Bloodlines and the Color Line.* Kent, OH: Kent State UP, 2012.

Gantos, Jack. *Joey Pigza Swallowed the Key.* New York: Farrar, Straus and Giroux, 1998.

Hemingway, Ernest. "The Good Lion." *The Complete Short Stories of Ernest Hemingway: The Finca Vigía Edition.* New York: Scribner, 1987. 482–84.

Lerer, Seth. *Children's Literature: A Reader's History from Aesop to Harry Potter.* Chicago: U of Chicago P, 2008.

Mackenzie, John M. "Hunting and the Natural World in Juvenile Literature." *Imperialism and Juvenile Literature.* Ed. Jeffrey Richards. Manchester: Manchester UP, 1989. 144–70.

Mandel, Miriam B. "Introduction." *Hemingway and Africa.* Ed. Miriam B. Mandel. Rochester: Camden House, 2011. 1–40.

Monteiro, George. "Hemingway Para Criancas (O Bom Leão e o Touro Leal) by Ernest Hemingway." *Modern Language Journal* 61.8 (1977): 433.

Nodelman, Perry. "Pleasure and Genre: Speculations on the Characteristics of Children's Fiction." *Children's Literature* 28 (2000): 1–14.

Ostry, Elaine. "Magical Growth and Moral Lessons; or, How the Conduct Book Informed Victorian and Edwardian Children's Fantasy." *The Lion and the Unicorn* 27.1 (2003): 27–56.

Reynolds, Michael. *Hemingway: The Final Years.* New York: Norton, 1999.

Richards, Jeffrey. "Introduction." *Imperialism and Juvenile Literature.* Ed. Jeffrey Richards. Manchester: Manchester UP, 1989. 1–10.

Roth, James M. "News from the Hemingway Collection." *Hemingway Review* 23.1 (2003): 137–39.

Stevenson, Robert Louis. *A Child's Garden of Verses.* 1885. Seattle: Laughing Elephant, 2009.

Stoltzfus, Ben. "The Stones of Venice, Time, and Remembrance: Calculus and Proust in *Across the River and into the Trees.*" *Hemingway Review* 22.2 (2003): 19–29.

Widmayer, Jayne A. "Hemingway's Hemingway Parodies: The Hypocritical Griffon and the Dumb Ox." *Studies in Short Fiction* 18.4 (1981): 433–38.

16

A "Very Complicated" Diet for a Lion

The Functions of Food and Drink in "The Good Lion"

KEI KATSUI

Food in Hemingway's Works

"Tell me what you eat: I will tell you what you are" (Brillat-Savarin 13). This celebrated remark of the French gastronome Brillat-Savarin may be applied to several protagonists of Hemingway's works. According to Linda Underhill and Jeanne Nakjavani, protagonists of Hemingway's works experience native cultures most completely through local food:

> By eating the food the natives eat, often even sharing the same bowl, bottle, or plate with them, the expatriate heroes take sustenance to strengthen themselves for an adventure in a foreign land and absorb the native culture through the food, taking part in the culture so as to experience the adventure truly, as a native world. (87)

Jake Barnes in *The Sun Also Rises*, for instance, enjoys French cuisine in Paris, drinks Spanish wine with Basques, and takes local food with people in Pamplona. Frederic Henry shares pasta with Italian soldiers in *A Farewell to Arms*, and Robert Jordan in *For Whom the Bell Tolls* eats a rabbit stew with the Spanish guerrillas. The various references to local food and drinks in these works show the protagonists' sympathy and understanding of different cultures.

In Hemingway's works food also serves to reveal the darker aspects of his characters. Hemingway's short story "The Good Lion" is one of the most striking examples of this relationship between food and the dark side of his protagonists. "The Good Lion" is a fable published in *Holiday* magazine in 1951 with another fable titled "The Faithful Bull." Although these fables are included in *The Complete Short Stories of Ernest Hemingway* along with Hemingway's other major short stories, they have been little discussed as literary works. Paul Smith states that "The Good Lion" and "The Faithful Bull" "have some slight biographical interest, but little to warrant their study as stories" (395).[1] Kenneth G. Johnston considers the lion and the bull as "thinly disguised, flattering self-portraits, tales of self-justification, probably intended to disarm, forestall and/or anticipate domestic and literary criticism. In fact, they may be read as fables for critics, past, present, and future" (149).[2] As Johnston's opinion suggests, "The Good Lion" and "The Faithful Bull" have been taken lightly because of their genre as a fable. "The Good Lion" is, indeed, dedicated to young Italian lady Adriana Ivancich's young nephew Gherardo Scapinelli, and also illustrated with charming paintings of animals by Adriana as for a picture book for children.

However, we should notice that *Holiday* is a travel magazine for wealthy men who seek high-quality trips, and it inserts numerous advertisements of luxury goods for adults, such as whisky and a motor vehicle. "The Good Lion," in fact, includes many references to cocktails and foreign food that may meet the tastes of readers of *Holiday*, not those of children. These facts indicate that even though "The Good Lion" seems a fable for children, it is actually written as a short story for adult readers, just like Hemingway's other narratives, which contain innumerable connotations and hidden meanings. Food and drinks in "The Good Lion," especially, have a significant allusion that discloses a conflict between the protagonist's appearance and inner desires. If we look more deeply into the representations of food and drinks in this work, it becomes clear that it is more than a biographical or self-justifying fantasy but is, to borrow the headline of "The Good Lion" in *Holiday*, a "very complicated" work "by a very complicated... American writer Ernest Hemingway" (50–51).

What Food Reveals

The title of the short story is "Good Lion," but why is the lion called "good"? To start with, I would like to consider the "goodness" of the lion in the context of food. The story begins: "Once upon a time there was a lion that lived in Africa with all the other lions. The other lions were all bad lions and every day they ate zebras and wildebeests and every kind of antelope. Sometimes the bad lions ate people too" (482). In contrast, the protagonist lion is mocked by the other lions because he had wings on his back and he "only ate pasta and scampi because he was so good" (482). This binary opposition seems natural and understandable from the point of view of a fable at first sight, but we should not overlook that there is no fundamental explanation of what "goodness" or "badness" means. The protagonist lion is called "good" because his diet meets the standard of Western culture, and the other lions are regarded as "bad" because their eating habits are contrary to Western morality.

At first reading, the lion's demand for Western food seems simply to show his "good" and cultivated nature rooted in Western civilization. Yet ironically, his tastes in food and drinks serve eventually to unmask the lion and to reveal his hidden desires.

In the beginning of the story, the good lion refuses to eat the Masai cattle, which are a favorite of the other lions, but he prefers "some tagliatelli" and "a glass of pomodoro" like an Italian (482). His unique wings on his back are always mocked by the other lions, and his persistent preference for Western food act as a trigger for his separation from the other lions. The lioness says, "Who are you that you think you are so much better than we are? Where do you come from, you pasta-eating lion? What are you doing here anyway?" (482). As the lioness's words suggest, the good lion's refusal to eat animals and his inclination for Western food are represented as signs of his arrogance in placing Western above African culture. In fact, he boastfully replies to the lioness that his father is king of Venice and all pigeons and bronze horses in Piazza San Marco are his father's servants and proudly adds, "There are more palaces in my father's city than in all of Africa" (483).

His contempt for Africa and its culture becomes obvious when he flies away from the other lions, which are offended by the good lion's arrogant boasting. Flying over angry lions, the good lion says to himself, "What savages these lions are" (483), and says goodbye to them in "beautiful Spanish" and "exemplary French" as "a lion of culture" while the other lions "all roared and growled in African lion dialect" (483). His arrogant reply and attitude toward the other lions, which is set off by his stubborn fondness for European food, show that he thinks highly of European food, culture, and language and also has a sense of discrimination against those of Africa, even though he is mentioned as the "good" lion in the story.

Compared with other Hemingway heroes, such as Jake Barnes, Frederic Henry, and Robert Jordan, who habitually share local food with local residents and try to absorb foreign cultures, the good lion may seem a rare and curious character in its refusal of African food and culture. Nevertheless, in comparison with other Hemingway protagonists who visit Africa, the good lion's insistence on Western food is not so peculiar. For example, Harry in "The Snows of Kilimanjaro" drinks "whiskey-soda" (*CSS* 40) in the middle of the savanna, and when his wife shoots a Thomson's gazelle, she says to Harry, "He [Molo]'ll make you good broth and I'll have them mash some potatoes with the Klim" (46). In short, even though Harry does eat a Thomson's gazelle, it is cooked as "broth" in the Western manner. Mashed potatoes with the "Klim" (a powdered milk sold by Merrell-Soule Company that was popular in America since 1920) also remind us not of African local meal but of modern American dishes. In "The Short Happy Life of Francis Macomber," the protagonist Macomber asks his wife and Robert Wilson whether they drink "lime juice or lemon squash" after the hunting in the savanna, and then they choose to drink "a gimlet" (*CSS* 5). Not only their drinks but also their food is served in the Western style. When Macomber eats an eland, he is seen "cutting the eland steak and putting some mashed potato, gravy, and carrot on the down-turned fork that tined through the piece of meat" (10).

Furthermore, in *Green Hills of Africa*, the protagonist, who clearly reflects Hemingway himself, eats only meals cooked in the Western manner, such as "the fresh butter ... Grant's gazelle chops, mashed potatoes, green corn, and then mixed fruit for dessert" (29). He also drinks "a gimlet" and even partakes of "a special dish of Viennese dessert" (28–29) despite the fact that he stays in Africa. A more significant point is that Hemingway in *Green Hills of Africa* does not eat local food with local residents, and not only that, he gives his Western food to the Masai:

> Then I had M'Cola open the two cans of mince meat and the plum pudding and I cut these into rations and passed them out. I had heard and read that the Masai subsisted only on the blood of their cattle mixed with milk, drawing the blood off from a wound in a vein of the

neck made by shooting an arrow at close range. These Masai, however, ate bread, cold mince meat and plum pudding with great relish and much laughter and joking. (*GHOA* 286)

At first sight, it would seem that Hemingway is resisting prejudice against the Masais' dietary habits by showing their willingness to eat Western meals. However, if the eating of foreign food means the absorption of the foreign culture, we may observe that Hemingway does not adapt himself to African culture by eating the Masais' food with them but rather tries to assimilate the Masai to Western culture by giving his food to them.

In these three works set in Africa and written in 1930s, the protagonists' insistent preferences for Western food and unconscious resistance to African culture are represented as natural and reasonable attitudes for those who are sophisticated and experienced Westerners. On the other hand, writing about sixteen years later, Hemingway may intentionally emphasize the arrogant, narrow-minded, and discriminative aspects of the good lion by describing his persistent fondness for Western food and his strong reaction against other lions' eating habits. Jayne Widmayer calls the good lion "a hypocritical griffon" (433), and states that the "wickedest lioness ... represents everything a lion really is. Blood is caked on her whiskers and her breath smells bad 'because she never brushed her teeth ever'" (434). That is, it is only natural for African lions to eat animals and even human beings, dripping blood from their mouths. In other words, animals and humans are local food for African lions, and their way of drinking blood is surely equivalent to Spanish people's manner of drinking wine from a wineskin.

Widmayer regards the fables as follows: "[T]he fables are not self-serving allegory; they are instead satiric attacks on pretensions and affectations. And more remarkably, the fables are Hemingway's own parody of Ernest Hemingway" (433). Indeed, Hemingway traveled in Africa in 1933 and enjoyed the safari as well as the good lion. Hemingway, who lived in Paris in the earlier part of his career and visited Spain frequently to see bullfights, could also speak French and Spanish just like the good lion. A dry martini made with Gordon's gin, which the good lion orders in a bar in a later part of the story, is, needless to say, one of Hemingway's favorite cocktails. Therefore the good lion, who so clearly reflects the tastes of Hemingway and his protagonists, may be an ironical self-parody of the typical Hemingway hero and of Hemingway himself: a mirror reflecting Hemingway's and his heroes' sense of superiority and unconscious rejection of African culture that are hidden beneath the persona of the experienced traveler.

Hidden Thirst

Not only food but drinks also serve the significant function of disclosing the good lion's hidden thirst, as it were. After the quarrel with the other lions, the good lion flies to his hometown, Venice. Although he always refuses to eat animals and humans in Africa, when he visits Harry's Bar, he orders the "Hindu trader sandwiches" (484). The reason he asks for human sandwiches is explained as follows: "[T]he good lion had flown all the way from Africa and Africa had changed him" (484). In this scene, we can interpret "Hindu trader sandwiches" not as real human sandwiches but as a kind of exotic ethnic food. In fact, the proprietor Cipriani is not surprised by this order and replies, "No, but I can get some." To which the good lion replies: "While you are sending for them, make me a very dry martini. . . . With Gordon's gin" (484). Widmayer notes that the lion "shows his friends the enlightening advantages of travel. . . . So he orders a Hindu trader sandwich and a very dry Gordon's martini. He is happy because in Venice, unlike in the jungles of Africa, he can indulge himself in his affectations and can impress people by them" (434). In short, the good lion tries to show off his experience in Africa by ordering an exotic African meal for a lion although he never ate a Hindu trader in Africa.

However, we should not jump to the conclusion that travel has changed the good lion. Let us now look more carefully at the good lion's preference in drinks. When the lion was in Africa, he "would sit and fold his wings back and ask politely if he might have a Negroni or an Americano and he always drank that instead of the blood of the Hindu traders" (482). A Negroni is a cocktail made of gin, vermouth, and Campari, and named after the Italian Count Negroni who was fond of the cocktail. An "Americano" is also a cocktail composed of Campari, sweet vermouth, and club soda. Although it was invented in Italy in 1860 as Milano-Torino, Italians noticed that many Americans enjoyed this cocktail, and thus it has been known as an Americano since the 1900s. When the good lion asks for these Italian cocktails, we instantly regard him as a cultured being possessed of Western values.

These cocktails, however, also drop a hint about his hidden aspect. There is no doubt that the names Negroni and Americano remind us of Negroes and American people. Furthermore, the dark red color of these cocktails created by the Campari also makes us think of the color of blood. That is to say, while the good lion asks for cocktails that underline his refined taste, the names and the color of the cocktails imply that he might want to taste the blood of Negro and American people instead of that of Hindu traders.

What is more, the good lion shows his fondness for "pomodoro," or tomato juice, in Africa: "One day he refused to eat eight Masai cattle and only ate some tagliatelli and drank a glass of pomodoro" (482). The tomato juice, superficially, suggests that the good lion is a "good" and safe creature who prefers vegetables to meat or blood, but the red color of tomato juice is immediately associated with the color of blood. Thus, although the good lion apparently refuses to drink human blood and emphasizes his devotion to Western culture by his choice of drinks, the wordplay of "drinks" implies that he actually desires to drink human blood like the other lions in Africa.

The consumption of human blood is definitely against the ethics of Western culture, and is regarded as a "bad" or "wicked" act. At first glance, the good lion shows no interest in drinking human blood in Africa and asks politely for drinks that are fit for a civilized creature. However, the drinks for which he asks are redolent of images of human blood, having significant dual functions. First, the drinks act as "masks" to impress readers with the lion's "goodness" in line with Western morality and culture. The same drinks also serve the function of revealing his secret, or unconscious, "thirst," which is prohibited as "bad" according to traditional Western standards.

Not only the good lion but also many Hemingway heroes are attracted by "bad" habits, although they usually suffer internal conflict and disguise their desire. For example, Frederic Henry and Catherine Barkley in *A Farewell to Arms* are steeped in the bliss of premarital sex while they fear punishment from God. There are also many connotations of homosexual affection between Jake Barnes and Bill Gorton in *The Sun Also Rises* and between Frederic and Rinaldi in *A Farewell to Arms*, although their affections are concealed beneath their friendship. Add to this the transgendering between Frederic and Catherine insinuated in *Farewell to Arms* and between David Bourne, his wife Catherine, and Marita featured in *Garden of Eden*. What is an interesting and, to borrow Hemingway's phrase, "complicated" point is that drinks not only act as things that save the appearance of the lion as a civilized creature but at the same time act as things reveal his true desires.

Gilded Wildness

In this last section, I would like to focus on the meanings of the good lion's order in Harry's Bar in Venice. As the good lion comes back to Venice, he visits his father, the winged lion in Piazza San Marco, and exchanges a couple of words with him as follows:

> [T]he horses still had their feet up and the Basilica looked more beautiful than a soap bubble. The Campanile was in place and the pigeons were going to their nests for the evening.
> "How was Africa?" his father said.
> "Very savage, father," the good lion replied.
> "We have night lighting here now," his father said.
> "So I see," the good lion answered like a dutiful son.
> "It bothers my eyes a little," his father confided to him. "Where are you going now, my son?"
> "To Harry's Bar," the good lion said. (CSS 483)

As we can assume from the descriptions of Venice such as "the horses still had their feet up" and the "Campanile was in place," the good lion sees that the town has not changed and tries to show his father how he has "changed" through his travel in "very savage" Africa. His father, however, does not seem very interested in what his son says, and starts to talk about the "night lighting" in Venice, which does suggest the change of the town. Thus, as soon as the good lion gives short and rather perfunctory responses to his father, "like a dutiful son," he moves on to Harry's Bar, where he can satisfy his desire to feel and show his "change" in contrast to unchanged people:

> In Cipriani's nothing was changed. All of his friends were there. But he was a little changed himself from being in Africa.
> "A Negroni, Signor Barone?" asked Mr. Cipriani. But the good lion had flown all the way from Africa and Africa had changed him.
> "Do you have any Hindu trader sandwiches?" he asked Cipriani. (484)

When Cipriani asks him whether he wants a Negroni, which can be assumed to be the good lion's favorite, the good lion emphasizes his change by ordering "Hindu trader sandwiches." This scene has a symmetrical aspect with the scene in Africa. On one hand, in Africa the good lion refuses to drink the blood of a "Hindu trader" and asks for "Negroni" in order to express his sophisticated Western value. In Venice, on the other hand, he declines a "Negroni" but orders "Hindu trader sandwiches" to show how he has acquired the wild and exotic customs of Africa.

His order, which is intended to show off his "wildness," ironically implies that his "wildness" is not true but rather gilded. Actually, his order is not for a block of raw meat or blood, which may fit in perfectly with an African lion's taste, but rather for "sandwiches" and a "martini," a standard menu that refined Westerners prefer. Even though the good lion intends to display his change and wild exoticism as a traveler by ordering "Hindu trader sandwiches," "sandwiches" and a "martini" suggest that his "wildness" is limited to the standard of the Western culture. That is to say, like the drinks in Africa serve a function as a "mask" to emphasize the good lion's cultured taste that meets the Western ethic while revealing his hidden thirst, food in Venice may act as a "mask" of his exotic "wildness" although they hint at his cultural boundaries as a Westerner.

In conclusion, we can see that food and drinks in "The Good Lion" have ironical dual functions. The lion's persistent preference for Western food and drink can be read as a self-critical caricature of the heroes of Hemingway's 1930s works set in Africa who conform to a Western standard. On the other hand, the same drinks that the good lion asks for in Africa reveal that he secretly cherishes a desire that acts against the Western ethic, and which is typical of so many of Hemingway's protagonists. Moreover, the food in Venice is represented as a tool for showing off the good lion's exotic tastes, although the same food suggests in the end that he has not absorbed African culture fully and that his taste is quite conventionally westernized.

In Africa, drinks such as a Negroni, an Americano, and a glass of *pomodoro* act as things that save the appearance of the lion as a civilized creature, but at the same time they act as things that reveal his true desires. In Venice, food apparently disguises his "wildness" as they suggest that his "wildness" is bound by Western culture. Food and drinks in this work are a kind of "mask" that has two sides: it disguises the protagonist's appearance while it discloses his concealed aspects. Although this is a very short story, and has been neglected as a literary work, it contains several complex aspects common to other of Hemingway's major works. Food and drinks in this fable in particular play an important dualistic role of expressing the dilemma and contradiction of the protagonist. Considering the ingenious connotations of food and drinks, it is entirely fair to say that "The Good Lion" should not be ignored as a trivial story for children, but deserves to be investigated as a literary work and also a microcosm of Hemingway's "complicated" works.

Notes

1. As a part of "biographical" aspect of "The Good Lion," we can find Hemingway's reminiscence about a lion in a bar:

> Back in the old days this was one of the few good, solid bars, and there was an ex-pug who used to come in with a pet lion. He'd stand at the bar here and the lion would stand here beside him. He was a very nice lion with good manners—no growls or roars—but, as lions will, he occasionally shit on the floor. This, of course, had a rather adverse effect on the trade and, as politely as he could, Harry asked the ex-pug not to bring the lion around any more. But the next day the pug was back with the lion, lion dropped another load, drinkers dispersed, Harry again made request. The third day, same thing. Realizing it was do or die for poor Harry's business, this time when lion let go, I went over, picked up the pug, who had been a welterweight, carried him outside and threw him in the street. Then I came back and grabbed the lion's mane and hustled him out of here. Out on the sidewalk, the lion gave me a look, but he went quietly. (Hotchner 46)

Hemingway tells this story to A. E. Hotchner in 1950, only a year before "The Good Lion" is published. This memoir is located in "Harry's New York Bar" in Paris, where Harry MacElhone works as a bartender, and its name instantly reminds us of Cipriani's "Harry's Bar" in Venice in "The Good Lion." The "very nice lion with good manner" in this episode also resembles the "good" lion who tries to behave "politely" in the fable. Although there is no certain evidence to support the truth of this episode, this memoir gives us a hint that Hemingway might be inspired by his real experience in a bar. At the very least, this episode suggests that the story of a lion in a bar had matured in Hemingway's head for one year at least.

2. Johnston interprets the good lion who flies away from angry lions as Hemingway's flight from spiteful criticisms:

> Again this may be seen as a flattering self-portrait of a dedicated writer who faithfully adheres to his own distinctive style and subject matter, de-

spite rejection by editors, hostile attacks by reviewers, and laughter and scorn from former friends. (Johnston 154)

Johnston also states that the model of lioness in the fable could be his former wife Martha Gellhorn; Diana Trilling, who criticized his work in the *New York Times Book Review*; or Gertrude Stein, whom he attacked in his works (154).

Works Cited

Boreth, Craig. *The Hemingway Cookbook*. Chicago: Chicago Review Press, 1998.

Brillat-Savarin, Jean-Anthelme. *The Physiology of Taste*. 1825. Trans. Anne Drayton. New York: Penguin, 1970.

Cipriani, Arrigo. *Harry's Bar: The Life and Times of the Legendary Venice Landmark*. 1996. New York: Arcade Press, 2011.

Hemingway, Ernest. *The Complete Short Stories of Ernest Hemingway*. New York: Scribner, 2003.

———. *A Farewell to Arms*. 1929. New York: Scribner, 2003.

———. *For Whom the Bell Tolls*. 1940. New York: Scribner, 2003.

———. *The Garden of Eden*. 1986. New York: Scribner, 1995.

———. "The Good Lion." *Holiday* 9 (March 1951): 50–51.

———. *Green Hills of Africa*. 1935. New York: Scribner, 1998.

———. *The Sun Also Rises*. 1926. New York: Scribner, 1970.

Hotchner, A. E. *Papa Hemingway: A Personal Memoir*. 1955. Cambridge, MA: Da Capo Press, 2005.

Johnston, Kenneth G. "The Bull and the Lion: Hemingway's Fables for Critics." *Fitzgerald / Hemingway Annual* (1977): 149–56.

Smith, Paul. *A Reader's Guide to the Short Stories of Ernest Hemingway*. Boston: G. K. Hall, 1989.

Underhill, Linda, and Jeanne Nakjavani. "Food for Fiction: Lessons from Ernest Hemingway's Writing." *Journal of American Culture* 15 (1992): 87–90.

Widmayer, Jayne A. "Hemingway's Hemingway Parodies: The Hypocritical Griffon and the Dumb Ox." *Studies in Short Fiction* 18.4 (1981): 433–38.

Contributors

Ruggero Caumo was the barman at the most famous bar in Venice, Harry's Bar, which Hemingway frequented during the late 1940s and immortalized in *Across the River and into the Trees*.

Mark Cirino, professor and Melvin M. Peterson Endowed Chair in English at the University of Evansville, is the author or editor of several books, including *Ernest Hemingway: Thought in Action*. He is the host of the popular Hemingway Society–sponsored podcast, *One True Podcast*.

Cam Cobb is associate professor in the Faculty of Education at the University of Windsor, Canada.

Kirk Curnutt is professor and chair of English at Troy University in Troy and Montgomery, Alabama.

Scott Donaldson is the Cooley Professor of English Emeritus at the College of William and Mary in Williamsburg, Virginia.

Marina Gradoli is emerita professor at the University of Perugia in Italy.

Giacomo Ivancich served as Italian ambassador to South Africa, UNESCO, and Denmark. He and his family were friends of the Hemingways beginning in the late 1940s.

Kei Katsui is lecturer at Kwansei Gakuin University in Hyogo, Japan.

Alberto Lena is research fellow in the School of History, Journalism, and Media Studies at the University of Valladolid, Spain.

Adam Long is director of the Hemingway-Pfeiffer Museum at Arkansas State University.

Davide Lorigliola is a scholar at the Municipality of Lignano Sabbiadoro and the Società Filologica Friulana. He lives in Udine, Italy.

Miriam B. Mandel is senior lecturer (retired) in the Department of English and American Culture at Tel Aviv University in Ramat Aviv, Israel.

Mark P. Ott is the author of *A Sea of Change: Ernest Hemingway and the Gulf Stream, A Contextual Biography*, and co-editor of *Ernest Hemingway and the Geography of Memory: New Perspectives*. He is also the editor of the "Teaching Ernest Hemingway" series for Kent State University Press, and most recently served as Program Advisor for Ken Burns and Lynn Novick's documentary, *Hemingway*. He is the Head of School at The Kiski School in Pennsylvania.

Sergio Perosa is emeritus professor of English and American literature at Ca' Foscari University in Venice, Italy.

Piero Ambrogio Pozzi is a translator and scholar who lives in San Pietro All'Olmo, Milan, Italy.

Michael Kim Roos is professor emeritus of English at the University of Cincinnati Blue Ash College.

John D. Schwetman is assistant professor in the Department of English at the University of Minnesota Duluth.

Rosella Mamoli Zorzi is professor emerita of American Literature in the Dipartimento di Studi Linguistici e Culturali Comparati at University of Venice Ca' Foscari in Venice, Italy.

Index

Abruzzi (Italy), 89, 108, 128, 134–35
Across the River and into the Trees (Hemingway): Alvarito in, 156; bridges in, 155; calculus of, 163, 170–71, 174–75n3; Cantwell as "code hero" in, 146; Cantwell's critiques of generals in, 149–51; Cantwell as insider in, 148–49; Cantwell as intellectual in, 151–52; Cantwell's love for Venice in, 1–2; dialogue in, 1; EH on, 163; elevator scene in, 172; *Gran Maestro* in, 24–25, 147–49, 203; iceberg principle in, 165, 170; Italian translation of, 177, 179, 190–93; Jackson in, 147–48; picturesque in, 65n8; "pitted compatriot" in, 148; publication of, 195; Renata, beauty of, in, 147; Renata, naming of, 154, 159; stones in, 155, 168, 170, 185; style of, 200; Torcello in, 58–59; Venetian setting of, 3, 55, 145; writing of, 23
"Across the Street and into the Grill" (White), 195–213
Akeley, Carl, 111
Alighieri, Dante, 106, 152, 160, 171
Anderson, Sherwood, 33, 44, 195, 209n2
Antongini, Tom, 168
Ascham, Roger, 48

Bainsizza Plateau, 88–89, 92
Baker, Carlos, 71, 128, 129, 133, 161, 185, 196
Balestra, Gianfranca, 97
Barbusse, Henri, 97, 116
Barrès, Maurice, 50
Barthou, Jean-Louis, 37
Beegel, Susan F., 218
Beerbohm, Max, 197
Benini, Isi, 72
Bergman, Ingrid, 15
Bernardis, Aldo, 72

"Big Two-Hearted River" (Hemingway), 200
"Bird of Night" (Hemingway), 171, 174
Bissolati, Leonida, 85
The Black Pig (Notari), 96–107, 108, 123n1
Blake, William, 170, 182–83
Blanche, Antoine, 97–98
Bonadeo, Alfredo, 85
Bone, John, 37
Borgatti, Renata, 44
Bosha, Francis J., 211n13
Braddock, General Edward, 87
Brecht, Berthold, 92
Briggs, Julia, 221
Brillat-Savarin, Jean Anthelme, 230
Bromfield, Louis, 195
Browning, Robert, 6, 33, 54, 55, 64, 66n12
Bruegel, Pieter, 160
Brusadelli, Giulio, 146
Bump, Marjorie, 35, 36
Butts, Dennis, 221
Byron, George Gordon, Lord, 6, 48–49, 64, 66n12, 152, 157

Cadorna, General Luigi, 77–78, 82, 85, 87, 88, 91–92
Cain, William E., 136
Calzavara, Vittorio, 24–25
Camastra, Nicole, 134
Campbell, Joseph, 160
Campbell, Kenneth, 200
"A Canary for One" (Hemingway), 3
Caorle (Italy), 58, 64, 70
Caporetto (Battle of): *A Farewell to Arms* and, 78–93, 127, 130, 136, 137, 140, 177–78; Hemingway and, 22, 26n3; Pivano and, 177–78
Caporetto (Italy), 77

Capote, Truman, 201–2
Carducci, Giosuè, 100
Carso (Italy), 87, 92, 185
Casamassima, Mario, 73
"Cat in the Rain" (Hemingway), 3, 45
Chambers, Robert, 196
"Chapter VI" (Hemingway), 3
"Chapter VII" (Hemingway), 3
Chateaubriand, François-René de, 53
Chesterton, G. K., 33
"Che Ti Dice La Patria?" (Hemingway), 3, 4
Cipriani, Arrigo, 21
Cipriani, Giuseppe: "The Good Lion" and, 225, 227–28, 235, 237, 239; Harry's Bar and, 21, 22, 26n1
Cirino, Mark, 185, 209n1
Clegg, Jeanne, 59
Codroipo (Italy), 70, 71, 72, 186
Comisso, Giovanni, 78
Connable, Dorothy, 168
Cooper, Gary, 15
Cooper, James Fenimore, 48
Cooperative Commonwealth, 31, 33
Coren, Alan, 197
Cortina d'Ampezzo (Italy), 12, 13, 44–45, 58, 65, 69–70
Corvo, Baron (Frederic Rolfe), 51, 54
Cowley, Malcolm, 111
Coyne, Jerry, 113, 114
Custer, George Armstrong, 150

D'Annunzio, Gabriele: ARIT and, 19, 64, 168–71, 175, 183–85; FTA and, 89, 93; WWI and, 79–80, 83, 85, 88, 90
D'Aronco, Gianfranco, 72
Darwin, Charles, 111, 113–14, 123n3, 124n10, 223
da Udine, Tino, 71
Da una felice Cuba a Ketchum (G. Ivancich), 15
Davis, Jack, 206
Dawkins, Richard, 113, 114
Dennett, Daniel, 113, 114
De Robertis, Giuseppe, 87–88

De Simon, Adamo, 70, 71, 72
Dewey, John, 226
Dickens, Charles, 197
Dietrich, Marlene, 15, 19, 181–83
Diliberto, Gioia, 35, 43
D'Olivo, Marcello, 72, 73
Dorman-Smith, E. E. ("Chink"), 30, 37, 40, 41, 146
Dostoevsky, Fyodor, 209n5
Dudley, Marc, 218, 219–20
Due Spadi (hotel), 37
Dunant, Henry, 138–39, 141
Duse, Eleonora, 160, 168, 170, 175, 185

Eider, Will, 206
Eisenhower, Dwight David, 149, 206
Eliot, T. S., 34, 208
Ellis, Havelock, 111, 123n5
Emmanuelle II, King, 85
Ermacora, Chino, 72
"Ernest Hemingway Special" (recipe), 23
Excelsior (hotel), 25, 26n11

"The Faithful Bull" (Hemingway), 13–14, 218, 231
A Farewell to Arms: art in, 97; disillusionment in, 29; elevator scene in, 172–73; execution in, 90; Fascism, and, 77; food in, 230, 233; inspiration for writing, 4; Italian setting of, 3; knowledge in, 110; man from Pittsburgh in, 140; priest in, 82; quest for wisdom and happiness in, 109; reading in, 97; realism in, 89; Rinaldi in, 106–7, 114–15, 128; sex in, 236; translation of, 77, 177–78. *See also* Caporetto (Battle of)
Ferrata, Giansiro, 178
Fielding, Henry, 196–97
Fitzgerald, F. Scott, 197
Fiume (Italy), 69, 80, 83
La Floridita, 22–23
Foch, General Ferdinand, 84, 87
Fonzi, Bruno, 178
Ford, Corey, 207
Ford, Ford Madox, 124n9
Fortuna, Loris, 72
For Whom the Bell Tolls, 23, 195, 205, 230, 233
Fossalta di Piave (Italy), 30, 37, 81

Franchetti, Baron Nanuck, 13, 70, 71
Franco, General Francisco, 86
Frescura, Attilio, 81
Freud, Sigmund, 53
Friuli (Italy), 12, 13, 68–74, 78, 79, 186
Frost, Robert, 130–31, 133

Gaines, William, 204, 210n8
Gamble, Jim, 30–32
The Garden of Eden (Hemingway), 236
Gardner, Ava, 15
Gatti, General Angelo, 79, 82
Gellhorn, Martha (third wife), 124n9, 240n2
Genoa (Italy): EH and Hadley travel to, 42; EH and Mary travel to, 69, 71, 73; EH reports on economic conference in, 36, 37, 82, 83
Gentile, Emilio, 89
George, David Lloyd, 37
Giotto, 147, 170–71
Godolphin, Francis R. B. (Frisco), 41
Goldstein, Irene, 33, 35
"The Good Lion" (Hemingway), 13, 218–28, 230–39
Gorizia (Italy), 88, 130, 131–32, 134, 136
Goya, Francisco, 71
Graziani, General Andrea, 91
Greco, El, 71
Greenblatt, Stephen, 48
Green Hills of Africa (Hemingway), 22, 26n5, 233–34
Gritti Palace Hotel: ARIT and, 182, 185, 202; Calzavara and, 24; EH as patron, 12, 13, 26n8, 58, 65n2, 71, 73; location of, 194n6; Schrafft's as opposite of, 206
Guttuso, Renato, 178

Hammond (Indiana), 162
Hanneman, Audre, 200
Harry's Bar in Venice: ARIT and, 182; EH's enjoyment of, 55; EH's unpublished writing, in, 14, 239n1; G. Ivancich, and, 12; "The Good Lion" and, 218–19, 225, 227, 228, 235, 237; location of, 26n4; view of EH by employees of, 22
Le Havre (France), 12, 71, 73, 179
Hemingway, Ernest: alcohol and, 22, 24; erysipelas of, 70; Fascism, feeling toward, 4, 85; knowledge of history of, 81; lost suitcase of, 39–40, 42–43; marriage of, 36; Native American heritage of, 174; Nobel Prize and, 26n7, 196; plane crashes of, 5, 12, 17, 23, 26n7, 71; pseudonym of, 38; reading of, as a youth, 220–21; Ruskin and, 64, 66n11; sexual activity of, 42; travel and, 217; Venice, love of, 5; WWI wounding of, 3–4
Hemingway, Grace Hall (mother), 80
Hemingway, Hadley (first wife): ambitions of, 35; beauty of, 34–35; engagement with EH of, 34; EH meeting of, 29; EH's trip to Italy, opinion of, 31–32; father's suicide and, 35; independence of, 34; lost suitcase and, 40, 42–43; pregnancy of, 45; sensibility of, 33; Isabelle Simmons, friendship with, 41; travel in Italy with EH of, 37, 44–45, 69; trust fund of, 36; Agnes von Kurowsky, attitude toward, 39
Hemingway, John Hadley Nicanor (son), 38, 41
Hemingway, Madelaine (sister), 35
Hemingway, Marcelline (sister), 35
Hemingway, Mary (fourth wife): ARIT and, 19, 23; EH European travels with, 69–73 EH missing, 65n2; Ivanciches and, 12, 13, 15, 16, 17
Hemingway, Pauline Pfeiffer (second wife), 45
Hemingway, Ursula (sister), 35, 36
Hickock, Guy, 4
Hinkle, James, 116, 123n2
Hitler, Adolf, 83, 86
Hofmannsthal, Hugo von, 53
Ho guardato il cielo e la terra (A. Ivancich), 17
Horne, Bill, 38
Hotchner, A. E.: *Adventures of a Young Man* and, 210n9; EH conversations with, 69, 195, 200, 239n1; EH correspondence with, 181; "In Harry's Bar in Venice" and, 209n1
Hotel Danieli, 25
Howells, William Dean, 61
Hudson, W. H., 111, 123n5

Hugo, Victor, 162
Hutcheon, Linda, 202
Huysmans, Joris-Karl, 104

Iacobaci, Giuseppe, 179
"In Another Country" (Hemingway), 3, 171
"Indian Camp" (Hemingway), 200
"In Harry's Bar in Venice" (Hemingway), xiin1, xiin2, 64, 209n1
Isella, Dante, 178
Isonzo (river), 131
Isonzo, Battles of the: *FTA* and, 84, 129, 135–36, 139; history of, 78, 87, 88, 130, 133
Ivancich, Adriana: *ARIT*, allusions to, in, 160, 181–82, 184, 186; *ARIT*, inspiration, as, 70, 160, 177; *ARIT*, suppression of and, 177; artistic talent of, 16; aunt to Scapinelli, as, 231; fables, as inspiration for, 13–14, 231; gossip concerning, 14, 17, 19, 146, 177; illustrations of, 218, 231; last meeting with EH in Venice of, 73, 187; meeting EH, 13, 16, 70, 71, 185; memoirs of, 15; Montale, helping EH meet, 12; opinion of *ARIT* of, 17; trip to Cuba by, 17, 186
Ivancich, Carlo (father of Adriana), 11
Ivancich, Francesca (sister of Adriana), 13, 15
Ivancich, Gianfranco (brother of Adriana), 12, 13, 14–15, 16, 73

Jackson, Stonewall, 151, 173, 186
James, E. L., 197
James, Henry: *The Aspern Papers*, 51; Beerbohm and, 197; *Daisy Miller*, 203; EH and, 64–65; "The Grand Canal," 50–51; Torcello, views on, 59, 62; "Venice," 61–63; "Venice: An Early Impression," 62; *The Wings of the Dove*, 51
Joffre, General Joseph, 87
Johnston, Kenneth, 231, 239–40n2
Johnston, Liver Eating (John), 148
Jones, James, 210n11
Josef I, Emperor Franz, 138

Keats, John, 42
Kechler (family), 12; history of, 69, 68–73
Kechler, Alberto, 70, 72

Kechler, Carlo, 69–71
Kechler, Federico, 69, 72, 73
Kefauver, Estes, 204
Kert, Bernice, 15
Knodt, Ellen Andrews, 140
Knowles, A. Sidney, 146, 150, 157n1
Krigstein, Bernard, 206, 210n11

Lampedusa, Giuseppe Tomasi de, 93
Lardner, Ring, 197
"The Last Good Country" (Hemingway), 36
Latisana, 70, 72, 185–87
Lawrence, D. H., 112
Lecomte, Madame, 205
Ledda, Elena, 184–85
Lewis, Sinclair, 64, 66n12, 197
Lignano Sabbiadoro (Italy), 68–73
Lisca, Peter, 146–47, 154–55, 157n3, 161
Locanda Cipriani, xi, xiin2, 23, 58, 61, 63
Locchi, Vittorio, 88–89
London, Jack, 111
Lupino, Ida, 160
Lynn, Kenneth, 35

Macdonald, Dwight, 196, 198, 207–8
MacElhone, Harry, 239n1
Malaparte, Curzio, 81
Maldini, Sergio, 71
Mandel, Miriam, 123n1, 127–28, 129, 146, 218
Mann, Thomas, 48, 51, 53–54, 185
Mantegna, Andrea, 97, 162–63
Marinetti, Filippo Tommaso, 85, 98–99
Marlowe, Christopher, 48
Marvell, Andrew, 97
Mason, Frank, 38
Matteotti, Giacomo, 80
McAlmon, Robert, 42
McDowell, Edwin, 196
McKelly, James C., 197–98
McLain, Paula, 39, 43
McPherson, David, 47–48
Melville, Herman, 52
Menand, Louis, 196, 198–99, 200
Meredith, James, 161, 171
Merkin, Fanny, 197
Mestre (Italy), 136, 152, 162
Meyers, Jeffrey, 43, 146

Michelangeli, Enzo, 98
Milan (Italy): Adriana lives in, 17; EH convalescence in, 3, 29, 30, 86; EH interview with Mussolini in, 38–39; EH travel to, 32, 33, 37, 91; *FTA* and, 115, 172–73
Milne, A. A., 197
Mondadori, Alberto, 178–79, 194n2
Mondolo, Onelia, 72
Montale, Eugenio, 12, 160
Monteiro, George, 218, 219
Moore, Clement Clarke, 201–2, 208
Moore, Thomas, 48
Moorhead, Caroline, 139
Moreland, Kim, 137
A Moveable Feast (Hemingway), 45, 124n9
"Mr. and Mrs. Elliot" (Hemingway), 202
Mussolini, Benito: EH's feelings toward, 38–39, 84–85, 92; *FTA* and, 77; historical role of, 78–81, 84, 90; Torviscosa and, 72
"My Old Man" (Hemingway), 3, 44

Nakjavani, Jeanne, 230
Napoleon I, 48
Napoleon III, 150
Nashe, Thomas, 48
"A Natural History of the Dead" (Hemingway), 3
Neroni, Nick, 29, 33
Nervi (Italy), 187
Nivelle, General Robert, 87
Notari, Umberto, 98–107, 123n1
"Now I Lay Me" (Hemingway), 2, 3

O'Brien, Edward, 44
The Old Man and the Sea (Hemingway): A. Ivancich and, 18; EH's comeback, as, 196; EH's conception of, 17; success of, 23; translation of, 177–79, 187–89
Oliver, Charles, 156
O'Neil, Barbara, 41
O'Neil, Dave, 41
Orlando, Vittorio, 83
"Out of Season" (Hemingway), 44, 171

Padua (Italy), 70
Parker, Dorothy, 207
Pasubio (Italy), 3, 185

Patrick, John, 210n9
Patton, George, 149
Percoto (Italy), 71, 72, 187
Perelman, S. J., 207
Pfeiffer, Virginia (sister-in-law), 168
Phelan, Janet, 41
Pierce, Dick, 32
Pius X, Pope, 100
Pivano, Fernanda, 58, 65n2, 177–80, 187–93
Plimpton, George, 201
Pound, Ezra: *Cantos*, 52, 54–55; EH's lost manuscripts, opinion on, 40, 42; expatriate, as, 33; influence on EH, as, 36; Rapallo and, 42, 44
Pound, Dorothy, 42, 44
Pozzi, Piero Ambrogio, 18–19, 20
Proust, Marcel, 52–53, 54, 161–62, 170–71
Putnam, Samuel, 80

Quinlan, Grace, 35, 36

Rapallo (Italy), 42, 44–45
Remarque, Erich Maria, 92
"The Revolutionist" (Hemingway), 3, 162–63
Reynolds, Michael, 42–43, 77, 128, 135, 140
Ribalaigua, Constantino, 23
Rilke, Rainer Maria, 53
Rommel, Erwin, 149
Roosevelt, Theodore, 111, 123n5
Rose, William S., 61
Ross, Harold, 198, 211n13
Ross, Lillian, 171, 174, 209n5
Rossi, Ermete, 102
Rossi, Piero, 78
Rubens, Peter Paul, 97
Ruskin, John, 49–50, 52, 53, 55, 59–61, 63–65, 66n11
Russo, John Paul, 153–54
Russo, Puccio, 178
Ryall, William Bolitho, 36, 38, 39, 44

Salandra, Antonio, 85
Sampson, Edward C., 197, 202–3
Sandburg, Carl, 33
San Michele al Tagliamento, 11, 16, 70, 185, 187

Scapinelli, Gherardo, 13, 218, 231
Scarsini, Carlo, 71
Schio (Italy), 37
Schwarz, Jeffrey, 137
Seefeldt, Michael, 148–49, 152, 154
Shaffer, Andrew, 197
Shakespeare, William, 47, 64, 97, 171
Shaw, Irwin, 70, 71
Shelley, Percy Bysshe, 49
Sherborne, Michael, 117–19
"The Short Happy Life of Francis Macomber" (Hemingway), 233
Simmons, Isabelle, 41, 44
"A Simple Enquiry" (Hemingway), 3
Skinner, Cornelia Otis, 197
Smith, Bill, 34
Smith, David C., 116–17
Smith, Doodles, 33–34
Smith, Katy, 34–36
Smith, Paul, 231
Smith, Walter Bedell, 150
Smith, Y. K., 32–34
"The Snows of Kilimanjaro" (Hemingway), 3, 201–2, 233
Sokoloff, Alice, 43
"Soldier's Home" (Hemingway), 128
Sonnino, Sidney, 85
La Spezia, 81, 91
Spiegelman, Art, 210n11
Steffens, Lincoln, 36, 39
Stein, Gertrude: EH's correspondence with, 42; EH's satires of, 195, 209n2; expatriate, as, 33; *Geography and Plays*, EH's review of, 112; "The Good Lion" and, 240n2; influence on EH, and, 36; White's parody of, 198, 210n7
Stevenson, Robert Louis, 221–22, 224–26
Stewart, Donald Ogden, 123n6, 197
Stoltzfus, Ben, 136, 154–55, 161, 172
Stoneback, H. R., 123n2, 124n10
Strater, Mike, 42
Strunk, William J., 198
"Summer People" (Hemingway), 34, 36
The Sun Also Rises (Hemingway), 22, 200, 205, 230, 233, 236

Tagliamento (river), 11, 78, 90–91, 93, 186
Thompson, Mark, 85, 87, 91
Thurber, James, 198–202, 207–8
Tintner, Adeline, 161, 168, 174n1, 185
Tintoretto, 64, 147
Titian, 2, 97, 148
To Have and Have Not (Hemingway), 200
Tolstoy, Count Leo, 209n5
Torcello (Italy), 23, 58–66, 152–54, 157n3
"Torcello Piece" (Hemingway), xi–xii, 63–64
Toronto Daily Star, 4, 36, 38–39, 91
La Torre Bianca (A. Ivancich), 14, 15, 16, 18
The Torrents of Spring (Hemingway), 112, 209n2
Torviscosa (Italy), 72
Tracy, Daniel, 206, 207
Tracy, Spencer, 23
"Translations from the Esquimaux" (Hemingway), 171, 174
Treviso (Italy), 24–25, 78
Trieste (Italy), 79, 85, 186
Trilling, Diana, 240n2
Trogdon, Robert W., 200
Twysden, Duff, 45

Underhill, Linda, 230
Updike, John, 208
Usinger, Fred, 26n10
Usinger, Lena, 24–25, 26n10

Valle, Gino, 72
Valpolicella (wine), 5, 26n6, 182
Venice: death, and, 53–54; history of, 47–48, 65n5, 153; paradox of, 51; post-war life in, 11–12; La Serenissima, as, 48; St. Mark's, 54, 170, 180, 185, 227, 232, 237
Venus Rising from the Sea (Titian), 2, 155–56
Verduin, Kathleen, 146, 152
"A Very Short Story" (Hemingway), 3, 44
"A Veteran Visits the Old Front" (Hemingway), 4
Villiers, George, 194n5
Vittorini, Elio, 58, 65n3, 70, 160
von Clausewitz, Carl, 92

Von Kurowsky, Agnes: breakup letter to EH and, 30; EH's wedding and, 36; engagement of, 39; expectations of by EH, and, 29; feelings toward by EH, 35, 39; Milan and, 3, 30; prayer at the Duomo, refusal to, 32; "A Very Short Story" and, 44
Wagner-Martin, Linda, 77, 90
Wallach, Ira, 204–8, 210n10
Wallach, Eli, 204, 210n9
"A Way You'll Never Be" (Hemingway), 2, 3
Wells, H. G., 97, 108–24
Wertham, Fredric, 204
"Where the Fight Was," 171, 173–74
White, E. B., 195–211

Whitman, Walt, 161–62, 163, 166–68, 170–71
Widmayer, Jayne, 219, 234, 235
Williams, Steve-Stewart, 113, 114, 121
Williams, Tennessee, 210n9
Winwar, Frances, 168
Wirth, Joseph, 37
Wood, Denis, 131
Wordsworth, William, 7–8, 42, 49

Yeats, William Butler, 98
Young, Philip, 3

Zambelli, Luigi, 69

www.ingramcontent.com/pod-product-compliance
Lightning Source LLC
Chambersburg PA
CBHW031806220426
43662CB00007B/541